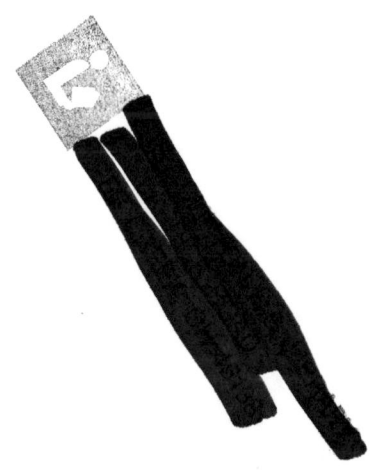

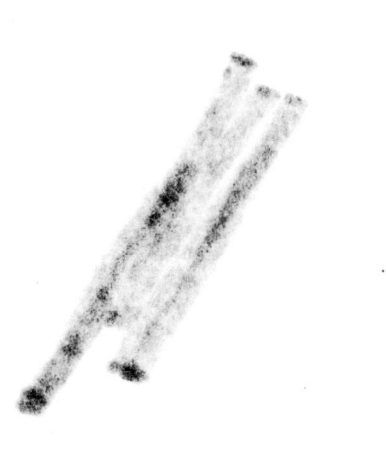

EXPLORING CAREERS IN CYBERSPACE

EXPLORING CAREERS IN CYBERSPACE

By
MICHAEL FULTON

The Rosen Publishing Group, Inc.
NEW YORK

Published in 1998 by The Rosen Publishing Group, Inc.
29 East 21st Street, New York, NY 10010

Copyright 1998 by Michael Fulton

All rights reserved. No part of this book may be reproduced in any form without permission in writing from the publisher, except by a reviewer.

First Edition

Library of Congress Cataloging-in-Publication Data

Fulton, Michael, 1968-
    Exploring careers in cyberspace / by Michael Fulton. — 1st ed.
       p. cm.
    Includes bibliographical references and index.
    Summary: Provides background information on the Internet and such related careers as programmers, writers, designers, sales representatives, and "Cyber-bosses," and includes interviews with people working in the field.
    ISBN 0-8239-2633-8
    1. Computer industry—Vocational guidance—Juvenile literature. [1. Computer industry—Vocational guidance. 2. Vocational guidance. 3. Cyberspace.] I. Title.
    HD9696.C62F84   1997
    004.67'8'02373—dc21   97-28847
                                                                         CIP
                                                                          AC

Manufactured in the United States of America

About the Author

Michael Fulton is a high school literature teacher who resides in New York City. He is an avid reader and writer of poetry and enjoys experimenting with haiku.

Cyberspace appeals to his wanderlust, fulfilling his need to explore the globe and allowing him to stay in contact with his friends around the world.

Acknowledgments

I would like to thank every person mentioned in this book. Each of you has taken time out of your busy days to sit down with me and share your thoughts. Your stories and insights will serve the reader well.

Special thanks to Patra McSharry Sevastiades for her editorial guidance. And a warm thank you to my friends for their support and patience while I brought this book to fruition.

Contents

Introduction Where and What Is Cyberspace? 1
1. How the Web Was Won 6
2. Before You Start 20
3. Programmers 23
4. Writers and Producers 34
5. Designers 42
6. Sales Representatives 52
7. Cyber-Bosses and Other Cyber Gurus 56
8. Entrepreneurs: Cyberspace Working for You 70
9. What You Need to Do Now 81
10. "DIY": Books, Software, and Web Sites 100
11. Conclusion 105
Glossary 107
Index 111

Introduction: Where and What Is Cyberspace?

Howdy, space partners, and welcome to *Adventures in Cyberspace*. Let us begin by taking inventory of ourselves.

When you were small, you crawled and then struggled to walk, falling and bruising yourself as you went along. You learned to ride a bike, falling and bruising yourself as you went along. You learned to do a cartwheel and to skate. You have skied and built ramps to jump things.

What does this have to do with cyberspace? Basically, you are a born stuntperson. When it comes to deciding on your career, you can choose: Will you wear a blazer and read through sales reports all day? Will you sit in an office making calls to potential life insurance policy holders? You can do all of these things—and you can choose a career that allows you to exercise your more audacious essence. Cyberspace offers just such creative outlets.

Think about it. You cannot take an entry-level job with a bank and expect to keep being promoted until you are the bank's president. Your progress will probably be limited to a certain level of achievement. In cyberspace there is no limit to the success that you can enjoy. Anyone can be an expert, and everyone has a chance to be successful.

Cyberspace is everywhere you look—*http://www.ohmygosh.com/*—and, although you may have yet to see it, you still want to get a piece of the pie. Cyberspace is both hot *and* cool. In the age of the information superhighway, your Web page may be as important as your address.

So grab your résumé, put on your power suit, and head out the door. But to where? Is the information highway far from the expressway? Which exit, and is there parking? Will it be a long commute?

OK, so you have no idea where cyberspace is. Pay close attention. It's both everywhere and nowhere. The first step in getting there is defining what cyberspace is.

"Cyberspace" is a term coined by the author William Gibson in his book *Neuromancer*. It is not so much a place as it is a workspace. It was created as a result of the network of computers that makes up the Internet. It is where computer users go to share and retrieve the information found on the World Wide Web. The terms "World Wide Web" and "cyberspace" are interchangeable to some degree. The Web is what fills cyberspace. And cyberspace is where the Web is floating, so to speak.

Cyberspace has been commonly referred to as a "fourth dimension," but this is not a very helpful term. It is difficult to provide a definitive answer to exactly what cyberspace *is*. It may be more useful to define this undefinable area in more fluid ways. I've interviewed numerous people who are currently enjoying careers in cyberspace. Following are the ways in which they define cyberspace. Their insights may help you create your own working definition.

How do you define cyberspace?

- I don't. It redefines itself everyday.   *Scott Brodeur*

Introduction: Where and What Is Cyberspace?

- A lot like Silly Putty. People want to do something, and they make it do what they want it to do. *Jinnah Hosein*
- A new marketing tool. *Isra Wattanasarn*
- A huge library. *Aryeh Goldsmith*
- One big net where everything's intertwined. *Christopher Park*
- The new frontier. The gunslingers have been pushed out, and the gold rush is on. *Bob Gale*
- A communal meeting place for the whole world. *Joe Schwartz*
- The coolest distribution network. *Jason Mulligan*
- Everywhere you are on the Internet, you are exactly the same distance away from every place else. You're inside looking out. *Arthur Perley*
- Free, fun, and different way of gathering information. *Jimmy Santos*
- The place where my generation doesn't have to play by the rules. *Trisha Smith*
- It's a create-your-own world. *Andrew Cary*
- A growing, changing, and exciting place that can't be defined. *Tricia Nelson*
- A totally different world than we live in. *Art Pardavilla III*
- The mecca of networking. *Kathryn J. Livornese*
- A most interesting contradiction. You can do whatever you want, but at the same time, you can do only a few things. *Maurice Williams*
- The world got a little smaller. *EB Stone*
- Where people meet inside the wires. *Lowell J. Gray*
- It's almost like electricity. You can't see it going

through the wires, but when you turn on that switch, the lights come on. *Brad Taylor*
- Going fishing. *Jeff Harrington*
- The ultimate integration of media. *Kermit Westergaard*

As you do further research, you will discover that this career area is fresh, exhilarating, and still in its infancy. In this book you will read again and again that it is up to you to do many things—beginning here by defining cyberspace. By the way, Ann Landers once defined the Internet as a place for "con men, the lonely, and the bored." Boy . . . who asked her?

When I asked one designer what her job is, she replied, "I wish I knew!" So, if you are a high-energy person who wants a hand in all aspects of the job and can work in surroundings that are still being defined and may undergo numerous redefinitions, then this may be your career field. You may be involved in designing your own position, as well as the workings of your office as a whole. Cyberspace is still the Wild West, according to Trisha Smith of New Jersey Online, and there is nothing else like it. The future is burning brightly, and so are its stars.

There is nothing boring about the field you have chosen to explore. And there is nothing common about the people with whom and the places where you may be working. Cyberspace is filled with young, creative people who demand a uniquely free work environment. From what I've seen, you probably won't have to cut your hair. Guys, your razor may sit idle for stretches of many days. You can expose your tattoos (in many cases they're a plus). And if black nailpolish is what you prefer, it will go unnoticed. The ties or hosiery that your mother stocked up for you for the job world will probably collect dust in your closet.

Introduction: Where and What Is Cyberspace?

As EB Stone, director of Long Island Internet Headquarters, points out, "The atmosphere of the company must be free so that people will remain creative, comfortable, and at their peak." EB has shoulder-length hair himself, and on the day I visited he was wearing clothes and earrings that would make the members of Metallica proud. Within the loose confines of cyber culture it's not how you look that will win you the job, but what you can do in cyberspace.

Cyberspace is about more than extensive computer knowledge. There will always be a demand for the accomplished hacker. However, creativity and good ideas are especially valued. As Kermit Westergaard, from Interactive Connection, told me, "There's not even close to the number of people that are going to be needed to provide creative content. In terms of interactive media, cyberspace is burgeoning." Artists, writers, entrepreneurs, and everyone in between the definitions can find their niche on the Web.

I have interviewed many people working in cyberspace. In the five chapters covering career options (chapters 3 through 7), I let them tell their stories. I have invited some of the brightest and most enthusiastic members of the cyberspace community to share their views and experiences with you.

The interviewees are excited to do so. They tell you about their careers and how they perform their tasks. More important, they will tell you what you need to know to break into the field of cyberspace. Listen to their sound advice. And please . . . enjoy!

1

How the Web Was Won

Cyberspace is the world created by the existence of the Internet, or Net. The Internet was developed over a forty-year period by scientists and researchers from many different sectors of society. It is the physical linking of computers through telephone systems that, in turn, form networks. The U.S. military, university research departments, and corporations have been involved in the development of the Internet.

The Internet is a communications network. For most people, seems to have spring up overnight. And it has taken on its own mythology because of its apparently meteoric growth. Since it is so effective and widespread, it is easy for some people to believe that the Internet must have existed in a secret form at some time.

THE MYTH

I was at the offices of New Jersey Online on Friday, August 23, 1996, when the entire Northeast region of the country went down off the Internet. A group of people were talking about it. I overheard one of them say that he thought the Internet could survive a nuclear war. His friend answered that she thought that was what the Internet was specifically built for.

A romantic notion of the U.S. military, brimming with secrets and capable of anything, has long fed our imaginations. Couple this with the unavoidable ignorance of mainstream society about the many quiet and anonymous advances in the sciences, and it is easy to understand why people can believably advance a story about conspiracies and the technological wizardry of the Internet.

Douglas E. Comer, a member of the Internet Architecture Board, was one of the original researchers involved in the formation of the Internet. He writes in his text *The Internet Book*, "The Internet had become a powerful force quickly. To newcomers, it seemed vast, strange and intimidating. Novices were shocked and ready to believe almost anything, including preposterous tales. Others were ready to invent a mythology that could explain it."

Comer recounts being in an elevator and hearing people speculate that the Internet was developed to "update the hotline" between the Kremlin and the White House. (For those coming of age in the post-Cold War era, it may be hard to imagine that such a hotline was once established to avoid nuclear war.) Needless to say, this too is myth.

THE REALITY

The Internet does have a military background, but it does not involve top-secret espionage or James Bond-like qualities. Yet, the Internet grew at such exponential rates, connecting so many people in so many countries, that it is a story quite deserving of boasting.

The United States Department of Defense began exploring the possibility of using computer networks in the late 1960s. The military funded research for creating networks and, by the late 1970s, had several in operation. But the networks they created were specific to their locations, and these locations could not communicate with each other. The military wanted to link their networks together into one inclusive system.

The Advanced Research Projects Agency (ARPA), established by the U.S. Department of Defense in the late 1960s, had developed the local networks. In the late 1970s they brainstormed a new approach to linking isolated computer networks. They called it the *internetwork*. The term was subsequently abbreviated as *internet*. ARPA's project and the system it developed as its prototype adopted the name and became known as the Internet.

The ARPA researchers evaluated software and computer applications that would allow the networked computers to transfer data among the sites. The product that resulted from this research is known as TCP/IP. *Internet Protocol* software, or IP, allows basic communication between networked computers. *Transmission Control Protocol* software, or TCP, provides additional functions to allow for communication. This software, in enhanced form, is now standard equipment in every computer.

Meanwhile, a few years earlier in the early 1970s, scientists at Bell Telephone Laboratories had built a new operating system for computers. They called it *The Unix Timesharing System*, or UNIX. It was given to universities, and the University of California at Berkeley became a major distribution facility.

ARPA decided to utilize the Berkeley software distribution network. They gave the university the TCP/IP software to incorporate into their version of the UNIX system. Soon computer science departments across the nation were using TCP/IP for teaching and research. Research possibilities and suggested improvements were made public. The Internet benefited invaluably from the attention.

By 1982, the Internet, still in its infancy, was operating reliably, and handfuls of academic and industrial research sites were using TCP/IP regularly. As Comer writes, "More important, the Internet demonstrated that the basic principles of internetworking were sound." By 1983, ARPA had expanded its efforts to include all U.S. military sites around the world, and the Internet had advanced from an experiment to a useful network for academia, industry, and the military. So much for the flights of fancy concerning a top-secret military operation. Comer states directly, "Although the military funded Internet research and eventually chose to use the Internet, internetworking was developed and tested at civilian sites."

In 1983 the Internet doubled in size. It nearly doubled again in 1984. The Department of Defense and the National Aeronautics and Space Administration (NASA) were now using TCP/IP and were supporting research for the Internet. The National Science Foundation (NSF) gave the technology the push needed to create a major new Internet. The NSF decided that the network should be extended to provide access to every science and engineering researcher in the United States. It would have significantly greater capacity to connect computer users.

The NSF disbursed its funds in the form of federal grants. These were given to companies that would bid to create the more powerful network. In 1988, IBM, MCI, NSF, and MERIT, a Michigan-based networking company, jointly established a new network that would form the backbone of the Internet. The NSF provided tax-payer dollars, MCI provided the transmission lines, IBM provided the routing computers and software, and MERIT operated the network, called the NSFNET.

By 1992, the Internet was experiencing rapid growth. It became clear that even the NSFNET would soon reach its capacity. Simultaneously, the U.S. government could not go on paying for the Internet. IBM, MCI, and

MERIT formed a nonprofit company called Advanced Networks and Services (ANS). During that year, ANS built a new network, known as ANSNET, that uses transmission lines with thirty times the capacity of the previous network.

Since then, the Internet has grown incredibly. In 1983, the Internet consisted of 562 computers. In 1993, the Internet connected 1,200,000 computers. The approximate number of computers in 1994 was 2,217,000!

Comer helps put this tremendous growth into perspective. He speaks of how, when you first access the Internet, you feel like a novice. In a matter of a year, however, you will have covered a lot of ground, having surfed innumerable miles of cyberspace. During that year, half of all Internet users will have just started to explore cyberspace. In fact, at any time during the period from 1983 to 1994 approximately half of the Internet's growth occurred during the previous year.

The Global Internet

ARPA's research was chiefly concerned with creating Internet access for U.S. participants. However, a few research networks included connections to other countries, including England and Norway, during the seminal stages of Internet development.

Once the software was developed that used the telephone system to connect computers, the Global Internet was quick to follow. The global voice telephone network was established to operate on a universal set of standards. Like any U.S. computer user, all one needed was a modem and the software to be connected.

1991 was the hallmark year for the Global Internet. The EBONE network was created. This European backbone network is the result of groups throughout Europe organizing themselves into a cooperative to form a high-speed Internet network. The Internet now connects countries on all continents. If you can make a phone call, you can send e-mail.

The Internet is a limited technology at this point. The TCP/IP software identifies each computer with a number. The maximum number of computers that the current program will accept is 4,294,967,296. That's a big number, but it's only two-thirds of the world's current population. People keep predicting the end of the Internet, and thus far they have been way off. Whenever an Internet technology approaches its limit, something more powerful has always been found.

Shaping the Web's Future

Americans have always been passionate about protecting their freedoms. Our cultural heritage is built on pioneers. America celebrates its nonconformists and even a few outlaws. We still cling to the image of the rugged individualist. Although the Internet was born free, more and more it is being introduced into the mainstream of our culture and being asked to mirror some of society's more rigid codes of behavior.

While advances in technology will see to it that the Web continues to expand, controversy exists over whether any forms of expression will be bridled. In many ways the Web's greatest strength, unregulated information, is also its greatest weakness. There are those in cyberspace who value regulation and search for standards limiting the Web's avenues of freedom. Let's explore the latest controversies involving the use of cyberspace.

Freedom of Speech

The most hotly contested issue facing cyberspace is that of free speech. At this point, the Web is an unregulated and uncensored network of communication. You may say anything on the Web that is currently legal and protected under the First Amendment. You could probably push that envelope a bit, if you so desired. Thus far, the Web's population of users have been deeply protective of their rights and will have none of them impinged upon.

But a growing concern in the general public is that there may be too much freedom. Some worry that indecency and flagrant lawlessness exist in far too great a proportion on the Web. They believe that rules and regulations must be imposed on cyberspace. Pornography and child pornography are most often cited as examples of the Web's failures to meet society's mores. *Wired* magazine refers to this as Net-porn hysteria. I have yet to see any pornography in cyberspace. I have never gone looking for it either. Let's just say that for the most part you do not simply come across it while you surf the Net. EB Stone says of the issue, "Cyberspace is like any other neighborhood. There are bad elements, and if you go looking for them, you will find them."

I suspect that relatively few people condone pornography on the Web. I do know that people are afraid of losing freedoms, though. People who have careers in cyberspace believe that it is best regulated from the inside. They think that the Web can and should function as an autonomous institution. The U.S. government is already developing legislation to regulate the Web. The Communications Decency Act failed to be voted into law in 1997; however, it is bound to be reintroduced as a bill before Congress. Its mandate was to regulate the content of the Internet. It proposed to abolish access to pornography and to prohibit profane and obscene language and material. Although its potential effects are yet to be fully understood and are not necessarily enforceable, it sends a clear message to users that similar laws may be forthcoming.

Judge Stewart Dalzell, writing for a Philadelphia federal court on June 11, 1996, wrote, "The government's asserted 'failure' of the Internet rests on the implicit premise that too much speech occurs in that medium. This argument is profoundly repugnant to First Amendment principles ... as the most participatory form of mass speech yet developed, the Internet deserves the highest protection from government intrusion."

The Web is a brilliant tool of communication. Too many regulations will hinder its effectiveness as a democratic tool. Users and devotees of cyberspace do not want to lose an egalitarian technology of inclusion to overzealous lawmakers. The lawmakers, on the other hand, do not want potentially dangerous, decadent, and degrading materials freely accessible to members of society not properly prepared for such messages and potential harm.

Is Big Brother Still Out There?

The next battle that is being fought in cyberspace is one of anonymity and encryption, or the ability to keep your e-mail address and other information secret. They are indelibly linked to each other and concern freedom of expression. You may be fighting for free speech, but you are far from free when you enter cyberspace. The fact is, every time you visit a Web site you have unwittingly given away a lot of information. You have left information about where you are from, what kind of computer you have, and what browser you are using. And possibly more information may be obtained from you without your knowledge.

When you send an e-mail message, you tell the whole story. You cannot remain anonymous. Your address is displayed right along with the intended receiver's. This was set up for ease of correspondence. But what if you want to post messages with impunity? What if you want to send vituperative messages without a return address? Many cyberspace users want unequivocal, uncrackable privacy. Many people, including our government, do not want that to be an option.

The U.S. government wants to be able to know who sends mail in cyberspace and what is in it. Software programs that allow you to encrypt, or make secret, your address, or anything else for that matter, are illegal in the United States. Some places around the globe are experimenting with using encryption techniques to send e-mail anonymously. Finland is at the cutting edge in this area. You can send an e-mail message with a forwarding address to a university in Finland. This institution will forward your mail anonymously.

The U.S. government wants to create a national encryption standard with a key escrow plan. This plan is like giving the government a spare set of keys to your personal data, whether it be financial, medical, or private communications. The government wants easy access to conduct investigations. Government law-enforcement agencies want to be able to conduct legal surveillance in the digital world of cyberspace much as they already can with telephone communications. The National Security Agency view seems to be that without a chance to eavesdrop, there is a possibility of disaster at the hands of hackers, malicious vandals, or worse, trespassing enemies opposed to the government.

Many citizens and members of government are convinced that wiretaps are crucial to the ability of law enforcement to protect society. The opposing viewpoint is that the government is sacrificing the individual's right to privacy for the sake of an erroneous idea of national security. Those who hold this opposing viewpoint fear that the government's encryption standard will be established in a way that will allow the government to break secret codes even without keys.

MONEY MATTERS
Regarding cryptography policy that protects financial transactions, it seems that the technology developed by Visa and Mastercard will become the standard. Thus far it has been referred to as Secured Electronic Transaction, or SET. It eliminates the need to have a merchant ever see your credit card number. With this program, you will swipe or type in your card number and it will appear in code. Not even you will see the number on your screen. The card number and amount will be sent directly to the merchant bank. The bank will then either authorize or deny your transaction with the business. The secure code will be known only to Visa and Mastercard—and, some believe, the federal government.

THE WEB'S TANGLES: ITS EVOLVING FUTURE
A few pages back I addressed the stuntperson inside you. Remember the falling and bruising I referred to? Keep that in mind. You are setting a course through unmapped territory, and that is daunting. Risk brings excitement. That is why we are exploring cyberspace anyway, right? The Internet has brought an enormous amount of hype, expectations, and confusion with its entrance into the economy. At the moment, quite a few observers are saying that the Internet is not living up to its promise.

Thus far, the Internet has had little effect on the public's consumption of traditional media, such as print, television, and radio. Web publishing in particular is feeling the pangs of being part of a developing industry. Because of the limited technology and the infancy of cyberspace, cyberspace ventures are having trouble competing with traditional media. Many cyberspace companies want to tap the cable television market with its music, movies, sports, and fashion. In cyberspace, however, the consumer must deal with the setbacks of download times, limited hardware capabilities, and line interruptions.

Cyberspace companies also have to deal with limited funds. The World Wide Web is free, and it will be difficult to change that. Whereas cable television has commercials and cable subscribers to pay for everything, cyberspace companies must battle to persuade companies to include banner advertisements on their pages. Attempts by cyberspace companies to have individuals pay subscription rates for visiting their pages have met with great resistance.

These obstacles have had an impact on the economy. In the last months of 1996 the NASDAQ, the technology listings for the stock market, experienced what is referred to as a market correction. The value of the NASDAQ listings fell 15 percent as a whole. This may reflect a waning enthusiasm for a technologies market that is filled with stocks, especially Web stocks, of inflated worth.

Until there is a clearer sense of what the consumer wants, Internet companies will be fighting to find their niche in the market. And with this search for a clearer vision come the inevitable fluctuations in Web employment opportunities. In 1995, there was an incredible demand for Web workers. Internet companies were hiring at a furious pace and at exorbitant pay rates. People with little or no experience were being hired at pay rates that were twice the entry-level salaries of traditional media positions.

Amy Yang, with whom you will spend some quality time in chapter 5, related a story to me. Amy's climb through the cyberspace ranks is a story that, until recently, was typical. The extent of her cyberspace experience was a few hours of study in college. She had taken a publishing course at the university that had included the Internet and the basics of HTML (Hyper Text Markup Language). She was hired more for her art background and sense of style than for her Internet experience. One day she was on the telephone with a client, who unwittingly informed her that she had been promoted to a new position: "*Well, I was just told that you were the manager . . .*" She had become a project manager and did not even know it.

But that is changing. Competition is fierce, and a sense of efficiency is being developed within cyberspace companies. It is increasingly obvious that profits are hard to come by in cyberspace. You are here to help the Internet find its legs. Cyberspace offers companies the freedom to publish many alternative ideas that traditional media would be unable to touch. Cyberspace gives a company freedom to give immediate news and sports updates. There are numerous opportunities for you to find your place on the Web. This is where your creativity and enthusiasm come into play.

Scott Brodeur puts it this way: "Two years ago, breathing could get you a job in cyberspace. Little or no online experience was necessary, but now cyberspace companies can be selective and demand skills." The employment opportunities are still out there. The money can still be made. Your imagination, talent, and drive must be readily apparent and ready to be applied.

Cyberspace is booming for many service ventures. Cyber-cafes are booming. Companies like Lotus are creating Web software that allows you to use cyberspace as a global office. Reservation-related businesses are the number one growth area online; business is quadrupling, and 80 percent of the market is still untouched. Biztravel.com is a company that delivers airline, hotel, and car-rental reservations over the Internet and has revenues in the double-digit millions.

If the future of cyberspace is really losing a bit of its luster, why is every major electronics corporation in a rush to catch up with their forerunners in the Web TV market? Why does the battle grow ever more heated between Microsoft's Explorer and Netscape's namesake browser? MCI has been developing answers to the technological challenges facing today's Internet. Their "Very-High-Performance Backbone Network Service," built on the existing fiber optics networks, is part of what is being termed the second-generation Internet. AT&T and Sprint are working toward President Clinton's "next-generation Internet" initiative that he announced in October 1996. The new Internet will have a capacity of more than 20,000 times the present capacity of most computer modems, and video will be integrated into the new network.

As one area of the Internet reaches its limit, another branch is sure to blossom. In a new industry, time will bring new opportunities and new hazards. The Internet may have lost a little pomp, but I contend that it has lost none of its power or mystique. What I believe has happened is that conventional wisdom has failed a limited number of cyberspace companies. Now is the time for you to choose the path less taken.

The New Millennium

New battles are certain to arise in cyberspace. The fact that there are ideas and values worth arguing for speaks of cyberspace's growing prominence in our lives. In his Internet initiative, President Clinton mandated that every school be connected to the Internet by the year 2000. The Web's ability to disseminate information promises to have a truly democratic effect on our population. The Web's usage will be bolstered and its mission enhanced.

As generations pass on, certain kinds of knowledge are lost. Perhaps less knowledge will vanish as more minds reach cyberspace. The vast library that is the Internet may prove to be the repository of human knowledge. It can act to preserve ideas, techniques, and information that would otherwise be lost. I have great hope for the future of cyberspace.

2

Before You Start

In this book you will learn about specific jobs in cyberspace. But no matter what job you may decide is right for you, a few suggestions will make your reading of this book even more valuable.

- **The Big Picture.** Learn as much as you can about *all* of the jobs available in cyberspace. As you read, think about the needs of cyberspace companies and about how a company benefits from the skills of the various employees. The more you understand the big picture, the better you will be able to present yourself to a company as someone who will benefit that company.
- **The Basics.** Some basic skills are important. The ability to write clearly and well and a knowledge of HTML and basic programming are musts.
- **Preparation.** Education—particularly college education—is essential. Knowledge of the Internet, computers, and various software packages is, of course, important. But it is also vital that you learn about the rest of life as well. Go to college and earn a four-year degree. This will make you a better problem solver and also a more well-rounded person.
- **The Internship.** One of the best and most common ways to secure a paying job in the field

of cyberspace is first to get an unpaid internship with a cyberspace company. This is usually a summer job. Although you will not receive pay, you will receive training on some of the best computers and software available. If you perform well at the company, they may offer you a paid position for the following summer. This is true no matter what type of job in cyberspace interests you.
- **The Résumé and Portfolio.** Although résumés and portfolios are only part of the job hunt, they are important. Prepare them and ask someone, such as a teacher or guidance counselor, to go over them with you. Preparation of résumés and portfolios is discussed at length in chapter 9.
- **The Job Hunt.** Searching for a job can take many forms. Pay attention to the stories of the people interviewed in this book. They will help you understand how best to proceed.

Chapter 9 discusses the job search in greater detail, as well as the setting up of your own homepage. Chapter 10 recommends books, software, and Web sites that will be of value to anyone wishing to get a better sense of the possibilities available in cyberspace.

Keeping pace with the changes on the Web is as difficult as keeping up with the fashion trends that find their way into your school hallways. I have tried to offer examples of Web sites for you to visit that will be available to you for years to come. Yet, with new companies entering and ever new ideas being experimented with, a steady supply of challenging and profitable positions is available in cyberspace. The rapid turnover rate for World Wide Web addresses is an inevitable result, as employees change jobs and companies change their pages to keep their sites fresh.

If an address in this book does not download it may be under renovation or it may have been set aside temporarily as features are rotated to keep sites interesting for the consumer. In rare cases, an address may have been permanently removed.

If a site discussed by a cyberspace employee is no longer available, rest assured that the advice given by the interviewee is nonetheless timely and sound.

Cyberspace is a wonderful and ever-changing place. Work hard—and enjoy yourself.

3

Programmers

Programmers form the backbone of their cyberspace companies. Their responsibilities cover all the bases in the daily operations of their company. Alan S. Ellman, owner and president of Interactive Connection, says, "Programmers are some of the most confident people in the world. I come from a family of doctors and surgeons, and I feel that programmers are more confident than doctors because each day programmers come to work, they solve new problems. Programmers can do anything; it's just a question of time and resources."

Programmers are the shop foremen of cyberspace. They keep the office productive and efficient. They develop new programs and adapt old ones. They troubleshoot and problem-solve. And programmers are compensated generously for their work. An experienced programmer can command anywhere from $70,000 to $100,000 a year. At the entry level a programmer can expect $30,000 to $45,000, depending on his technical skills and college coursework. Keep in mind, however, that the hours may be grueling.

WORK ATMOSPHERE
Interactive Connection is a company that creates Web pages. It also sells syndicated content to major corporations, which add this material to their own Web pages. Interactive Connection's client list includes such

household names as Ralph Lauren, Sports Channel, the *New York Times*, Univision, and Weider Publishing.

The offices of Interactive Connection are located in an expansive seventh-floor space on Fifth Avenue in New York City. Only antique columns interrupt the massive open space that would more resemble a roller rink than an office, if it weren't for the cubicles that form a maze for the visitor.

Upon closer examination the room begins to fit into the realm of cyberspace. I wouldn't try rollerblading there after all. Wires run everywhere. New hardware pops up in corners, and a lot of equipment is still in boxes. The atmosphere runs toward the eclectic. A few walls are decorated with jointed compound sculptures that seem to burst from inside the walls. The space provided for client and staff meetings contains dark wood furniture with aubergine upholstery.

The cubicles are decorated to fit the personalities of the people who work within them for the extended hours they spend there. A giant stereo system with tower speakers is found in Aryeh Goldsmith's space. Plastic toys and figures adorn Amy Yang's cube. One of the "walls" of Jinnah Hosein's cubicle is a plastic sheet because the wall was constantly being taken down to run more and more wires to keep up with the need. The sheet is somehow emblematic of the constantly changing world that is cyberspace. Posters and photos are the wallpaper elsewhere.

JINNAH: DISCIPLINE AND CURIOSITY

The programmers belong in this funky atmosphere. Jinnah, whom I met first, is the picture of Generation X grunge. With his shoulder-length hair and baggy clothes, he could easily be confused for one of the generation's minions. However, at nineteen, and already an indispensable summer employee with Interactive Connection, he is far from displaying the lack of direction that sometimes characterizes his generation. He is currently attending Vassar College and is, for the most part, a self-taught technician. To him, self-discipline is a key factor in being a successful programmer.

Jinnah began working with computers when he was ten years old. He had mastered the MS·DOS (the old Microsoft disk operating system) soon after. By the time he was thirteen, he was working summers with computers at his father's company. Each summer after that, he gathered more and more experience and knowledge. When his high school began installing its computer system, he worked with the company contracted for the job and was eventually hired by them.

The combination of networking and maintenance that the company taught him, and the self-taught expertise he had with UNIX and the system's administration, led him to study computer science at college. At Interactive Connection, he is involved with the daily maintenance of the server, and he provides programming for the Web pages the company develops. When the full-time staff runs into difficulties, he is called upon to assist them in developing programs to solve the problems.

Jinnah says that in order to become a programmer, you have to play around and ask yourself, "I have a task that I want to do. How do I get it done?" This curiosity is what makes for a successful programmer.

"You have to want to understand," Jinnah adds. "You have to ask questions and find people who can answer those questions." He believes that the computer has a rather basic methodology and that when you begin to understand it, all the pieces fall together. From that point on, you can begin to anticipate what another programmer might have done to achieve the result you want.

"There are things you can do to place yourself in the right place at the right time," he says, and I believe him, seeing how fast and far he has come. Almost a decade younger than me, he is in a position of responsibility at Interactive Connection. He recommends getting involved with your school's computer department and talking with your service provider's technicians to find solutions to any questions you have.

As for education, he believes that his liberal arts background at Vassar College has been most appropriate for his work. He thinks that having only a technical background is often limiting. Most helpful to him, outside of his technical expertise, have been discipline and his teaching skills. "The discipline that I need for this career comes from all ranges of education. My technical knowledge is useless unless I can assist others and explain to them what's going on." He is constantly being called upon to share his knowledge with the staff, so his language and writing skills are just as important as the programming languages he works with.

ARYEH: DILIGENCE AND THE ART OF PROGRAMMING

Aryeh Goldsmith, another programmer, is quick to explain that programming languages are not the basics of problem-solving. "They help to organize your thoughts and to focus you on working through the different steps, but programming can't be learned." Aryeh is a serious guy, so let me explain what he means by that ominous statement.

He is getting at the artistry behind computer programming. When you begin exploring computers in cyberspace, you have to learn the language that your computer speaks. All cyberspace programmers know

Unix, C, and C++ languages. You work to understand these languages so that you can see how your computer talks to itself. What you've learned is the architecture of your computer.

An artistic touch is needed to make that knowledge of computer architecture career-worthy. To be a programmer, you need to be able to use programming language to tell the computer what you want it to do. What Aryeh is saying is that this part—putting the language into practice—cannot be easily taught. "There's no one solution. Any way you get it to work is the right way."

Aryeh, too, is nineteen years old. He is studying computers at Brooklyn College. He wears his baseball cap backward and sports a goatee. Aryeh is philosophical about his work, if you haven't already noticed. Like his coworkers, it was his curiosity that brought him to programming. "I like to make and solve puzzles and create gadgets." Programming is an extension of this passion. He is currently at work creating a program to write guitar tablature on the Web.

Aryeh's official title at Interactive Connection is programmer/Web developer. On a daily basis he pores over the entire Web site and creates whatever scripts, or programs, are needed to adjust and improve the system. He writes "feeds" as well. Feeds are similar to templates, patterns used as guides to form a page. In this case, the feeds that Aryeh creates will make the Web site more useful to users. The feeds will form pages suited to the user's needs, categorize the subject matter, create links to other Web sites, and format graphics, or "gifs," as they are called on the Web, on the fly. All his company has to do is feed in a client's text for a Web site. Everything that was mentioned above will be created from that information, without anyone's touching another button. Aryeh's template lays it all out for them.

When I asked him what he had been working on recently, he told me the following story. Yesterday, a client had phoned in requesting that Interactive Connection remove the zeros that are placed before the months in the dates that appear on their Web pages. I was there on July 24, or (07/24), according to the old feed for the company's Web pages. So Aryeh had to turn to his feed and write a program that would search page by page and remove any zeros that preceded the first nine months of the year. "You take the task and break it into smaller and smaller steps, using the programming language to make the task understandable to the computer."

After some deliberation and many trials, he created a program. It first searched through the entire Web site and identified each page with an open parenthesis and a zero following it, or "(0." Next, he had the computer record the name of each file in which this "(0" format was found. Having located each instance of the offending zeros, he could write a program to have them removed. "And that's what I did, pretty much, yesterday," he said with his dry sense of humor.

This example illustrates what Aryeh means by saying that programming can't be learned. You can't teach the art of problem-solving per se. You can learn the basics of logical progression and can understand the principles guiding your computer's operating processes. After that, it's all about practice. The more you work with the language and tasks, the better you will be at creating programs to achieve the results you are seeking. As Aryeh so delicately puts it, "You need the butt for this career. You have to be able to sit there and work on a problem without getting discouraged." Diligence is what Aryeh cites as the key ingredient to success in cyberspace.

Aryeh says that he is constantly buying books, and that is how he has learned nearly everything necessary for his career. "When you want to learn a new language you buy a book, read it, work with it, and talk to other people." This is how he is staying ahead of trends with new programming languages, such as Java. He heard about it about two years ago from a professor. A few days later he bought the book and started talking to other people who had seen Java or were already working with it. He looked at other programmers' code and was soon working with it. "When you start working with a new or different programming language, you don't switch what you are doing or how you are thinking, you just switch the way you write it."

LEARN FROM OTHERS

Aryeh just mentioned another key to cyberspace programming: You can look at other people's code or programming. Netscape, the most frequently used Web browser, allows anyone who's surfing the Web to view the source of the page they are looking at. When you see a great-looking page on the Web, you can go to the "View" command on the menu bar at the top of the screen and drag to the "Source" command. Voilà, you can see the HTML that makes up the cool-looking page.

This is how almost everyone I spoke to got their start. It's not cheating. It's perfectly legal and acceptable to find out how another programmer did something unique. You can then try to use that technique to create your own stunning designs.

CHRISTOPHER: PRACTICE, PRACTICE, PRACTICE

Christopher Park's involvement with cyberspace began as a surfing hobby, and he rode the wave to a position of leadership. As systems operator at Interactive Connection, Christopher is top dog of the programmers.

He has his college degree, is well spoken, and at the ripe old age of twenty-three is a senior figure at the company. In no other industry can you find this combination of youth and success.

To break into a career in cyberspace, he recommends, "Set up an account with a Web service provider, take a look at what's out there, source other pages, and have fun with it." To make the transition from a hobby to a career, he just stuck to his own advice. Like so many others, Christopher is for the most part self-taught. "Computer science is largely like math, in that practice is the only way to get familiar with it. Don't be afraid or intimidated by it. Follow a logical pattern and keep plugging away at it."

Christopher arrives at work around 8:30 each morning and immediately begins his maintenance and troubleshooting regimen. He checks to see that each of the servers is up and running smoothly. He then turns his attention to whatever scripts and programs he has been working on. Any problems that arise during the day are also his responsibility—and, believe me, they arise. Christopher's was the one interview that was continuously interrupted as his coworkers came to him for answers to their troubles.

He told me about a program that he recently wrote that will make his life as systems operator a little easier. They have a "chron" at his office. It's a clock that keeps all of the computers and electronic devices synchronized, so that the entire operation runs together.

Christopher wrote a program to check that the ticker feeds, another element of their business, were always in sync with the rest of the system. (A familiar example of a ticker feed is the stock market quotes feed. When you watch the news on some television channels you can see the prices of stocks racing by as they are posted with up-to-the minute changes.) Since Interactive runs syndicated sites such as the *New York Times* Web page, they need ticker feed information to update their pages. If Christopher's program spots a ticker feed that is out of sync with the chron, it means that the ticker feed has been interrupted. Christopher's program will then e-mail him and cause his computer to beep to notify him that an e-mail message has been received.

Christopher enjoys his position because of the excitement and challenge of it. He feels that his job is new every day, and he's thrilled when he learns something new. The only drawback to his work has been the public's lack of familiarity with what the Web is best suited for. He thinks that many of Interactive Connection's clients have seen too many movies about the Web and that these businesses don't understand its limitations. His clients want real-time video and audio and fancy graphics work, which cannot always be done and usually isn't practical. Computers that most consumers have would not be able to download these pages because they would simply take up too much memory.

Freedom and Pressure
Programmers remind me of the independent filmmakers that you see on public television. They have better and more important things to think about than their own appearance. They are not slovenly or untidy, but most cannot be bothered with maintaining a corporate image. They are simply too busy getting and keeping things running to worry about such things. Neckties will not make them better thinkers, and with the hours that they sometimes work, their ties would simply get mangled.

Joe Schwartz, a cyberspace programmer with NPS Associates, *www.npsa.com/npsa/*, says that the freedom that programmers are given to dress as they choose lends a certain credibility to their work. "Scuzzy guys who are just into the machines lend credibility to the job, because that's what people expect to see. It's weird.... Because clients can't read computer code, they want to see computer trendiness in the programming pit."

Joe's job is currently situated in his boss' apartment in Brooklyn. He is the Windows programmer in a five-person office. His main responsibility is to write programs that allow a client's computers to work with cyberspace browsers. He enables a company's intranet (their internal computer network, linking computers in the office) to be plugged into the Internet, allowing office-wide access to cyberspace.

When I asked how he developed his computer skills, he joked that it was a result of a "lack of friends." He added, "If you're a kid that takes everything apart and puts it back together, you'll turn to computers sooner or later."

If the programmers are modest about the energy they pour into their work, their coworkers definitely are not. Amy Yang, a project manager with Interactive Connection, told me a story about a programmer who spent the better part of four days producing a Web site to get it done by the deadline. He couldn't be found on the day of the meeting with the client. Amy kept handling the phone calls from the client as calmly as possible, assuring the person at the other end of the line that the programmer would be in soon. Later that afternoon she spotted the groggy programmer walking by her cubicle. It turns out that he had spent the past three nights at work completing the project. He had just awoken from a much-needed rest following his third consecutive all-nighter. The client was well satisfied with the work, but it took a rather steep physical toll on Amy's coworker.

Is Programming for You?

Are you ready to help form the infrastructure of a company? You can be your own person and express yourself as you see fit. But you also have to possess the facility to put in grueling hours. In cyberspace you are given a lot of responsibility and then sometimes left on your own to pioneer your own answers. Discipline, diligence, curiosity, creativity, and practice are all required.

When I asked Joe Schwartz what nontechnical experiences in his life had been most helpful to him as a programmer in cyberspace, he answered that his days as a bike messenger and the lessons he learned from that job were most helpful. "I learned how to buckle down and get the job done. You can't really zone out or you'll get hurt or worse." Those words will either inspire or threaten you.

If programming does not sound like the job for you, you will be happy to know that there's much more to cyberspace than programming. Not all of the jobs involve extensive computer knowledge. Let's move along and visit some other careers in cyberspace.

4

Writers and Producers

Writers and producers give a Web site the interesting and imaginative flair that will keep surfers coming back after the visual thrills have lost their impact. They create the content that will be appropriate for this new medium. Their work has to be easily grasped and easily digestible. Simply reformatting a magazine for the Web will not pass muster in this heavily trafficked space.

Producers, like writers, are actively involved in creating original text for Web sites. The distinction between the two is that the producer is also responsible for creating additional material in the form of new features and pages. The writer brings fresh ideas to the column, and the producer develops still newer columns and pages.

Writers who are just entering cyberspace can expect to earn about $25,000 a year. The money grows steadily as you move toward the role of producer. Associate producers earn about $30,000, and an executive producer can be compensated at $100,000 a year.

THE WORKPLACE

Let's continue our exploration by visiting the offices of New Jersey Online (NJO), *www.nj.com*. NJO has combined journalistic excellence with the possibilities offered by cyberspace to create an online newspaper. New Jersey Online gets noticed: It receives approximately 50,000 users per month who read 800,000 to 1,000,000 pages per month. NJO won the 1996 NAA (Newspaper Association of America) Digital Edge Award for "America's Best Online Newspaper." The firm is located in Journal Square, Jersey City, New Jersey.

NJO's offices are a showcase of modern computer furnishings. The deskspaces are large, amoeba-like areas that allow you to swing about in your chair and find what you need. The writer's or producer's keyboard and mouse are suspended before him or her like a fighter pilot's joystick, floating and responsive.

The atmosphere is loose and brilliantly creative. At times the staff hums along in harmony, and at other times each person is lost in his or her own world. Imagine that you are a writer. You have a project, let's say it's updating the Maxwell's Web site, *www.nj.com/maxwells.*

Located in nearby Hoboken, Maxwell's is an alternative rock club. Their Web site is a big part of NJO's regional appeal. Your task is to write a review of a band that will be performing there in the near future. You put the disk into the CD drive, position your headphones, crank the volume to your damage level, and let the music shape the text below your byline. Where else are you paid to sit in absolute comfort and write your assessment of the latest bands? Let's hear what the staff writers have to say about their place in cyberspace.

ART: STAFF WRITER AND CREATIVE WRITER

Art Pardavilla III studied journalism in college. He wrote as both a columnist and sports editor. Art responded to an ad that NJO had placed in the Help Wanted section of the classifieds for a "Cyber Reporter." Soon after he was working in cyberspace as the sports editor at NJO.

It is fortunate that the atmosphere is comfortable, because Art's job is demanding. The hours between 7:00 a.m. and 9:00 a.m. are his toughest. When he arrives he takes the sports stories from the electronic news feed, which delivers up-to-the-minute stories, and edits them. He places the edited text in the HTML templates and then puts them on the server (NJO's Web site). He must then prepare the index for the sports stories, write the front page for the sports section, and sometimes write non-sports news. And there are plenty of times when he is involved in writing the headline for the whole site.

He creates links to each story so that readers can easily move from one story to the next, much like turning the page. He must then choose appropriate photos and graphics to use with the stories. He also comes up with his trademark catchy titles and headlines. Once he has finished all of this, he begins his tweaking of the sites—fine-tuning the presentation—to make sure all of his work is up and ready for people to read. By 9:00 a.m., he is done.

Art spends the rest of his day making sure the sports and news stay fresh. He checks the news wire every fifteen minutes and puts any breaking stories into the templates. He reads voraciously to earn his keep. In one day, Art will read either from hard copies or on the Web the *Los Angeles Times*, the *New York Times*, and the *Washington Post*, among several others. He is also responsible for cruising other Web pages and keeping track of what is new and exciting out there in space. Beyond all this, though, he cherishes the time that he spends working on his namesake column, "Art Naked."

It was always his dream to get some of his creative writing published. "Art Naked," *www.nj.com/artnaked*, is part of that dream. His column is a uniquely interesting tour guide of his world, complete with pictures of his friends and their exploits together. It's a perfect example of the kind of entertainment that one can find only in cyberspace. "I write raw, and that's a great thing. I don't think you could ever find my column in a newspaper. In cyberspace the gloves are off, and I can say and do whatever I want. I love working and putting stuff on the Net. It's what the alternative press was twenty years ago." Art recommends: "If you really enjoy the Web and computing and can combine good writing skills with an eye for design, being a staff writer for an online newspaper might be the perfect opportunity for you."

Tricia: Producer

This combination of the freedom to write in one's own style and to showcase one's artistic qualities also attracted two wonderfully talented producers to cyberspace.

"Jersey Girl," *www.nj.com/hot/jerseygirl*, is the fashion spokeswoman for NJO. Her alias is Tricia Nelson, and she is an associate producer. She is one of the first graduates of Columbia University's New Media Program, where she was fashion producer for the student on-line publication.

Tricia is most enticed by the flexibility that cyberspace offers. She can break a lot of rules that she would have to follow if she were working in print publications. "You can step right out of school and become an editor; that's unheard of in publishing. If there's a typo on a page, I can go in and fix it *after* it has been published. I can change a design an hour after it goes up. You are not locked into an inflexible way of thinking, and that's what I like about it!"

Tricia emphasizes that producers need to explore new ways of thinking and utilizing their communication skills. "You have to know how to think in 3-D," she says cryptically. "You have to use all of your senses at the same time. Be a forward thinker." For a Web page to be effective at grabbing the viewer's attention, you have to be more than a wordsmith. You have to think in terms of sight and sound in your presentation, as well as developing a unique writing voice.

Tricia recommends to people who are interested in writing or producing that they spend a lot of time surfing. "See what's going on, and realize the trends. It shapes your way of thinking, and you learn what sensory-type stimulants you have to work with." Tricia gives her forecast of trends in cyberspace: "I think the sites that are going to do the best in the next two years are the ones that are targeted to young girls, preteens to early teens. That's a market ripe for the tapping."

The fact that cyberspace is changing and dynamic just keeps things interesting, and Tricia wouldn't have it any other way. Her biggest fear about cyberspace is that it will get bogged down if people stick to old patterns instead of moving forward with the technology. "We must have higher expectations."

Trisha: Producer and Editor

"Cyberspace is our chance to be pioneers. We get to recreate the rules!" Trisha Smith is an exciting person, and she grabs your attention with bold strokes. If her striking, elbow-to-shoulder tattoo doesn't trigger a response, her enthusiasm for the weather will. Trisha made me realize that weather prediction is an art. "Trying to put up a weather predicting mechanism on the Web has never been done before." And she has just the creative energy to do it, at *www.nj.com/ros/weather/njo*.

As a producer and editor, she engages all of her faculties in her work. Trisha describes her challenge: conceptualizing what people would want in a five-day forecast. "Deciding what information is most useful and how to present it in a way that is easy to access is not a straightforward matter," she observes. Her facility for abstraction helps her to make her page interesting and useful. She can't offer either too much or too little information, so she has to interpret what will be best for her audience.

Trisha's education in dance has been helpful in her cyberspace career. "The dance experience helps when you're trying to think in a nonlinear way, and that's the mold that we're trying to break—the linear mold of journalism."

Trisha is inspired by the creative freedom of cyberspace. "There is a lot of room for self-starters and creative types." Her tattoo can tell us much about her. The design is of a dragon rising from ashes, like a phoenix. The dragon is a symbol of luck and change in Chinese culture. The idea that strength can rise from ashes speaks volumes of her will. "Everyone is overworked because big visions are hard to realize." She and her colleagues are helping to reinvent the journalistic wheel.

SCOTT: SENIOR PRODUCER

Scott Brodeur is also constantly on the lookout for new ideas and trying to develop new projects. He had been spinning comfortably along on that wheel for some time before cyberspace's call pulled him into the fray. Scott had written for numerous magazines and newspapers before NJO recruited him. He loves the rapid change that he sees daily. "Cyberspace is an ever-evolving, ever-changing medium. It's the first time in our history, I think, that we've ever had a medium that can reinvent itself without the exorbitant costs of printing."

As senior producer, Scott's responsibilities "run all over the place." He wears a lot of hats. He is involved in sports, news, entertainment, and features. His position as morning front page editor takes up most of his daily energy. Each morning at 7:00 a meeting is held about what news will be put up on the server. There is discussion about the headlines and what graphics will accompany each news story. In addition, one of Scott's most profound marks on NJO is his music column, jointly written by Scott and his colleague, Scott Hersey.

"Scotts on Sound," *www.nj.com/arts/music/sos*, has been referred to as "the Siskel and Ebert of music." It is an entertaining and sometimes bitter battle of opinions concerning new releases by a wide range of musical artists. The two critics give each other a week-and-a-half's notice of their choice of two CDs to be reviewed in the next issue. They write their reviews and e-mail each other with their retorts to one another's views over a four-day period. Scott listens to a CD at least three times and some songs as many as fifteen times before passing judgment. The writing for the upcoming page has to be done by Monday afternoon. Each week, on Tuesday evening, a new installment of four music reviews by Scotts Hersey and Brodeur is available to the Web-browsing public.

Writer's Block

Just as these writers and producers are drawn by the thrill of cyberspace's racing pace, they are also wearied by it. When they began New Jersey Online they put themselves under tremendous stress to be timely and get news up under a deadline. Now, Scott Brodeur says, as a story breaks an instantaneous response is *expected* of them, which adds even more stress.

Writing in cyberspace takes a lot of brainwork, some of which is unconventional. The thoroughly modern offices of NJO have all of the stresses and strains of a magazine or newspaper boardroom, but with a much smaller staff. Art says that his college experiences were most helpful in preparing him for this work. "Living on my own, carrying a full course load, and reporting full-time for the campus newspaper readied me for hard work."

The atmosphere among producers is only slightly less daunting than in the programming pit. Here, the challenge to make your work appealing to consumers is tantamount to securing your livelihood. Magazines and newspapers are far more convenient media for reading. The producer's job is to make his or her concepts and writing unique and intriguing so that an audience will take the time to download the producer's work. Writing is not exactly a contact sport, yet it will test your stamina. Read on to learn about the people who help bring writers' and producers' work to life by making their Web sites brilliantly attractive.

5

Designers

You probably consider yourself a creative person, which is why you are reading a book about careers in the field of cyberspace.

In addition, you may be less interested in limits or rules than many of your peers. Consider these questions: Are you a doodler? Do you constantly find yourself sketching, animating, or painting? Are you currently serving a detention for a caricature you drew of your biology teacher? If you have answered yes to any of these questions, then this is your chapter.

Designers capture a Web site's audience. They render ideas aesthetically pleasing. A designer works to keep the site fresh, developing new page layouts and color schemes and enhancing the logo.

A design director can command around $70,000 a year. An assistant design director works for about half as much. Project managers, depending on their workload, make anywhere from $25,000 to $30,000.

JIMMY: ASSISTANT DESIGNER

Jimmy Santos is an assistant designer at New Jersey Online. He considered himself an artist throughout his high school years, although he was not sure what he wanted to do with his talents. Jimmy was not really interested in becoming a starving artist. He decided to attend the University of Buffalo and study graphic

Designers

design. "I knew I wasn't going to be a painter. So I took it in another direction, where I used computers as my foundation and let the technology take me where it goes," he says.

By the time he graduated, he had been working heavily with print and graphic design and had moved toward multimedia applications and production. He went to work for a CD-ROM production company and acquired advanced skills with the latest technology. Jimmy saw the trend in the technologies shifting toward multimedia applications for the Web. He created his own CD-ROM, filled with examples of his work, and vigorously sought out an Internet career.

Jimmy loves working in cyberspace and at NJO. He loves the exciting atmosphere and the support he gets from working with such creative people. "I'm always learning from my peers. Once you're in a big boat, you've got to stay in, 'cause once you jump out you're swimming for your life," he says.

At NJO he's on the inside track and able to keep up with the pace of cyberspace. Our conversation was interrupted numerous times by coworkers who needed his assistance. Jimmy was asked to create various images, locate others, and give time estimates on designs.

His whole day is like that. He arrives at work by 7:30 a.m. and immediately begins the process of working on the morning updates, which must be launched by 9:00. Just as Art, the staff writer, uses the first part of his day to prepare the editorial content, Jimmy uses that time to prepare the design for the online newspaper. He prepares the graphics first.

"We have to make the graphics more interesting than what we get from the newspapers, which is simple gray scale stuff. We colorize and try to make them funky," Jimmy explains. He must then lay out the headlines and work with the font spacing on the page to ensure an aesthetically pleasing page. The remainder of his day is usually spent working on long-term projects.

He's currently involved in creating the Journal Square Interactive site. "We're trying to make a site for Journal Square, a publishing conglomerate, that will reflect on us, in terms of what we can do, what kind of designs we can come up with, and what we can offer. It's like a promotional piece," Jimmy says of his current project. After he has finalized the initial design, the difficult work begins.

As a designer, you have to compromise, sometimes changing your ideas to suit the producers, who may have developed that page, and the company directors, who have the final word on all projects.

"It's very tense. Just when you do something that's very appealing to you, you show it to the marketing people or editorial staff, and they say, 'Can you do this or that?' It's back and forth, that's how design works." He continues, "You have to fight back. You have to sell that job. You have to sell your design. You have to say why you did what you did. There's always a debate."

This work, known as editorial design, is demanding and can be disappointing at times. Editorial design entails matching the artwork to the text content. In other words, most cyberspace design complements a body of text or a company style. In cyberspace you may be designing to suit a specific aesthetic ideal. It is not a case of compromising your artistic integrity. Your role is to make a design that enhances the content of the Web page and that pleases many different people with differing tastes and needs. And if you think about it, a design that pleases the Internet market can be considered a masterpiece.

Jimmy sometimes finds it hard to swallow when he is asked to change a color or an important section of a logo he had labored over for some time. "I have no idea why they have the say and I don't. I just don't get that. I mean, you go to school for design, and you show your work to people who went to school for journalism, and it's just different how you interact," he says with honesty. "It always seems worth it, though, when the final product gets published."

Jimmy is constantly learning, relearning, and trying to keep up. He daily uses Quark, Illustrator, Photoshop, and HTML. "In two years you won't be using what you're using now. It's scary, but it's not a waste," he says. As cyberspace changes, so will Jimmy. He regularly updates his own skills as he updates the pages. And he would not change a thing. "Cyberspace is free, fun, and different," he says.

He thinks that cyberspace is a great place to work and that it will keep growing in popularity. He argues, "People are sick of TV, that's why the Internet is popular. It's the same concept as TV, but you have the control." Jimmy believes that cyberspace will eventually win the battle of media.

As for your own job search, he gives this advice, "Go all out and look for the best. Read and find anything computer-based, and don't stop at learning one program. Put together a portfolio."

In short, he recommends that you learn all you can about design programs and design. Locate the best Web sites and CD-ROMs. Acquaint yourself with books and magazines that update you on state-of-the-art computer technology and trends. He concludes, "If you have the gift or desire to design and draw, don't stop."

Amy: Project Manager

Amy Yang of Interactive Connection has a different perspective on a designer's work environment. She is on the frontlines of product design. Jimmy sits in a design room filled with scale models of action cartoon characters. He creates in an area designated for that very purpose. Amy, on the other hand, deals directly with Interactive Connection's clients. This leaves her with no zone of contemplative space. She has a wonderful sense of humor about her position.

When I asked Amy to describe cyberspace for me, she said, "A pain in the butt," and then she laughed. She was viewing it through the lens of her duties at work. "There's too much material to look through in a research sense." The Web's explosive growth is both bounty and bane for Amy. She found work in cyberspace, yet she sometimes finds it hard to work in a place of such abundance. "There's a lot of junk out there that you have to surf through," she adds.

Amy is an extremely talented and creative person. Her work space, her clothing, and her attitude are all evidence of her creativity. She studies photography and has brought her sense of design to Interactive Connection, where she works on up to four sites a day. She took a publishing course at the university where she learned the basics of HTML and has since worked her way up to the position of project manager.

Her responsibilities include gathering the graphics, text, and advertising for the site and then processing all of it, organizing it into a readable design. She uses these elements to create the layout and then has to place it in cyberspace. She has learned to match scripts, read image maps, and write advanced HTML.

"It's easy!" she says. "I like the fact that you're smarter than computers. You can make them do stuff. You control them. Once you figure them out, they work for you," she says. The day before I arrived, she had selected sixty images from a slide library for various Web pages that she would build. She spent all day processing them, producing computer-ready images, and then compressing them for use on the Web. She concludes, "Working all day, you quickly pick it up."

Amy works to meet the client's wishes and demands. She spends a lot of time on the telephone.

"You see what people A want, and you tell people B what to do. But sometimes I get different answers from different people at A, and then I have to check with people C," Amy says, her eyes crossed in exasperation.

MAURICE: DESIGN DIRECTOR

Both Amy and Jimmy have dealt with the difficulties sometimes associated with negotiating Web page design with clients. This seems to be a major drawback in this career area. But a seasoned professional in the design field brings a different perspective, viewing the process as a design challenge.

"That's what gives you the most satisfaction as a designer—that you have taken what other people could only talk about and made it something they can see," says Maurice Williams. Having regularly battled to maintain his designs at a print newspaper, his voice rings with ripened reasoning.

Maurice is the design director at New Jersey Online. He recently completed the task of redesigning the entire NJO site.

"Though everybody was happy with the final product, getting the design through management can be quite a task," he says. In all, the process took Maurice and his staff nearly six months to complete. The managers had different ideas about how certain features of NJO's service should be represented. Special attention was paid to features to ensure that they were given appropriate emphasis in terms of size and location on the pages. It was not easy for Maurice to provide results that would please all of the managers.

"It was really hard to please them and to maintain

something that I could be proud of at the same time," Maurice explains.

The fact is that cyberspace designers are often editorial designers, creating designs that emphasize the point of a story or feature. Maurice employs this distinction to make clear that an editorial designer promotes the text or the service itself. Maurice continues, "There's a certain level of talent that everybody has that can make something look pretty on the screen. But if a designer hasn't helped a writer get the message across, then he or she is not really an editorial designer."

Maurice is a professional, and he takes design seriously. He studied fine arts for two years at Howard University and then enrolled in Parsons School of Design, where he earned his BFA. He's not finished with school yet. He has considered holing up for a few years and studying art theory. "That's attractive to me because I've been involved in practical solutions for so long now. I'd like to go back to school and just sit around and think about letters and letter forms all day," he says.

Maurice spent three years working as a designer at the *Detroit News*. He worked on layout for the entertainment and lifestyle sections of the paper and eventually became art director for the features section. He was involved in the seminal stages of the *Detroit News'* Web site. A strike had been called soon after the idea of the Web site had taken hold, and the strike was the main reason that the site became a reality. The paper could still get out of the building and past the picket lines through cyberspace.

The newspaper was hesitant to let Maurice transfer from the features section to the Web site, and soon after, Maurice was recruited by NJO. As a designer, he had been working with desktop publishing platforms for years, and he found the transition to cyberspace simple. "It's a really easy step from creating graphics for a newspaper or magazine to creating them for the Web. You just have to learn a few extra parameters, that's all."

And the switch to cyberspace has brought him abundant satisfaction. "I really enjoy knowing that what I do on my screen will look the same for everybody who's going to see it. At the *News* you did an incredible amount of work and then you looked at the newspaper and you said, 'Is this what I did?' It's muddy. The color's off. The registration is crazy. You didn't have any idea how your work would look until it was printed, and then you would see this crappy thing printed on bad paper." Cyberspace has changed all that for Maurice. He continues, "I know now when I save a graphic and it's perfect to me, it will remain that way. No one will botch the printing or run it too fast. I know I have control."

Although he is happy to have escaped the production process of the printing presses, Maurice misses the organization-wide respect for deadlines that working with presses involved.

"At a paper, if you don't get it to the presses at a certain time, you're in trouble," he says. At an online newspaper, since things can always be changed it seems that no one ever has that same kind of deadline pressure. Design negotiation can go on for what may seem an eternity. Maurice continues, "I also get calls to make minor adjustments after the page is up. A lot of rules that apply to print media should apply here, or you'll never be done working on anything." Maurice cannot keep going back to old projects, however. He must move ahead toward the ideas that are still in the development process.

Maurice spends most of his day dealing with ideas in progress. "I spend three-quarters of my time looking at other people's work and correcting it, talking about it, defending it, and selling it. We're trying to do so much at once for this site that I'm having to go outside the company to get freelancers to do things. And while on the surface it seems like you're getting someone else to do it, which should mean that you don't have to worry about it, I spend almost as much time working with other people's designs as I would if I had designed them myself," says Maurice.

Beyond this he is concerned with the design aspects of the daily updates, like everyone else at NJO. At 9:00 a.m. it's sports, and at 2:00 p.m. it's news, not to mention the weekly and biweekly updates. And with the advent of the football season comes the grueling job of highlighting all the regional play. Maurice has a lot of fancy graphics and screensaver ideas for the upcoming season. To make both his life and the staff's lives easier, he has designed the pages with updates in mind. Each page has a template for use in updating.

"Basically, the most efficient way to do updates is to create something that has little boxes, little holes, and places to put things on the screen with few instructions. The staff can just plug things in, and it's still a good-looking page."

Maurice would like to redesign the entire site every six to eight months to keep it fresh and interesting to the audience. How the directors and managers will react to this is yet to be seen. Because it is Maurice's vision, it may well happen.

Choosing Design

Do you have the vision to create graphics that will grab people's attention and keep them returning to your work? Are you a team player willing to compromise with others? If so, think about pursuing the arts in college and build your portfolio.

Maurice advises, "You've got to be trained to take editorial concepts and illustrate them. You can apply natural talent to the work, but it's a skill that has to be learned and practiced. It's not something innate that you just know how to do."

6

Sales Representatives

Are you a born salesperson? Could you sell a sandbox to a person living in the desert? Could you convince a manufacturer of submarines to purchase your company's sliding glass doors? If you have answered yes to any of these questions, cyberspace has a growing need for you.

It is difficult to say how much you will earn working in sales. Owing to the hardships of entering a new market, most companies offer low salaries in addition to commissions on each deal made. The salaries vary according to your position. Selling advertising space for a company pays more than finding clients to open individual accounts with the service. You can be assured that as demand for the Internet grows most sales positions will operate exclusively on commissions.

Currently, few companies have the resources to hire employees to handle sales exclusively. At this stage in cyberspace's infancy, bosses and directors who have come to the Web from other business careers are performing the tasks of sales and advertising directors in addition to doing other work.

A Vision for Sales

As cyberspace companies grow, it will become necessary to have additional, specialized support for sales and advertising. While many other Internet service companies are just beginning to discuss the idea of hiring salespeople to expand their business, Long Island Internet Headquarters (LIIH), *www.pb.net,* already has a sales department of three full-time employees. Both Kathryn Livornese, president and owner of LIIH, and her colleague EB Stone are actively involved in making corporate sales the driving force of the company. In the last eight months the company has almost doubled its clients in the area of corporate Web site sales.

The key to their sales success is education, according to EB. "You can't just walk in here having sold car-peting elsewhere and do this job. You have to be educated about the Net," he says. In order to sell customers what they want and need, you must first know the hardware, software, and applications and be fluent in their use.

At LIIH, the goal is to bring the customer into their headquarters and sit him or her down at a computer. The sales staff then takes the time to show the client what is available on the Web and, specifically, what the client's competition are doing with their Web sites. Having had an overview of the Web and what can be done with a site, the client is given time to think about an appropriate design suggested by the sales representative to match the needs and budget of his or her company. The next step is to translate the client's vision into a site that will attract the attention of the consumer.

When I say an appropriate design, I mean that the salesperson must be aware of what Web applications are necessary for what the consumer wants, and which applications will fit within the client's time and budgetary limitations. For instance, having real-time video and Java applications on the page would be visually exciting, but they are expensive and require a good deal of memory space and therefore time for a consumer to download.

Kermit: Syndicate Sales

Kermit Westergaard is vice president of syndicate sales at Interactive Connection. Interactive Connection is moving into the future with bold plans to provide syndicated content for corporate Web sites. Kermit explained what sales in the field of cyberspace entail for him and his company, giving me an example of his company's sales and syndication process.

Kermit found a golf company's Web page in which the company included short biographies of its sponsored players. Kermit approached the company, telling them that he could provide statistics, articles, tour dates, and much more for each of their player biographies. Interactive Connection would then continually update and add to the content for that page. The site would be improved by the substantial content additions, and consumers would remember the page and products and return to the site again and again.

Kermit's position requires him to surf sites looking for mostly corporate pages that could benefit from content addition that could be consistently updated. He must then come up with suggestions as to how Interactive Connection could benefit the prospective client and must pitch the idea to the client.

Kermit observes, "The difficulty with advertising on the Web, as opposed to watching television commercials, is that people have to choose to view it. The site has to be stimulating to get noticed and to warrant return visits." Kermit continues, "We have alliances with contact companies and ticker feeds, so we can find information and tailor it for certain sites."

Isra: Promoting Web Sites

Isra Wattanasarn is the business director of Alpha Light Communications, *www.alphalight.com*. His company produces and markets Web pages for companies.

Alpha Light Communications is not simply sitting back and waiting around for the government to decide on encryption standards. It is involved in the traditional business of Web site design and hosting, coupled with a passion for marketing. "Our specialty is site promotion," Isra continues. "Making a nice site is getting easier and easier. What is difficult is bringing people to it. We actively promote by posting to relevant news groups and attending conferences, seminars, and roadshows."

KNOWLEDGE AND COMMUNICATION

As you can see, the normal requisites for working in cyberspace do not change in the field of sales. You must be articulate and personable. Your communication skills are your most valuable tool. You must be able to master new software programs quickly and to teach them to others. Your research and creative skills will be utilized as well, but this is where your familiarity with the Web will be essential. You will need to have done your homework on what is out there on the Web and what you believe can your company can do for other companies before you call on prospective clients.

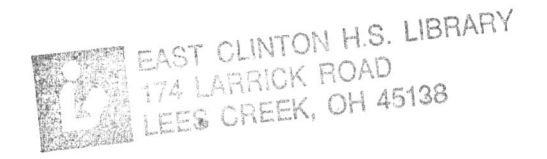

7

Cyber-Bosses and Other Cyber Gurus

I want to be a boss in cyberspace. The group of owners, managers, and directors that I have met are an exciting bunch. They do not seem to fit the "boss mold." These cyber-bosses are young and wonderfully articulate. In fact, I don't think I met anyone over forty. They are kept youthful by their world view.

Cyber-bosses bristle with energy and excitement about their own prospects, as well as those of cyberspace. They enjoy the vibrant atmosphere of cyberspace as much as the rest of us, relishing the rewards and hazards that are born of the changing technologies. They always keep one step ahead, anticipating consumer needs and shaping our experiences as they lead their companies forward in times that are unprecedented and wildly fickle.

Yet cyberspace can fit the description that F. Scott Fitzgerald applied to the city of New York: "It has a neurosis that most people mistake for energy." There are stress lines in cyberspace, perhaps more than in more established markets. It takes brains and bravado to be a pioneer. You must be a leader as well as a creator. This is a difficult and volatile mixture of assets. You must operate on a thin line between controlling your creative staff and not cramping their unique qualities. Cyber-bosses have to integrate business and market direction into an environment of ever-shifting courses.

PARTNERS ONLINE

My first stop is at Long Island Internet Headquarters. Their site, *www.pb.net*, was named "Best Home Page of an Internet Provider" by *2.ask.com*, a Web watchdog company. The "*pb*" in the URL is an abbreviation for the daughter company, named Point Blank, *www.pb.com*. This is LIIH's online BBS, or Bulletin Board Service. Their BBS was voted number one in the world by users polled in the May 1996 issue of *BBS* magazine. Talk about an award-winning outfit!

How is LIIH so successful when so many Internet service providers (ISP) come and go? President and owner Kathryn Livornese and colleague EB Stone have built a unique empire with their ingenuity and foresight. LIIH is a full-service cyberspace company. It offers Web site hosting and design, it is an Internet service provider, it provides commercial intranet and Internet consulting and installation, and it provides classes on the Internet for the general public.

LIIH has been rooted in the computer business for more than fifteen years. It is far ahead of the competition in many ways.

"I can't emphasize enough how my business background really facilitated our doing what we needed to do," says Kathryn. She is as business-savvy as they come. At present, Long Island Internet Headquarter is the only ISP owned solely by a woman. LIIH was also the first ISP with a storefront, a place where people can stop by and talk with someone face-to-face, in the United States. Why? you ask.

Uncommon Sense

Chalk this one up to Kathryn's business sense again. You see, you cannot simply walk into most ISPs. The overwhelming number of them are rooms stacked from floor to ceiling with servers, modems, and telephone lines. And when I say rooms, I mean anything from a closet to a small loft space. Kathryn says, "Anyone can have an ISP, but we believe in the personal touch. We must give what people need in the impersonal world of computers." Two-and-a-half years ago they purchased a storefront so that people could come in and speak with the staff at LIIH and have their questions answered. In fact, Kathryn and EB end up answering a lot of those questions themselves.

Kathryn honed her advantageous combination of computer and business skills through a variety of professional endeavors. She was one of the pioneers of computer networking in hospitals. As a health professional, she used computers for research and video transfer in surgical units. She also did programming and finance with a computer networking company for a few years. That was when she decided that she would follow the cyberspace trend and become her own boss.

EB came to cyberspace through the route of games. He was initially attracted by the fact that computers enabled him to play such great ones. He found himself spending a lot of time in front of the machine. Soon he was reading books and teaching himself how to navigate well beyond the highest levels of his games and right through the machine itself.

What brought Kathryn and EB together was their shared vision of how best to bring the experience of cyberspace to the public. They believe that this is why LIIH has thrived in a turbulent market. "You must have a shared vision to start a company. You have to work together, sure, but you also have to think together," says Kathryn. Their vision is developed and enhanced in a creative environment that is well governed by a business model. This may seem paradoxical. How can you give structure to freedom?

Team Players Sought

"As loose as the structure might be, you still have to follow it," Kathryn observes. In her view, you cannot simply gather four or five people together and call it a company. Being excited about cyberspace is not enough to maintain a business. You need a consensus of what your company goals are and how you will jointly go about achieving these goals. What Kathryn and EB have created is an atmosphere of exploration within the confines of having bosses who have the power to establish the rules of play.

"Business knowledge is what we find lacking in most employees," Kathryn continues. "People need to understand corporate structure." No matter how incredible your designs may look to you, your boss, who signs your paycheck, may feel differently. And it does not stop with your boss. The consumers' opinions matter. A company's purpose is to provide an efficient service for the customer. Every employee at LIIH is young and hip, but each of them knows how to work or, believe me, they wouldn't be able to get away with those hairstyles.

Now that Kathryn has made her philosophy clear, she can discuss other aspects of LIIH. Once you have a solid modus operandi (method of procedure), you can face challenges with systematic approaches.

"The Internet is about being you," Kathryn says about the laid-back atmosphere of LIIH. Jeff Faglio, who directs sales and marketing, remembers the day

Kathryn noticed that he had a hole in his ear for an earring and announced to him that it was perfectly acceptable for him to wear his earring to work. He was flabbergasted.

EB, who also wears earrings, could not agree more with Kathryn's ideas about freedom in the workplace. "Corporate culture must change to cyberspace culture, not vice versa, or they will lose their edge." EB believes it is necessary to maintain certain freedoms in order for a cyberspace company to remain on the cutting edge. "Anybody can code, but not everyone has the vision to work with the customer and create the logo. That is what's worth the money," adds Kathryn.

"I don't think you could talk to anyone here who would say that they don't love their job, and in how many companies are you going to see that?" says EB. And it must be that way for them to operate such a successful service-oriented company. It takes patience and insight to be able to work closely with customers and give them what they need. You must relate to the customers and interact with them on the appropriate level. EB continues, "You have to be well-rounded enough to see that once *you* were the guy who didn't understand 'double-click.' "

When EB and Kathryn put their heads together on this issue, they thought that the next trend for cyberspace was true support services. Kathryn says, "Training and education is where we're moving. Making it affordable for the average person to come in and see what this is all about is the first step." Their storefront, which they have recently expanded, allows them to teach numerous classes in cyberspace navigation and basic HTML. Enrollment for the classes is limited to twelve to maintain the personal touch that gives LIIH its edge. EB philosophizes, "There's no holding back the tidal wave of this thing now. Anyone who fears the Web or thinks that it's not for them isn't educated about it." He punctuates his point, "Knowledge is power."

Kathryn and EB have put a lot of time and energy into their business. When EB began dedicating his hours to cyberspace, he remembers, people told him that he had gone too far. He says that nowadays he turns to those same people and says, "You're becoming me." EB continues, "When Bill Gates was in school, people probably made fun of him for sitting in front of his computer all the time. Now everyone wants to *be* Bill Gates. Everybody wants to be the computer guy now." Kathryn says that she lives and breathes her work and that she does so by choice. "You have to be willing to work and learn and put in the time. I'll work sometimes fifteen, twenty hours a day."

All Work and Play

And that's not uncommon. Alan S. Ellman, president and director of Interactive Connection, says, "I work fourteen to sixteen hours a day, seven days a week. You don't feel it 'cause you love it. It's fun!" A serious look comes across his face, and he adds, "Typically, you won't be successful in life if you just put in an eight-hour day." And successful is definitely a term one can apply to Alan and his company. He is in the process of moving the New York-based company from its Fifth Avenue address to the World Financial Center downtown. Alan continues, "My hours increased, my income went down by two-thirds, but my quality of life has gone up."

Even though Alan's shirt is open at the collar and the atmosphere at Interactive Connection is loose and resembles a downtown bohemian scene, Alan thinks of cyberspace in terms of balance sheet variances and reconciliations, that is, with an eye to the bottom line.

While the company remains vital in the traditional business of Web page design and hosting, it is moving one step forward. It plans to market substantial informational content to existing Web sites. Interactive Connection has many external ticker feeds that bring a wealth of information to the company. It can search these pools of information and find content useful to other companies that do not have the capability to do such research on their own.

Hard Work and Success

As is the norm in cyberspace, Interactive Connection has a somewhat unstructured work environment. When Alan arrives at work, he gives the system a thorough assessment, looking for any trouble with the servers, lines, or programs. He usually has two or three appointments a day. As the sole director, he must deal with the investors, clients, and his twelve employees in New York on a daily basis. He also has a sales staff of three in California. "I do everything. Cyberspace is a twenty-four-hour-a-day, seven-day-a-week business, which makes it similar to broadcasting, but even more difficult because we don't have a twenty-four/seven staff [to share the workload as a broadcasting studio does]. I worry about every single detail."

Alan compared cyberspace to broadcasting because that is where he gained his sea legs for business. He put his MBA in accounting to work as director of finance for ABC Television. He came from a media and advertising background, and he has always been a hacker. "It made perfect sense to me that media/advertising should be delivered to your desktop," he says. He found that by utilizing video and graphics you could take a magazine off the shelf and place it on the computer screen. His vision grew from that point to a company that is not only profitable but projects a doubling in growth of sales each year. "People need information, and cyberspace is the most efficient way of getting it."

He likes to compete and take risks, and that is why he enjoys what he calls "the grassroots feel" of this industry. "In cyberspace small companies can compete with larger ones and win markets and take over business just because they're smart and they work hard," Alan says. "I come from a very structured, suit-and-tie background." This newly formed, level playing ground makes it possible to experience success in a far more thrilling and quick way than climbing the traditional corporate ladder.

Billboarding the Superhighway

Isra Wattanasarn of Alpha Light Communications is another individual who has approached cyberspace from a business background and vantage point. He views the Web as a business venture. He is using his MBA business skills in combination with his marketing savvy to be in the game when cyberspace commerce pushes forward. He believes that very soon new business ventures will experience explosive growth.

"From a business standpoint there are two things holding back the Web. Companies don't like to advertise on the Web, because there is no reliable method to track hits. The second thing is the comfort level with encryption technologies," Isra explains. Commercial cryptography is the business of converting information, in this case financial and medical data, into secret and secure code. Larger corporations, such as IBM, are now waging media campaigns to assure Internet consumers that their respective encryption codes are secure. But until the consumer has the confidence to send his credit card number into cyberspace, commerce on the Web will be limited. There are people putting every ounce of their energy into tackling this issue, so this roadblock will soon be removed. And so should the problems with accurately accounting for the number of hits, or visitations, that a Web page draws. Some companies have recently released software for tracking hits that can be independently verified by analysts.

So when the floodgates of commerce are fully open and consumers are pouring money through the Web, Isra will be involved. "No one has the advantage of being an old-timer in cyberspace. It is so new that you can have expertise or, at least, equal expertise with anyone else in business," he says with great enthusiasm. "You can be a big shot while you're still young."

Punching the Clock
Isra shares Kathryn Livornese's belief in the necessity of the business manager. He believes that his designer, who is brilliant when it comes to design, would run the business into the ground with his lax business practices. When his designer has stayed up for a few nights finishing a project and hasn't clocked his time, how can Isra accurately bill the time or create estimates for prospective clients? You don't want to lose money if you are up nights working!

Isra tells the story of the foresight that the creators of the Netscape browser possessed. The team of seasoned designers brought together by Jim Clark sought out Jim Barksdale to be CEO. They recruited him to drive the corporation forward so that they could retreat into the programming pit and effectively ignore the business aspects of their new venture. "In order to succeed, a company needs a plan. Then a manager has to be chosen who will have the seniority to run the show," Isra concludes.

It's not that easy to develop the groundwork for such a new and changing field. The youth and energy of cyber-bosses are not so much a blessing as a necessity for running a business in cyberspace. They are not only running a new business, but developing wholly new business practices.

THE TAMING OF THE NEW

Andrew Cary, production manager of New Jersey Online, was wearing a tie the day I met with him. It was the only tie to be seen on a cyberspace employee during my interviews. The blatant gesture at professionalism was not an expression of insecurity but a desperate attempt at giving his title some credence, however superficial. He says with a great sense of humor, "There's the ideal role of the production manager, and then there's the reality. In the same way that cyberspace offers opportunity, it's very chaotic, and structures aren't in place to make sure things happen in an efficient way."

Andrew's primary function as a manager is to set up a production system. "The job of manager has never really been defined or structured in a real way. We need more time to think things out and set up a system." Andrew kept smiling through our talk. I asked him how he copes with the stresses of prioritizing the paper deadlines as well as defining his role as a leader. He left us with this advice, "Don't be overwhelmed by it. It is all so new, you can't keep up with it. Don't be discouraged."

CYBER GURU

Peter Levitan is a seasoned business veteran with a determined vision for NJO. His voice is quite different from Andrew's.

It's not a question of confidence or enthusiasm, which they both share. It is a matter of perspective. While Andrew is now finishing his master's degree, Peter has the mature experience of having been a professional for many years. He is now marketing director at NJO and has an aggressive and upbeat style. His office has an Asian feel to it, with a minimalist decor and a sliding door frame covered in a diaphanous material resembling rice paper. He is trendy and well dressed. His words are sage, and his voice fills the room.

"I'm a sucker for new ideas—I'm the early adopter type. I like a fast-changing environment. You can't make a decision about cyberspace that will last for much more than a month or two, because everything is changing completely," he begins. Cyberspace suits him, and he suits cyberspace. When I inquired about his responsibilities, he answered, "Everything . . . from seeing that the air-conditioning repairman shows up, to the profit and loss statements." He handles advertising sales, shapes the editorial and design product, develops new features, and the list goes on.

"We'd like to be perceived as an indispensable information resource," says Peter. "We expect 30 percent growth each year and that's pretty impressive, as there are very few content businesses that are profitable."

Peter has plans to keep NJO on top of the curve for some time to come. "I believe in local," he says. He means that NJO wants its information to be fully applicable and relevant to as many users as possible.

"Local is the killer application. Our next step is building a statewide database and getting very local. I want to get each of the five hundred towns in New Jersey online."

How do you get such attention from an audience that might not know you exist? Peter replies, "We must get more useful. Being simply a news source or having cute features won't make it. We have to make the Web more utilitarian—make it more of a usable medium than an indiscriminate surfing tool. I want NJO to be like the *Yellow Pages* of the Internet."

WEBMASTER
Brad Taylor, the WebMaster at the Metropolitan Museum of Art in New York City, observes, "I would like to see some organization of the Web. Not regulatory organization—almost like a *TV Guide* listing of the contents." He would like to see an index or card catalog to help people narrow their searches and better handle the scope of the Web's resources. "The search engines are a first step, but they are not enough," he adds.

Brad can speak in terms of big issues and enveloping concerns. As the WebMaster of the Museum, he runs a one-man production, placing in cyberspace the Web pages of one of the world's most important cultural institutions. He was hired to host a Web site. He has been involved with conceptualizing, brainstorming, developing, and building this site. It was made public on October 16, 1995. "It's fun working in cyberspace. What better thing can you ask for? It's in the news every day. And you find a wealth of information out there."

The Met, as it is known, is a self-supporting Web entity with a T1 line, which means the museum is its own ISP, directly connected to the Internet. And Brad does it all, every day. He has to check the Web server, maintaining it and making sure the logs are up to date. He records the "stats," the number of hits that the site has had and which HTML documents have been viewed by users. He spends a lot of time answering a portion of the e-mail and forwarding the rest to the appropriate departments. He makes small system updates and any necessary corrections. He monitors the security of the transactions server, which is used for financial transactions, and the site in general. He implements policy and procedures for in-house Internet training of staff. As needed, he creates Internet accounts for the staff. And he works with the departments to get new materials to enhance and update the site.

Pleasing Them All, All the Time

This is where Brad's job truly challenges his intellectual capacities. He must juggle the needs and interests of the entire museum. He may be the monarch of the Web page, but the Met is an expansive institution with a multiplicity of voices. Each must be represented. His Web pages must embody the diversity that makes the institution great. He works in conjunction with committees from the editorial, education, visitor's service, development, and communications departments in order to design content for the site. The masterpieces that you see on the site are chosen by the curators of the museum's eighteen art departments. And the legal department has to arrange for copyright permissions to feature works by certain artists: American artists who have been dead for less than seventy years, and European artists who have been dead for less than ninety years.

This is where his experience and education in consulting and project management are invaluable. "It's a huge project. I'm tying together a lot of different departments with different technologies," Brad says. As a consultant he is used to listening to what people need and then developing solutions to fit their needs. "It's a lot to think about. You have to be able to see what must come first and implement from there."

Brad is in the process of expanding the education section of the site to make it increasingly interactive, interesting, and informative. He's building a Frequently Asked Questions page (FAQ) and working with Java. The latest technologies for secure electronic transactions are of great interest to him, as the site receives about fifty such transactions a week. They include purchases and membership applications, and he believes that such transactions will grow exponentially as the technology improves. He would like to do more special events promotion, including bringing a curator of an upcoming exhibit into cyberspace for a live chat. He's definitely not sitting still.

Brad is happy to be involved in such serious work. He jumped at the chance to work for the Met and to leap into cyberspace. "The standard today is old hat tomorrow. People say, 'Have you heard of X?' 'No, I'm just trying to keep my head above water keeping things running,'" Brad admits. "Being the WebMaster is becoming a jack of all trades and a master of none. You're sort of putting bandages on it to get everything together and working."

Becoming a Cyber-boss

Cyberspace is a wonderful and harried world in which to lead a company. To stake your claim it takes unique talents and a lot of energy for work. Do you look forward to attaining a position of leadership in cyberspace? Cyber-bosses are an energetic, articulate, and educated bunch of pioneers. You have your work cut out for you if you want to get them to pay attention to your ideas. Do you want to know how you can brighten your prospects for a career like theirs? Turn that page!

8

Entrepreneurs: Cyberspace Working for You

Everyone in this book works *with* cyberspace, but not everyone works directly *for* it. In the chapters that you have read so far, the persons involved have been working for cyberspace in related industries, such as Web production and support. They are making a career out of the work they produce for the Web.

This chapter is about people who are making careers by having cyberspace work for *them*.

FOOD FOR THOUGHT

In urban areas a burgeoning new service opportunity has been born out of the cyber-craze. Cyber-cafes are popping up left and right in the cityscape, and they are outgunning the traditional coffeehouses in popularity. You can e-mail your lunch order ahead of time, and when you arrive, your sandwich will be at your table. You can fuss over a frappe while you file transfer philosophy (FTP) from Finland.

Let's take a stroll to the Internet Cafe in New York's East Village. The Internet Cafe is a comfortable place. It is more reminiscent of a setting from a Colette story than a glass and steel Silicon Valley nouveau lounge. It has a cozy, den-like feel. Internet Cafe maintains its bohemian feel with a pleasant blend of aromatic coffees and cool jazz. The bookshelves, magazines, and newspapers are easily accessible. Homer, a regal golden retriever, lounges about.

The Internet Cafe is the brainchild of Arthur Perley, who owns and operates the establishment. Arthur has arrived at this position in cyberspace through, in his own words, "a convergence of circumstances." He's a bright guy who has enjoyed really good luck. He was hired by IBM in information services back in 1981, and he rode out the computer revolution as an insider. He learned and matured alongside the rest of the industry in positions where he was not only the first to know, but the first to know how. "I had been doing systems development for some time, and I started to hear the drumbeats of the Internet. I knew that it was the coming thing," Arthur says.

He also had artistic ambitions. He had been pursuing photography and writing as serious hobbies. He recognized the new creative energies and possibilities that were opening up in cyberspace. Then he saw his countercultural heroes—such as Timothy Leary and William S. Burroughs—jump onto the Web. That was the last incentive he needed. He had been in the business world long enough; he wasn't going to miss the chance to be a part of the next Beat Generation.

Arthur began developing some ideas that had been churning in his head since the enormous boom in the personal computing market. "I had this idea of a public space where people could get their hands on the technology," Arthur notes. "By 1994, personal use was driving the computer markets. The high-end multimedia were now being built for home use. That signaled to me a fundamental change."

When you are at work, Arthur pointed out, you have a staff of technicians to help you with your computing difficulties. And he knows how often they are called upon to solve troubles; he was a corporate technician. The fact that high-powered, multitasking machines were now being made and marketed for personal computing meant that a lot of people would be using them without the constant support that they would get in business. Arthur continues, "Computers are complex things, and most people understand only very little of what their computer is capable of and how it works. People can come in to the Internet Cafe and explore the technology. They can find someone who has the answers without going to a store which, obviously, has another agenda."

He brought all of his ideas together in the form of a cafe. The cafe atmosphere would be conducive to exploration and the asking of questions. Food had always been a favorite hobby of Arthur's; he even referred to himself as a "foodie." He went on to say that in a former life he was a chef in San Francisco. I was not quite sure whether he meant that he cooked before he became a computer professional or that this was his second tour on the planet. In any case, Arthur and his partner Elizabeth Groeneman carefully searched for local vendors, bakers, and purveyors to supply their cafe with the finest quality foods and coffee. Arthur interjects, "People are surprised by it, frankly—the amount of attention we pay to our menu."

E-Mail Boxes Etc.

"We have a high concentration of young and creative people in the East Village, and I wanted to attract them," Arthur says. The Internet Cafe has many distinguishing features. Beyond providing workstations for customers to access cyberspace, it has a full library of computing software (Quark, Photoshop, Illustrator, and Pagemaker), including the major office tools for word processing. The cafe is also a server, providing full

Entrepreneurs: Cyberspace Working for You

Internet service without dial-up. The cafe staff design and support Web pages, but the cafe does not host individual dial-up addresses. What grabbed my attention was the fact that it hosts e-mail accounts for a nominal monthly fee. This means users can maintain e-mail correspondence without owning a computer. They set up a box and pay the maintenance fee. Then they pay for the time that they are on the cafe's computers checking and sending messages. Arthur refers to what he is building as "sort of an E-Mail Boxes Etc."

And the cafe has been conducive to cyberspace exploration. Business is booming. Arthur says, "The Internet is a big deal. What's surprised me is that in the time that we have been open, the attention paid to the Internet has not gone away. It's just the opposite: It's grown immensely! It used to be you could pretty much get a handle on what the Internet was—its size, shape, its components, and what was out there. And now it's totally impossible." And that is good for business. The cafe passed the break-even point a while ago.

Arthur has recently begun teaching classes at the cafe. He teaches an Internet basics course, which involves learning about its origins and capabilities and provides instruction on navigating and using Internet tools. For a reasonable price you get a two-hour class and an additional hour of computer time at the cafe. He is also teaching a beginner's course in HTML and will soon commit to an advanced course.

The Internet Cafe has made good business sense for Arthur. If this kind of business appeals to you, he recommends leasing the hardware so that you will have your money free for other uses. He is considering turning to a company for sponsorship to bring in all new hardware for the cafe. He runs the business with six employees, including his business partner, Elizabeth, who is also the manager. "I'm totally caught up in this," he says, as he explains his 120-hour workweeks. The cafe is open from 11:00 a.m. to 2:00 a.m., and Arthur can be found there for most of those hours. Where he found time to write a book, I have no idea, but Arthur's book, *The Kid's Guide to the Internet,* is now available.

He wants to move the Internet Cafe forward by further expanding its access to the Internet's possibilities. He wants to bring the cafe closer to the creative energies in its East Village neighborhood. "Cyberspace is being underutilized for creative purposes," Arthur says. "I want to tie performances and presentations into the Web," he continues. Artists can use text, graphics, and with CU–SeeMe reflectors can use live video interaction as part of their truly multimedia expressions. Arthur looks forward to people's using the cafe as a studio and the Web as a huge performance space.

Studio Space

Jeff Harrington, a cyberspace programmer at the Children's Television Workshop (CTW), who is also a composer, is doing just that. He is using cyberspace as his family's museum, gallery, and concert hall, *www.parnasse.com.* And what a family he has! Jeff's wife, Elsie Russell, has been painting since she was four. She was a welcome guest at Picasso's home as a young girl. Elsie's father, Alfred Russell, was a renegade member of the abstract art movement that delivered Jackson Pollock into fame and a few of Alfred's works into museums, including the Museum of Modern Art in New York. Elsie's mother, Andree Deschannes, is also a painter, and her classically styled canvases can be gazed upon at the parnasse site. Numerous compositions, ranging from chamber pieces to dance-oriented jazz, each written by Jeff, can be downloaded and enjoyed.

Entrepreneurs: Cyberspace Working for You

Jeff also has a wonderful job. He creates CD-ROM games involving the *Sesame Street* characters. He was showing me a new CD in which you can direct one of the characters around a yard and enter the house, tree fort, etc., and learn the alphabet, how to count, how to tell time, and how to create masks in the separate areas. Jeff is also the sole online programmer at CTW. He had recently created an online coloring book and a puzzle in Java for the CTW Web site. When you complete the *Sesame Street* character puzzle, disco music sounds and the character dances. This is really fun stuff!

He has limitations attached to his programming, however. "Since our page is geared toward an audience of three- to seven-year-olds, we have to give the illusion of zero download time," says Jeff. The complicated puzzle and coloring book take only seven seconds to download. During longer download times Jeff employs what he calls "teasing mechanisms." Using simultaneous processes, he will have a goofy screen pop-up with one of the characters waving hello on it, so the monitor can hold a child's brief attention span during the download. If the download is for a complicated game, he will have the game's functions download incrementally, so kids can start playing right away and more features will become available as they continue playing. Jeff Harrington is a programmer's programmer.

He combines his computer skills with his music to help him develop new melodic possibilities. He refers to his music as "contrapuntal." I ask him about this term. "My counterpoint technique refers to taking more than one melody, setting them against one another, and trying to mesh them. I'm looking for the melodic combinatorial possibilities." This is about as avant-garde as it gets. Jeff takes different melodies and overlaps them, looking for points of musical consonance, creating an entirely new melody based upon these musical matchings.

Jeff wrote a program to systematize the process. "The program can take up to six melodies of 5,000 notes each. Using a brute force search space, it combs through the music looking for note combinations, by passing dissonant combinations and trying to find consonance," Jeff explains. "I started small in basic language. Then I moved to C, using only two voices of ten to twenty notes each, and beefed it up from there."

Family Portrait

Jeff's decision to create the parnasse site has brought his family recognition and growing fame. The page is named after Mont Parnasse, where Apollo was said to reign with the Muses, the nine sister goddesses in Greek mythology that provide the inspiration for song, poetry, and the arts and sciences. The site receives approximately 500 hits a day. During the school year the site receives sudden bursts of 300 hits as instructors have entire classes log on to the page. "My art and my wife's art are of interest to a minority of people, and the Web is just the perfect way to outreach to the micromarket—to reach an esoteric audience. We create such rarefied stuff it's never going to be that popular or commercial. By using the Web we don't have to worry about dying unknown. In the micro-community that the Web is turning into, we already have a certain amount of fame. In May 1996 we won 'cool site.'" This is a distinction awarded by the Yahoo search engine, *www.yahoo.com*.

His wife's art is receiving bountiful recognition. Elsie is the only living artist whose work is included on an upcoming mythology CD-ROM, "The Genealogical Guide to Greek Mythology." Galleries are approaching her to do shows, a company wants to produce museum-quality posters of her works, and she has been approached for purchases. Jeff has had his music performed all over the planet. In Moscow, a pianist publicly performed his works. A Siberian musicologist who attended the performance borrowed the score. That instructor now uses Jeff's music to teach counterpoint to his classes. "I think it's wild that Siberian graduate students are being tested on Harrington's Counterpoint Techniques," Jeff admits.

A recent performance of his music in South Carolina was very well attended and received. Jeff has never met the musicians or the organizers. One of the musicians downloaded the MIDI file and liked it, so he downloaded the postscript (score) and started playing and practicing the piece. The trio that performed the chamber piece is thinking of taking the performance on tour! "Because the Web is free, it encourages play. People download stuff and look at it, and if they like it, they'll do something serious with it," he says. "People go for the music first." He is listened to, not because of his reputation, his friends, or record company propaganda, but because people enjoy his music. Jeff has learned of performances in Arizona, Colorado, and New Zealand, as well.

How will he keep public attention heading for his page? "Think of it as being on a publishing schedule," he says of the necessity of freshening the pages. He trys to bring in new capabilities and additions to his site. "I use teasers to bring people to the art and music." He has recently created "Dr. Webowitz," a program that searches for key words in your text and then asks you pointed questions in return, much like a stereotypical psychoanalyst. It's fun, and it will link you to the other parnasse delights. If someone searches for psychology and arrives at Dr. Webowitz, they may follow the links to the real substance of the parnasse site. Jeff continues, "Give away cool stuff so people stop by." He has taken the art images from the pages and created downloadable screensavers from them. He changes them regularly so that people will return to the site for another one and, more than likely, peruse the site again.

"I like the unpredictability of it," Jeff muses about cyberspace. "I like never knowing what's in the mailbox . . . people playing my music, you writing a book, someone enjoying the art."

OPEN MIC

This quality, the unpredictability of what cyberspace can offer, is the main attraction of cyberspace for many. The uncharted future of cyberspace bolsters the optimism of these forward thinking entrepreneurs and artists. They can foresee its promising and instrumental qualities and envision its agreeable and lucrative offerings.

Bob Gale believes that from this chaos of the unpredictable will come a sense of community or, at least, communities. He is looking to find and expand an audience for poetry and spoken performance, much as Jeff has found a niche market for his art.

Bob is eloquent. Words are of great importance to him, and he wants to find others equally earnest about language and make sure that they are heard. Bob is president of London Productions, a print and online company that, in his words, "highlights the variety and vibrancy of spoken word talent." Bob says, "London Production's mission is to create artistic, cultural contexts bringing together people of diverse backgrounds." He seeks to expand the audience of poetry and spoken word performances by offering an increasing array of talents. His Web site is the Spoken Word Universe, *www.spoken.com*. He also operates a newspaper called *Shout!* and manages the performance group "Cacophony Chorus."

Bob has turned to cyberspace to expand his offerings. He says, "I am looking to unite, build, and expand the spoken word community by publishing information and resources, providing access for audiences and artists, increasing standards of excellence, networking communities and individuals, and promoting diversity and variety." He continues, "Our Web site is an extension of our print newspaper, but it aims to be more. We want it to be a gateway to other resources on the Net, while developing a sense of community between various users."

Waxing Poetic

It should come as no surprise that Bob gets poetic about his new workspace. "Cyberspace has been, and always will be, like any other tool—an extension of human minds and limbs. But unique to cyberspace, these interacting tools have begun to create almost a sense of alternative consciousness that is wrapping itself around the planet in an unseen dimension. It has its own primitive culture that we can dip into, contribute to, influence, but not control."

Bob says, "I have always been more interested in the cultural and social aspects of the Net than in the technical side of things." He continues, "Individuals can make an impact at the time of technological paradigm shifts. When the Internet changed from a solely text-based medium to the hypermedia of the Web, individuals could make a difference. The appearance of numerous personal homepages and self-published Web magazines attests to that fact." Bob wants to ensure that Web technology's ability to unite remote access users does not simply leave us with the feeling that we are all isolated users of an impersonal network. He wants to see the Web go further and unite users into communities of interest and shared resources. Bob believes that the art of the spoken word has the ability to personalize the shared expanses of cyberspace.

"While it's no replacement for human touch, spoken word has the ability to create a sense of community in a world where most of our stories are overly mediated," he says. Bob's pages have grown to a point at which they now receive several thousand hits a day. He thinks that soon these neighborhoods on the Web will be self-reliant and self-sufficient entities. "Successful online communities will exist with no corresponding or supporting offline community. In fact, offline folks who try to translate their efforts to cyberspace will by and large fail. Creativity and improvements will come from the Net itself," he concludes.

That is some pretty heady talk brimming with dollar words. Bob's words are also sound career advice. Cyberspace entrepreneurs must be concerned with the purpose and philosophy of their business. You do not instantly turn a profit. You do not have the same forms of feedback and recognition in a cyberspace career as in other businesses. If you start a business, you need to believe in what you are doing.

Do you have an idea that you have been itching to try? Stoke the coals of that smoldering idea and put it into action. Chances are, if you think the idea or the service is missing, so do thousands of other Web users. And they may be waiting for someone to bring it to fruition so they can appreciate it. Cyberspace is a resource and business opportunity for all fields.

9

What You Need to Do Now

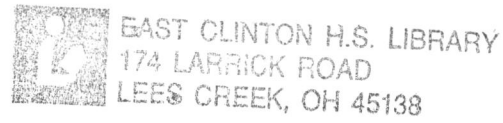

[Library stamp: EAST CLINTON H.S. LIBRARY / 174 LARRICK ROAD / LEES CREEK, OH 45138]

Cyberspace is relatively uncharted territory for the career seeker. That presents both wonderfully exciting opportunities and terrifying adventures for you. In some ways, there are fewer expectations and in others, many more. It is not as simple as getting a degree in cyberspace studies. That isn't possible and might never be relevant. The information and tools that make up cyberspace change too quickly. Technological knowledge is useful but is not as important as the ability to be creative and enthusiastic in the midst of continuous change.

You won't need much technical knowledge beyond a basic understanding of HTML, especially in the nonprogramming positions. So many editing programs are available that will ready your text and graphics for the Web that you can get by with knowing how to use the programs. As Tricia Nelson told me, "HTML fluency gets less and less relevant every day." What everyone interested in a career in cyberspace does need to do is start exploring the World Wide Web.

Scott Brodeur says the Web is very DIY. You've got to do-it-yourself. Everyone interviewed in this book got started in cyberspace by diving in and doing it themselves.

Take advantage of the "view source" option. "Pay a lot of attention to what's out there and try to mimic it," says Scott. "Target what you like, and be able to explain to an employer clearly why it is that you like it."

Getting Started

First, you must get a computer and a modem and set yourself up with an Internet service provider (ISP). Be careful to choose an ISP. For instance, America Online (AOL) is an online entertainment service that allows you to access the World Wide Web, but it is not a true Internet provider. When you use AOL, you are dialing into AOL, not the Web. You cannot create your own homepage and view sources with the AOL browser. Check in smaller community papers and browse through the Yellow Pages of the telephone book for an ISP. The price range for an Internet account is currently between $10 and $30 a month.

The prices vary for a few reasons. Companies differ in size and number of clients, so some companies can charge lower prices and still turn a profit. Some companies limit the number of hours each month that you can log on to the Web. And companies vary greatly when it comes to the level of service that they provide users.

Talk to people who already have accounts, and ask questions about their ISP. You should inquire about how easy it is to connect to the Internet during the hours you wish to surf. Too many busy signals tell you that the ISP may be overextending its client base. You should find out whether or not users think that they receive all of their e-mail. Also, you should find out whether the ISP staff is available for help during times when you are able to contact them.

I am very happy with the service I receive with my company. I include information about their rates and

What You Need to Do Now

services so you can have an idea of what to expect from a full-service ISP.

My Internet service provider is an ISP offering leased-line and dial-up connections in the New York City vicinity (212 and 718 area codes). A *leased-line connection* is a line that is dedicated solely to your use. A *dial-up connection* is a connection made by your computer and modem to your ISP's server.

You will be dialing in on a 14.4 or 28.8 modem, so you need only PPP access.

I. For 28.8 Analog PPP/Shell Accounts, the costs for use at my ISP are as follows:

- $16.95 per month:
  flat rate for twenty hours of use per month, $1.95 per hour thereafter
- $25.00 per month:
  flat rate for unlimited use per month
- $222.00 per year:
  flat rate for unlimited use per year

Standard services offered include:

- 5-megabyte storage space
- UNIX shell access
- personal homepage (limit: 1 megabyte storage; no business sites are permitted for this account)
- e-mail
- Usenet News
- Gopher
- other Internet services

II. For Integrated Service Digital Network (ISDN) Service Dial-up Accounts (64K or 128K), the costs for use are as follows:

- $29.95 per month: flat rate for 40 hours of use per month, $1.95 per hour thereafter
- $299.00 per year: flat rate for 40 hours per month for one full year
- $49.95 per month: flat rate for 100 hours of use per month, $1.95 per hour thereafter

Standard services offered for ISDN are identical to those described above for 28.8 accounts. ISDN offers significantly faster transmission times over existing telephone lines but requires a special modem.

III. For Dedicated Connections Accounts, lines that are direct connections to the Internet, the costs for use are:

- T1 (1.54 Mbps) $1,200 per month: nonresellable; $1,000 installation fee
- 56K $595 per month; $495 installation fee
- 128K ISDN $495 per month; $395 installation fee
- 28.8 analog $250 per month; $295 installation fee

No matter what kind of account you have with an ISP, you must be able to run Netscape software, which you will receive with your Internet account. When you dial your ISP via your computer, you will be connected to their service through your telephone connection. Log on to Netscape, and you're in cyberspace.

As for buying a computer, that is a whole book in itself. Find out which computers cyberspace explorers are using. Ask the staff at your school or your local ISP what they recommend. You will need to consider two

What You Need to Do Now

things. One is your budget, and the other is a clear understanding of what you will be using the computer for. These are personal issues that only you can answer. You can easily spend up to $7,000 on a new computer. Are you going to be multiprocessing with the latest publishing, engineering, and advanced graphics programs? Not in the beginning, that's for sure! If you are buying the computer to browse the Web and construct personal Web pages, you will probably be able to find a suitable computer for about $2,000. Check the papers and ask around first. You'll be amazed by the number of people looking to upgrade their systems and sell their current equipment.

Once you're online, then the work (or should I say, fun?) begins. Just explore. Let one site lead you to another. Following a link from one page could lead to another country or farther.

No matter where you go and where you end up, this is how you will get the wings that will propel you on your job search. Surfing the Web is a major part of what those people who are already working in cyberspace are doing on a daily basis. The only way to keep up and stay ahead is to know what is out there. Get well acquainted with what is happening, making a list of your favorite sites. Your next step will be to create your own.

Raising Your Homepage

In order to break into cyberspace, you *must* have your own Web page, called your homepage. Building and rebuilding your homepage is where you will get the practical skills you will need for your job search. Take that list you were making of interesting sites, and view the sources. Everything you need to figure out about how that site was made will be on the screen before your eyes. It is written in the HTML code that you've been hearing so much about. If you don't understand it, print it out and then surf to one of the many online HTML information pages. Try this one: *www.ncsa.uiuc.edu/General/Internet/www/HTMLPrimer.html.*

You'll probably start with just text. It's fun to see your own words published on the Web. Andrew Mathis, an assistant producer at NJO, says, "You can vanity publish on the Web. Setting up homepages is so easy that an infant could do it, and boom, you have your own vanity press." Start experimenting with different font styles (bold, underlined, italics) and using tables to create an interesting layout so that your page is visually exciting.

Then try adding gifs. You don't need expensive scanners anymore. Take some photographs using the photo CDs (or photo diskettes, if you do not have a CD-ROM) and you're ready to transfer graphics to your page. Any better photography store can now place your files on disk or CD at a rather nominal cost.

The latest rage is the animated gif. The animated gif is a graphics frame where the pictures keep changing. They are all over the Web, so if you have been surfing, you will already have seen them. If not, you can always find one on Art's sports page at NJO. They look like ancient movie technology or those wacky moving billboards. How do *you* create an animated gif? Use "view source" and try out the code for yourself. Remember, it's a DIY world.

Once you are satisfied with your page, ask for feedback from friends and other visitors. Cyberspace is a tightly knit group of mostly friendly and helpful people who are more than willing to give advice. What you will more than likely receive is invaluable commentary, instruction, and knowledge.

Freelance cyberspace writer Jason Mulligan recommends placing a message asking for advice and comments on your page. "You may think your page is really silly, but suddenly you will have a thousand hits a week with specific feedback."

WHAT ARE BOSSES LOOKING FOR?

Remember Peter Levitan, the man of vision and the marketing director at NJO? At the Christmas party last year, he promised me that he would make me and my page, *www.nj.com/arts/marquee/haiku*, famous. And now look at me: I have written a book! Peter also has a lot to say about how you should approach your career in cyberspace.

"Entry-level job seekers have to exhibit an interest in the subject before they walk in the door. They must come prepared to explain very succinctly what they like about cyberspace and why they want to be involved. If they have worked as an intern one summer doing something at an Internet site, that's very appealing. It demonstrates interest and shows they're coming with some information about it."

This is why you need to construct an excellent homepage. You will put the page's URL on your résumé. You will put your résumé on your page. In fact, you might construct a job-search page. Along with your résumé you can include a bit of your biography. You may want to include stories about how you became involved with cyberspace and what you are looking forward to learning and doing at a company. You can include some of your art or creative writing to demonstrate other qualities that might interest prospective employers.

Take out that list of interesting sites that you are using as inspiration while you build your site. Review the sites and develop your ability to speak eloquently about them; put into specific terms what you like about them.

This is excellent practice for an interview. It can be quite difficult to explain what it is that you like about something that catches your attention. Ask yourself questions about the pages. Is it the writing, the layout, the use of color, or the way the graphics have been manipulated that makes the site worthy of your regard? Your ability to express yourself confidently will show your preparedness for the job. Peter advises, "Look at your top ten sites, study them, and see why they set themselves apart. Apply those rules to your site and be able to articulate your decisions."

Alan S. Ellman, the owner of Interactive Connection, looks for just that ability to articulate. "I look for intelligent people. I don't necessarily hire on the basis of a set of skills, because I believe that anybody can learn anything." How does he find qualities like intelligence and aggressiveness? He tests your ability to think on your feet. Like all bosses, he is looking for responsibility and enthusiasm. If you just started thinking about cyberspace the morning of the interview, these bosses will know.

Alan adds, "If you ask someone to describe themselves in five words and they say the same words again and again, they can't solve problems. You must instill confidence in the room, and in me, that you can take the ball and run with it."

Alan reminds potential interviewees of one more point: "The biggest thing is to figure out what is missing from the Internet."

Rebel with a Cause

This is a key idea in setting yourself apart from the pack. The act of imitating is essential when you enter cyberspace, but your ultimate goal is to create a vision of your own. As your comfort level grows and as you mature as a cyberspace viewer, you must look at other pages and not only stay abreast of the latest designs, but adapt them in original ways. EB Stone reaffirms, "Be creative.

What You Need to Do Now

Be cutting edge. Everybody has the same machines and can be taught how to use them. I don't think I can teach them how to be cutting edge." It will be relatively easy for you to figure out what is going on in Web page design and cyberspace in general. The difficulty lies in bringing new ideas to the Web. Developing original content is your ultimate goal. Andrew Mathis advises, "You have to be impressive. That one little trick that you can do, that no one else can do, is what is going to land you that job."

And once you have that idea, adapting it efficiently to the Web can be a challenge. Jeff Harrington, from the Children's Television Workshop, adds, "Newcomers to cyberspace must recognize the bandwidth limitations and how to work within those boundaries. They must be able to design content in small file sizes." In other words, your idea can't take up too much memory space or no one will be able to download it.

Keep looking, viewing, learning. If you have been thinking critically about the work you have been doing and the work you want to continue doing professionally, you can soon begin interviewing for a job with confidence. Take the time to know what you are talking about and to learn how to talk persuasively about what you know.

RÉSUMÉ AND PORTFOLIO

When you walk down the corridor of a business school in the early spring, you hear constant chatter about résumés. "How's your résumé?" is a communal beginning point of interaction, much like "Hello" and "How are you?" For those of us in cyberspace, the greeting modulates to "How's your homepage?" Of course, you will have to make a résumé and stick it on your homepage, but your true calling card will be your work.

Anastasia Victoria Michaels
32 Levan Road
Livonia, MI 48154
(313)555-0024

OBJECTIVE

To secure an internship at a cyberspace-related company.

EDUCATION

University of Michigan, Ann Arbor
Anticipated graduation date: May 2002
B.A. English

RELEVANT EXPERIENCE

University of Michigan Bookstore, Ann Arbor, MI
Sales Assistant, 1997–1998
- Assisted customers with purchases
- Maintained and controlled merchandise invoices
- Monitored and maintained supply of physical plant
- Installed and updated computer system daily

Office of Jay Packard, M.D. Livonia, MI
Administrative Assistant, 1995-1996
- Assisted with patient registration
- Processed patient and insurance billing
- Created and maintained patient files

ADDITIONAL INFORMATION

- Day Camp Counselor, Ellwood YMCA
- Member, National Honor Society, Adlai E. Stevenson High School
- Member, Varsity Track and Field
- Member, Varsity Basketball Team

What You Need to Do Now

Spend time on the hard copy of your résumé and make it sublime. Add graphics, print it on boldly colored paper, and be as creative as you want to be. Just make sure it properly showcases your unique personality.

Maurice Williams, the design director at NJO, advises, "I just went through a long hiring process. I could easily dismiss three-quarters of the applicants on the basis of their résumés, because they didn't look good. If you're a designer and your résumé doesn't look good, then you're not thinking. You're sloppy."

And take note of this cautionary advice. Maurice continues, "I ask applicants to send faxes. What that means is that you have to know what faxes well. You can't fax me paper with flecks of gold in it. It has to be a strong design that works in black and white and that isn't overly detailed, or it must be a very clean, traditional résumé look."

Create a portfolio of your work both in cyberspace and in hard copy. Have your Web pages printed out on a color laser printer and carry them in an attractive binder. Carefully select your favorite drawings and writings and include them. Place any academic awards and your transcripts in the binder as well. Present your talents in an exciting and concise way so that prospective employers can see the extent of your skills in a slick and speedy fashion.

Maurice says, "Suppose you want to work for NJO. A really cool thing to do is to redesign NJO. Choose one of the pages, make it look better, and write something about what you're thinking. Then e-mail it to me. I would definitely look at it, and it would really catch my eye."

Maurice observes, "Cyberspace is making it so much easier. For other media you drop off your portfolio, and when you pick it up you never know if it was looked at or even if they're hiring. Now you can simply e-mail your portfolio to places that you want to work." Your portfolio will shout where a simple résumé whispers.

Check out these examples of online résumés that were chosen by Maurice:

- *www.mmdstn.com*
- *www.users.interport.net/~jillyp*

And be sure to drop by Justin Hall's homepage to view his interactive résumé, *www.links.net*.

What Do You Need to Know?

As you have read in previous chapters, you will need particular skills for each type of job in cyberspace. Beyond the specifics of each job description, there are some universal skills that you should develop. Everyone I spoke with mentioned the importance of writing. Writing skills will limit or enhance any other talent you have. Writing skills are profoundly important if you want to explain yourself and your new ideas either orally or in any format on paper. You may be writing code, but if you cannot explain your idea, it is of little value. You do not have an idea until you can clearly express it.

Practice writing during your job search. Write out your ideas about what you expect to learn and what you want from your future. Isra Wattanasarn says, "Get your writing skills up. Read a lot, and more than cyber-stuff. *The Campaigns of Napoleon* was a book that really helped me improve my writing skills."

Bob Gale warns, "Overspecialization can lead down the wrong path. Job candidates should have a holistic understanding of their product, audience, and resources." This is excellent advice. Know as much as you can about *all* of the tasks that make a successful cyberspace company. Reading this book is a great step. You have heard about the responsibilities of several types of cyberspace employees. Take that into consideration.

Bob continues, "In cyberspace the various steps of creation, production, distribution, exhibition, and marketing become blurred. Folks who want to work online should have editorial and design knowledge, including copyediting, graphic layout, and color composition. Knowledge and understanding of HTML and basic programming is essential." Jump in and explore the aspects of each cyberspace career. Use Bob's list as a syllabus of things you want to learn at your internship.

The Internship

The single most used example of how to enter cyberspace is the internship. You simply have to get one!

An internship rarely pays. You will want to get one during a summer break from college or even high school so that the following summer you will be invited back with pay.

If you are saying to yourself, "Why should I work for free?" let me correct the impression. You are not working for free. You are working on top-of-the-line computers and learning the latest programs and applications for free. As EB Stone points out, "Interns don't work for nothing. They gain information that they can't get anywhere else. That's the value of an internship."

One of the best aspects of the internship model is that every company wants to bring in interns. It is a win-win situation. You get the business experience you need, and the companies get your energy and expertise. Peter Levitan adds, "Interns are cheap talent. The World Wide Web is one of the more unique businesses where the interns may actually know more than the salaried employees." When I asked him if he would have any reservations about hiring high school students as interns, he said, "No problem. There are kids in high school who have been building Web pages for two or three years."

Summer employees can be invaluable. Although Jinnah Hosein works at Interactive Connection only during the summer, the other programmers rely on him heavily when they get stuck. He is salaried now and is invited back during each of his school breaks. Once you are an intern, make yourself indispensable. Display your energies and skills. You will learn more and attract the right kind of attention.

How do you get an internship? It is the same process as getting any other job. You get to know as many people as possible who are involved in cyberspace. Trisha Smith advises, "Getting a job is about knowing people. Learn the names of people who are doing what you might want to do from discussion groups and list servers on the Web. Learn their e-mail addresses and contact them. People get back to e-mail."

Ask anyone and everyone if they have an opening for an intern. Check papers of every size, and call any company that deals with computers and cyberspace and request an interview. Internships are also available through school placement offices. There has been a steady increase in the number of companies making inquiries into finding young and talented people at both the college and high school level.

You may also wish to speak with employment agencies that have established contacts with cyberspace companies. Although such agencies usually do not list internships, a recruiter who is actively involved with many cyberspace companies may know of a company that has some need for interns.

It really becomes a game of odds. The more contacts you make, the better your chances of success. The more no's that you collect just put you closer to the one yes that you need. Being in the right place at the right time requires vigilance.

Jimmy Santos says, "It took me months and months of interviews to get a position. The more interviews I went to, the more I learned, and I got better at them." He continues, "Take your interviews as great learning experiences. I kept saying to myself, 'One day one company will say yes,' so I went to one more." All it takes is one yes.

EDUCATION

In cyberspace it is assumed that you will go to college. Yes, you want to get involved in cyberspace before the waves of employment and the trends are over. That is why you need the internship.

But this career field calls for a thoroughly educated individual. You can be involved now, but to stay involved and to remain on the edge you have to educate yourself continually, and a four-year degree is evidence that you can do just that. Jeff Harrington adamantly states, "Everyone should be required to learn about art, literature, and music. They form the backbone of culture. A life without that kind of stuff is empty."

You do not necessarily need to study computers in college, either. If you are not going to be a programmer, you might enroll in one or two computer courses related to publishing or multimedia. As Albert Einstein said, "Imagination is more important than knowledge." Go ahead and study poetry, dance, and sculpture. Consider a degree in microeconomics, chemistry, or psychology. Your bachelor's degree is to help you remain competitive in the future by helping you to become a well-rounded and thoughtful individual. College provides experiences in a broad range of disciplines. You will be able to draw from these to build new ideas for your company, which is a skill that will be highly valued.

As Kathryn Livornese stated repeatedly to me, "You must be able to get answers, so you have to be research- and solution-savvy. Sometimes to solve a problem you have to build a bridge that goes six miles out of the way to come back." As the market is flooded each year with a more and more highly skilled and educated workforce, you will not be left behind if you have had a solid education.

Resist the urge to join the cyber-workforce immediately. "Stay in school. You have your whole life to make money. Once you start working, you're going to work forever," Brad Taylor says. He continues, "There's more to college than just learning academics. It's learning life. Going away and learning how to live is a whole learning process beyond school."

Alan Ellman caps the discussion with this insight: "College teaches us to look at situations and to come up with solutions. A college degree shows prospective employers that you've been independent and can deal with life's problems. It also provides an excellent base for making contacts."

Colleges and universities are filled with other bright minds and experiences. The people that you meet there can be the key to your career. My own entry into cyberspace occurred with the help of meeting Scott Brodeur while we were both enrolled at the university. We were exchanging ideas at a campus eatery, and he said that I should send examples of my work to NJO. The rest is history.

One of the more popular cyberspace success stories is that of Justin Hall. His story is inspiring for anyone looking for a career in cyberspace. Visit his homepage, read his story, and view his résumé, *www.links.net*. You

What You Need to Do Now

will see how he has used cyberspace much to the advantage of his youth, intelligence, and aggressive self-promotion. Just remember, underneath all the play is a hardworking young man.

When Justin was fourteen, he was a software salesman. He was making forty dollars an hour teaching about software by the time he was fifteen. He has worked with computers in various capacities ever since. When he enrolled in Swarthmore College he discovered cyberspace and became "a card-carrying member of the digital revolution." He used his homepage as an interview tool and landed himself an internship with *Wired* magazine. I don't even want to venture a guess as to how many people are daily visitors to his page nowadays.

Freelance Opportunities

Many cyberspace employees do not go to work each day. A great deal of what we see on the Web is delivered to cyberspace by freelance employees. A freelance employee never has to show up at work. In fact, several of the features and columns found at online service sites are frequently written by freelance employees, and the same can be said for design and programming code work.

Let's say a freelancer, you, contacts a producer at the online service and promotes an idea for a new series. If the company expresses interest in placing your idea on its site, you will probably have to meet with the producer at that point to negotiate your contract.

The freelancer is awarded a contract and then sells his or her ideas for the individual installments to a cyberspace company. He or she then provides the company with each new installment as frequently as was agreed to in the contract. The updates could come from home, the beach, or an airliner. Where there's a telephone, there's a way.

Freelance work makes sense to a growing industry. A new company without the resources to maintain a large staff can save a lot of money by utilizing freelance employees. The company does not have to pay substantial hourly wages, full-time salaries, benefits, or bonuses of any type for freelance work.

Get Ready, Get Set

Plan out your job search. Articulate your objective, your goal. Determine what your strategy will be, then execute your plan. Build a portfolio and carry it with you. Select your interview clothing with an eye to fitting in with the style of your potential employer. Write an interview script and rehearse it—in front of a mirror or in front of others. Practice presenting yourself in the best possible light. At the interview, handle yourself with confidence.

If You're Thinking of Setting Up a Business

As long as there are telephone lines in your neighborhood, you can set up shop on the Internet. You will need to dial in to a local ISP or become your own ISP. There is a good deal of expense in becoming your own ISP, however.

You can run your business from home as well. Keep in mind that when you are connected to the Internet you are paying for a telephone call for the length of time that you are surfing. So you want to be sure you are making a local telephone call instead of a long-distance one.

Just Do It

I'll give Trisha Smith the last word in this chapter: "It's important to know what you want when you job search.

Define what you want out of cyberspace, and be flexible in your attempt to get there. Switch your internships so that you go to different companies each summer until you find the type of work you want and where you would be happy."

10

"DIY": Books, Software, and Web Sites

DIY. It's the rallying cry for each of you as you prepare to close this book. Do It Yourself. Everyone will be asking, "Do *you* DIY?"

This may be the most important chapter for your cyberspace career. Remember, you are an enthusiastic self-starter. This means that you are going to have to teach yourself.

Don't fret. You can do it.

BOOKS

Most of the people interviewed in this book have said that they prepared for their careers by reading numerous books and that they will continue to do so to keep up with the software and programming changes in cyberspace. Go into your local bookstore and check out the rows upon rows of Internet-related books. You may at first be immobilized by the overwhelming selection. They all look the same and have similar titles, and you know better than to judge a book by its cover.

However, let me point you in the direction that the cyberspace professionals in this book have successfully taken by suggesting several titles that they recommend.

"DIY"

- If you are just starting out on your pilgrimage to cyberspace, I recommend the Dummies Press from IDG Books (*www.idgbooks.com*). Theirs is the best-selling computer book series in the world, and with good reason. The books are funny, informative, and clearly written for those of you in the beginners to intermediate skill levels. The covers are black and yellow, and each of the titles has the words *for Dummies* in it. The series now has 255 texts, with thirty-three of them specifically about the Internet.
- Brad Taylor, the Metropolitan Museum's Web-Master, recommends the titles offered by O'Reilly & Associates, Inc. (*www.ora.com*). He uses them exclusively and says, "They're well documented and very easy to read." They have ten Internet programming titles and six more titles for using the Internet. They also have twenty-five programming titles (NT, C, C++) with an additional eighteen for Unix and four more for Java. Their Web page was listed as one of the "Top 100 Sites on the Web" by *PC Magazine*.
- Brian Kress, the book buyer at New York University's Computer Store (*www.bookc.nyu.edu*), recommends a new line of computer books for those of you who are looking forward to entering cyberspace as graphic artists/designers. The series is called The Visual QuickStart Guides by Peach Pit Press (*www.peachpit.com*). The books are designed for quick and simple exposure to graphic arts software to get you working with the programs as soon as possible.
- The Macmillan Information Super Library (*www.mcp.com*) includes the books most often mentioned by programmers as especially useful.

101

The *Unleashed* series is published by Sams.net Publishing. It comes highly recommended for everyone from the casual to the accomplished user. Forty-five titles dealing with Internet communications, networking, and programming are currently available. It is an expensive series, but the books are exhaustive in their efforts to bring you comprehensive information. Also distributed by Macmillan are the books by Que Publishing. Que has an extensive library of Internet titles for the accomplished to the expert user.

Software

There are dozens of software products currently on the market to help you create Web pages. Often referred to as authoring tools, they are basically templates that allow you to point and click information into the appropriate spaces or to cut markup language commands and paste them into your scripts as needed. The programs make Web page construction as easy as writing a paper on your word processing software. You can create, edit, and update your page like a professional in a matter of hours. Microsoft's "FrontPage," Claris' "HomePage," Symantec's "Café," and Adobe's "PageMill" and "SiteMill" are all popular software packages that allow you to make elaborate and elegant Web pages with simplicity and speed.

But you do not need to purchase software for page construction. Many packages are available free or as shareware at the Shareware Web site (*www.shareware.com*). There are even demonstration applications available for the previously mentioned packages.

Surf for Turf

There are numerous other Web sites in cyberspace to help you DIY. You don't even have to buy books or

"DIY"

expensive software for HTML and Java programming languages. Some Web sites offer instruction, examples, and downloadable editors to help you get your markup language error-free and functioning. Try connecting to any of the following links for even more information on getting started.

123—Easy!
spring-board.com/123easy

National Center for Super Computing Applications
www.ncsa.uiuc.edu/General/Internet/www/HTMLPrimer.html

Yale Center for Advanced Instructional Media
info.med.yale.edu/caim/stylemanual

University of Minnesota
web66.coled.umn.edu/Cookbook/contents.html

Indiana University
www.indiana.edu

The HTML Guru!
members.aol.com/htmlguru

And keep surfing to look for new ideas. Just look at "view source" to see how the programmer designed the page and then try it for yourself.

Even accomplished programmers view the sources of pages that intrigue them. It is standard industry practice and works to keep the Web increasingly better-looking and ever-changing. Since anyone can see what you've done, you must continually strive to do better and stay ahead of your imitators. A very popular quotation of Picasso's is, "Good artists copy, great artists steal." What more sanction could you need?

In addition, be sure to visit some of these interesting sites.

Yahoo's Cool sites—*www.yahoo.com*
Best of Web—*wings.buffalo.edu/contest*
Cool Site of the Day—*www.infi.net/cool.html*
Whole Internet Catalog—*nearnet.com/*
Useful Things—*www.telport.com/useful.
   html*
Hot on the Web—*kzsu.stanford.edu/uwi/reviews.html*

Keep browsing through space, sometimes with no goal other than spanning the world. Your "bookmarks" (saved pages) will probably grow.

At the same time, it is important to take time to create order in your world as well as on the Web. Your goal is to relate well to others and be a team player. Hone your diplomacy skills too. Cyberspace will still be there when you're done.

11

Conclusion

As you have seen in this book, you will be pushing yourself constantly to search for fresh insights and bold new ideas. Working faithfully within the vision of a specific company, you will be exploring, stretching, and redefining the parameters that exist in its business practice. You will be improvising like a jazz musician. Even with a score in front of them, the best jazz musicians make the music leap right off the page by deliberately inventing their own animated interpretations of the tune. Stanley Crouch eloquently describes jazz in his recently published book, *All American Skin Game*:

> Each performer must bring technical skill, imagination and the ability to create coherent statements through improvised interplay with the rest of the musicians . . . The improvising jazz musician must work in the heat and the pressure of the moment, giving form and order in a mobile environment, where choices must be constantly assessed and reacted to in one way or another.

That pretty much says it all concerning your potential role in cyberspace. Just replace "musician" with "cyberspace employee" and "music" with "artistic Web pages." You want to be the Wynton Marsalis of the Web. You want to develop an original vision and be able to express it, even in the confines of an established business structure, much as Marsalis can make his trumpet's distinctive tone and style sing within the patterns of a Duke Ellington standard.

You are going to have to learn most of what cyberspace is about on your own by exploring. In reality, though, any career success that you experience will ultimately be up to you alone. Work hard. Learn all you can. Educate yourself. This is your chance to experience the flush of an emerging industry. This is your chance to compete in a market where everyone has an equal opportunity. No one has a better chance than you.

Besides, in cyberspace, you are not preparing yourself for the job market as much as you are preparing the market for you. You are creating a portfolio in cyberspace to grab people's attention and rattle their notions of what Web pages are. You are not waiting for trends. You are setting them. You are not getting an edge on life. You are putting an edge on life.

It's just the beginning.

Glossary

browser The software application that you use to surf the Web. Netscape, Hot Java, and Microsoft Explorer are a few examples of graphic browsers that allow you to locate and access information from the Web's resources. Today's advanced browsers also allow you to display graphics and photographic images, as well as play sounds or display videos. Visit *sunsite.unc.edu/boutell/faq/www_faq.html* for information on browsers available for your computer.

C Computer programming language developed by Dennis Ritchie of AT&T Bell Laboratories. It was developed in the early 1970s in connection with the Unix Operating System. During the 1980s nearly all applications for personal computers were written in C. It has been described as "terse, elegant and deceptively simple" by Charles Petzold of the *New York Times*. It is a powerful and versatile language allowing for a variety of problem-solving solutions. Because of its power, Petzold also says, "It's almost impossible to write a bugfree program in C." By the way, C got its name from an earlier program called B.

C++ An extension of C that was developed at Bell Laboratories by Bjarne Stroustrup in the 1980s. C++ brought about object-oriented programming. Objects are reusable computer codes that serve as the building blocks of programs. Objects are added to make computer codes easier to maintain and reuse. C++ also makes it easier to avoid infestation by bugs.

CU–SeeMe Computer application that facilitates using the Internet for videoconferencing. This application turns the Internet into an inexpensive and relatively simple global videocommunications network. It was developed at Cornell University and is available free from White Pine Software.

download To retrieve information from the Web. When you wish to examine a document on the Web, you download that document using its URL.

e-mail Abbreviation for electronic mail, a service that allows one to send messages and graphics to another person or group of people. As technology improves, so does the service. You can save all of your mail, incoming and outgoing. You can reply to letters without creating a new address form and create aliases to avoid having to remember e-mail addresses.

FTP Acronym for File Transfer Protocol, an Internet service that allows transfer of copied files from one computer to another. While the amount of resources available through FTP is staggering, you must know exactly what you are looking for, as the files and directories are described beyond their file name.

hacker Person who is inclined to spend more time with a computer than most people. Hackers have developed an extensive language system to complement their behavioral code. For a humorous look at the jargon file, check out Eric S. Raymond's *The New Hacker's Dictionary.*

homepage Your homepage is your personal URL, your vanity plate, on the Web. Homepage is also the term for the starting point of a cluster of Web pages. In this case, it serves as a cover page or a table of contents for sites that span many Web pages.

HTML (Hypertext Markup Language) Used for creating hypertext on the Web. Hypertext refers to the language that marks the structural parts of a document: paragraphs, lists, headings, block quotations, and others. The computer can then understand the logical structure of the document.

interactive Functioning as a two-way communication system that includes responses by the user.

Java Computer language that is similar to C++ but has distinctions that make it simpler. It was developed by Sun Microsystems, Inc., in the early 1990s. Basically, the language grabs programs from other more powerful computers that run Web sites and returns the information to your personal computer. Its applets (little applications) can be used on Web pages along with text and pictures. Javascript, as the applets are called, allows the pages to be more animated and interactive by moving the focus of interactivity from the servers to the browsers. You can create animated icons and automated data gathering for your Web page without having to be a master programmer. Javascript runs on any platform, meaning that it is equally suited to Macintosh, Windows, and other systems.

links Connections between one hypertext document and another. Also referred to as hyperlinks, these special HTML codes tell the browser where to go and what to do. Links typically appear as buttons or graphic elements and as highlighted, colored, or underlined text.

online Being connected to the Internet. The term is also applicable to checking e-mail.

page, Web page, and site Interchangeable references to a single hypertext document on the Web.

server The workhorse or primary computer that provides services or resources to client computers.

URL (Uniform Resource Locator) The pathway used to find a particular page on the Web. Commonly refered to as the address, the URL is a short character string that identifies a particular document and its location on the Internet.

Web, World Wide Web, and www Interchangeable references to the computer files that are accessible through the Internet. All URLs on the Web begin with the prefix *http://*

Index

A
Advanced Networks and Services (ANS), 9–10
Advanced Research Projects Agency (ARPA), 8, 9, 10
advertising, 16, 46, 52, 63
Alpha Light Communications, 54, 63
America Online (AOL), 82
Analog PPP Shell account, 83
anonymity, 13
"Art Naked," 36–37

B
Barksdale, Jim, 64
Bell Telephone Laboratories, 8
books, 21, 29, 45, 100–102
Brodeur, Scott, 2, 17, 39–40, 81–82, 96
browser, 13, 18, 29, 32, 82
Bulletin Board Services (BBS), 57
business manager, 64

C
cable television, 16
card catalog, 67
careers, 1, 4, 5, 12, 42, 80, 81
Cary, Andrew, 3, 65
CD-ROM, 43, 45, 75, 76
Children's Television Workshop (CTW), 74–76, 89
chron, 30–31
Clark, Jim, 64
classes, Internet, 57, 60, 73
code, program, 29, 60, 63, 85–86
column, Internet, 34
music, 40
Comer, Douglas E., 7, 9–10
commissions, 52
Communications Decency Act, 12
communities, online, 80
computer, 2, 5, 7, 8, 10, 11, 13, 20, 25, 26, 27, 31, 58, 62, 82, 83
architecture, 27
buying, 84–85
Computer Store, 101
creativity, 4, 5, 17, 33, 42, 46, 55, 80, 81, 88
credit card, 15, 63
Crouch, Stanley, 105
curiosity, 27, 33
CU–SeeMe, 74
cyber-bosses, 56–69
cyber-cafe, 17, 70–74

D
Dalzell, Stewart, 13
deadlines, 49
dedicated connections, 84
Defense, U.S. Department of, 7–8, 9
Deschannes, Andree, 74
design, editorial, 44, 48
designer, 4, 42–51
dial-up, 72–73, 83
diligence, 33
director, 47–51, 61, 66
do-it-yourself (DIY), 81, 86, 100–104
download, 16, 31, 41, 74, 77, 89
"Dr. Webowitz," 77–78
Dummies Press, 101

111

INDEX

E
EBONE, 10–11
editor, 38–39
education, college, 20, 26, 95–96
Ellman, Alan S., 23, 61–63, 96
e-mail, 11, 13–14, 31, 40, 83, 91, 94
encryption, 13, 14, 55
entrepreneur, 5, 70–80
Explorer, 18

F
Faglio, Jeff, 59–60
feeds, 27, 28
file transfer protocol (FTP), 70
freedom of speech, 11–13
freelance, 97–98
Frequently Asked Questions (FAQ), 68

G
Gale, Bob, 3, 78–80, 92–93
Gates, Bill, 61
Gibson, William, 2
gif, 27, 86
Global Internet, 10–11
Goldsmith, Aryeh, 3, 24, 26–29
golf biographies, 54
graphics, 27, 31, 43, 48–49, 62, 75, 81, 86, 88, 91
Gray, Lowell J., 3
Groeneman, Elizabeth, 72, 73

H
hacker, 5, 14, 62
hairstyle, 5, 24
Hall, Justin, 96–97
Harrington, Jeff, 4, 74–78, 89
Hersey, Scott, 40
hits, 64, 67, 76, 80, 87
homepage, 21, 79, 82, 85–87, 89, 97
Hosein, Jinnah, 3, 24–26, 94
hosting, Web site, 55, 57, 62, 67
Hyper Text Markup Language (HTML), 17, 20, 29, 36, 45, 46, 60, 67, 81, 85–86, 101, 103

I
IDG Books, 101
Illustrator, 45, 72
information superhighway, 2
Integrated Service Digital Network (ISDN), 83–84
Interactive Connection, 5, 23–31, 45–47, 61–63, 88, 94
Internet Architecture Board, 7
Internet Book, The, 7
Internet Cafe, 70–74
Internet Protocol (IP), 8, 9, 11
Internet service provider (ISP), 57, 67, 82–84, 98
  costs, 83–84
internship, 20–21, 87, 93–95
intranet, 32, 57

J
"Jersey Girl," 37
job
  entry-level, 87
  hunt, 21, 45, 81–99
  interview, 87–88, 94–95
Journal Square Interactive, 44

K
key escrow plan, 14
Kid's Guide to the Internet, The, 74
Kress, Brian, 101

L
languages, programming, 27–28, 76
  C, 27, 76, 101
  C++, 27, 76, 101
  HTML, 17, 20, 29, 36, 45, 46, 60, 67, 81, 85–86, 101, 103
  Java, 29, 53, 68, 101, 103
  NT, 101
  Unix, 27

INDEX

leased line, 83
Levitan, Peter, 65–67, 87, 93
links, 36, 85
Livornese, Kathryn, J., 3, 53, 57–61, 64, 96
London Productions, 78–80
Long Island Internet Headquarters (LIIH), 5, 52–53, 59–61

M

Macmillan Information Super Library, 101–102
marketing director, 65–67
Mathis, Andrew, 86, 89
Maxwell's, 35
media
 interactive, 5
 multi-, 43, 71, 74
 traditional, 15, 16, 17
Metropolitan Museum of Art, 67–69, 101
Microsoft, 18, 25
modem, 10, 18, 82, 83–84
Mulligan, Jason, 3, 86
Museum of Modern Art, 74
music, 74–78

N

NASDAQ, 16
National Aeronautics and Space Administration (NASA), 9
National Science Foundation (NSA), 9
National Security Agency, 14
Nelson, Tricia, 3, 37–38, 81
Netscape, 18, 29, 64, 84
network, 6, 7, 8, 9, 10
 fiber optic, 18
networking, 25, 58
Neuromancer, 2
New Jersey Online (NJO), 6, 34–41, 42–45, 47–51, 65–67, 86, 87
newspaper, online, 34–41, 78–79

NPS Associates, 31–32

O

opportunities, employment, 15–17, 18
O'Reilly & Associates, 101

P

Pagemaker, 72
Pardavilla, Art III, 3, 35–37, 43, 86
Park, Christopher, 3, 29–31
Peach Pit Press, 101
Perley, Arthur, 3, 71–74
Photoshop, 45, 72
poetry, 76
pornography, 12
portfolio, 51, 89–92
practice, 29–31, 33, 92
privacy, right to, 14
problem-solving, 28
producers, 37–41, 44
production manager, 65
programmers, 23–33, 101
project manager, 17, 32, 45–47

Q

Quark, 45, 72

R

regulation, government, 11–12, 13–14
résumé, 2, 21, 89–92, 96
Russell, Alfred, 74
Russell, Elsie, 74, 76

S

salaries, 23, 34, 42, 52
Santos, Jimmy, 3, 42–45, 47, 95
Schwartz, Joe, 3, 31–32, 33
search engine, 67
Secured Electronic Transaction (SET), 15
self-discipline, 25, 26, 33
server, 25, 30, 36, 40, 67, 72–73, 84

Index

Sesame Street, 75
shareware, 102
Shout!, 78
skills
    basic, 20
    communication, 37, 55
    design, 49, 93
    editorial, 93
    language, 27
    updating, 45
    writing, 92
Smith, Trisha, 3, 4, 38–39, 94, 98
software, 8, 9, 10, 14, 20, 21, 102
Spoken Word Universe, 78
Stone, EB, 3, 5, 12, 53, 57–61, 88–89, 93
storefront, 57, 58
surfing, 29, 34, 38, 54, 86, 103–104
syndicate sales, 23, 54
systems operator, 29–31

T

tattoo, 4, 38–39
Taylor, Brad, 4, 67–69, 101
TCP/IP, 8, 9, 11
technology, 11, 15, 16, 68, 81
template, 27, 36, 50, 102
text, 74, 81
ticker feed, 27, 54, 62
training, in-house, 68
Transmission Control Protocol (TCP), 8, 9, 11

U

Uniform Resources Locator (URL), 57, 87

Unix Timesharing System (UNIX), 8, 25
updates, 17, 43, 50, 54

V

view source, 29, 82, 86
Visual QuickStart Guides, 101

W

Wattanasarn, Isra, 3, 54–55, 63–64, 92
weather prediction, 38–39
Web, 2, 5, 11–13, 18, 27, 29, 37, 43, 46, 70, 71, 76, 82, 91
WebMaster, 67–69, 101
Web page, 2, 23, 28, 36, 38, 47, 54, 62, 68, 73, 85, 88–89, 91, 102
Web site, 13, 21, 27, 28, 32, 34, 41, 42, 48, 53, 57, 67
Westergaard, Kermit, 4, 5, 54
Williams, Maurice, 3, 47–51, 91–92
Windows, 32
Wired magazine, 12, 97
World Wide Web, 2, 16, 21, 81, 82, 93
writers, 5, 34–41

Y

Yahoo search engine, 76
Yang, Amy, 16–17, 24, 32, 45–47

ENDORSEMENT

If you are an aspiring leader, or a leader who aspires to a higher level of greatness, read this book! If leadership is about unleashing human potential, *not* reading this book would be a great injustice to both you and all those you would lead.

At a time when fear, divisiveness, and distrust are amplifying the dark, aberrant, self-centric aspects of the collective human soul – at a time when critical-thinking, personal responsibility, and moral fortitude have been buried under a blanket of political correctness, crowd-sourced morality, and a mindset of entitlement; a time when it seems that the preferred weapon against endemic injustice is even more injustice – we find a world in which the very definition of "leadership" seems to have been lost in an abyss of malpractice.

Thankfully, there are thought-leaders among us who see the current state of affairs simply as the "darkness before the dawn" and who have great wisdom to impart to those who would lead us towards a brighter future. Dr. Melodye Hilton is one of those thought-leaders.

In ***Higher Living Leadership***, Dr. Hilton invites tomorrow's leader to think differently. Her invitation is not based in idealistic theory and philosophy, but rather, is inspired by, and rooted in real science, yet speaks to true heart of leadership and human potential.

Peter Demarest
Co-Founder, Axiogenics, LLC
Co-Author, ***Answering the Central Question***

DEDICATION

I would like to celebrate the countless emerging and established leaders who have chosen to take *the road less traveled,* challenging themselves to raise the bar of leadership. I honor those who choose to think deeply, work responsibly with passion, and serve a cause greater than themselves. This book is for you.

I am truly a blessed woman because I am surrounded by true friends, too many to name, and family that encourage me to release my heart and impact my world for good. Thank you, Katie Stansfield, for your support as we build together and package trainings that impact people worldwide. To my daughter, Rebecca, I am so proud of you and am overjoyed that you carry my leadership and training passion…I love you! To my son, Joel, who has partnered with me for many years in investing into up-and-coming leaders, you are truly a rock of stability and a wealth of wisdom. I love you! To my daughter-in-love, Erin, who knits our family together—we'd never go on vacation if it wasn't for you! I love you! To my beloved and valued grandchildren: Ayden, Laila, and Maxwell who are being groomed to release their contribution to the world without fear, I love each of you. To my husband, Steven, the greatest cheerleader in my life who, for over 40 years, has said no matter the cost, "Go for it!" "I believe in you." "Just do it!" I love and honor you!

Table of Contents

ACKNOWLEDGEMENTS	i
INTRODUCTION: Higher Living Leaders Purpose	iii
Chapter 1: Leadership Reformation	1
Chapter 2: Validation Quotient: Validation	13
Chapter 3: Signature of Value	31
Chapter 4: Higher Living Leadership: Head-Hand-Heart	42
Chapter 5: Intra-Leadership	63
Chapter 6: What was I thinking?	75
Chapter 7: Invisible Motivators: Values	90
Chapter 8: Discovering Personal Purpose	102
Chapter 9: Higher Living Leaders: Empathy	116
Chapter 10: Builders of Trust	126
Chapter 11: The Greatest Form of Honor	146
BIBLIOGRAPHY	159
ABOUT THE AUTHOR	171
NOTES	177

ACKNOWLEDGEMENTS

Isaac Newton said, "If I have seen further than others, it is by standing upon the shoulders of giants." I want to thank the *giants* in my life who have supported and encouraged the writing of the book. Thank you to my friend and skilled neuroscientist and microbiologist, Andrea Ham. Thank you for ensuring the accurate representation of objective scientific facts to support the leadership principles of *Higher Living Leadership*. Thanks to Christina Bates, of Bates Consulting, who spent months reviewing and editing my book. Thank you to Jeanenne Sweatman for the hours of editing and insuring the accuracy of the references, I love your building heart. Thanks to Peter Demarest, author and expert in Axiogenics, who took his valuable time to review the manuscript with his value centric passion.

INTRODUCTION

Higher Living Leaders PURPOSE

Culture is a reproducible system of beliefs that shape the actions of individuals. It communicates to others what are, and are not acceptable beliefs and actions. Culture tells you what is right or wrong and what you must do to "fit in." We learn our culture through instruction and observed behavior.

Most would agree that we live in a global culture where there is a widespread epidemic of mistrust. Decisions are often stress-filled and fear-driven and the most common mentalities are self-serving and self-gratifying. At the same time, there is a remnant of emerging and established leaders who combat this epidemic by serving as catalysts for positive change in their realms of influence.

Even in the midst of the challenges of our world's culture, these leaders refuse to focus on, and in turn perpetuate what is wrong. Instead, they deliberately choose to view the future through lenses of hope for families, communities, organizations, and nations. These leaders embody the concept that I have coined as,

"Higher Living Leadership."

Higher Living Leadership thrusts us beyond our individual successes and helps us to make the most of our opportunity to influence our culture. This is a vital responsibility that today's leaders must both recognize and exercise. In order for our efforts to continue beyond our lifetime, we must purposely plant seeds today; we must be an incubator of validation to shift the cultural atmosphere. These kinds of leadership endeavors will prepare a generation of courageous trailblazers; the goal being to embolden them to go farther, achieve more, and give more as power and influence are used for the greater good.

In summary, *Higher Living Leaders* skillfully set the stage for emerging leaders to have a platform to positively impact their world.

Governmental leaders do not dictate culture; instead it is shaped by society's loudest and most influential voices that ultimately shape legislation. Therefore, we should not look to our governments to solve all the world's problems. Doing so not only neglects our responsibility as citizens, but also abandons our obligation to inspire, influence, train, and mentor those who *do* shape culture.

Science has proven that the neural pathways of our brain are constantly changing as a result of belief conversions, behaviors, or the environment. Similarly, history has revealed that the beliefs of citizenry lead to rapid changes in culture.

CULTURAL DEGENERATION

During the course of my lifetime, I have observed how rapidly culture has changed from one generation to another. The expression "generation gap" is commonplace to represent the drastic difference between a young person's worldview and that of his or her parents or grandparents. The decades of the sixties and seventies—my generation—witnessed a Cultural Revolution that was, in many ways, won at society's detriment. We were activists with a cause to liberate *our and future generations from anything binding us to traditional morals, values, and responsibilities.* Our mantra was, "if it feels good, do it!"

What were we thinking?

Every child is born with innate contributions in order to serve his or her world. When his or her unchanging purpose enjoys its place of expression, he or she will encounter a fulfilled life as they serve a cause greater than themselves.

The optimum environment for a child's development is one where they are understood and raised to maturity (fully adult) by emotionally healthy and full-grown, giving parents. These parents are not driven by meeting their own needs, or by fear-driven selfishness, but to lead for the good of their children.

Today, the opportunity for a healthy upbringing is rarely a child's experience. The sad reality is that a self-serving mentality and deterioration of morals and values has brought about a new cultural norm. This was not a premeditated abuse of power but has propagated injustice nonetheless. Our nation's sons and daughters are surviving rather than thriving, feeling numb regarding their own lives. They are searching for some sense of personal fulfillment and finding themselves powerless to impact their world. The self-centered and personally irresponsible attitudes and actions of previous generations have shifted cultural norms, silencing healthy voices and distorting the treasure within our children.

Benjamin Franklin once said, "I conceive that the great parts of the miseries of mankind are brought upon them by false estimates they have made of the value of things." Allegorically speaking, we placed a high value upon our freedom to eat all the "candy" we wanted. Yet now we grieve the idea that today's generation is riddled with "cavities" and "diabetes" as a result. We lived only for the moment, and failed to consider or recognize the consequences for future generations.

Freedom in the absence of accountability produces internal chaos and consequences that are incongruent to the very nature of our humanity. External achievements without internal order leave us constantly searching for more; we are never satisfied. External power without internal control positions us to hurt those we love, and to damage our own self-worth. Injustice is the outcome, and it permeates our world. It is a direct outcome of selfishness—caring only about what we want at the expense of others. As a result, we devalue human life knowingly or unknowingly by means of prejudice and hatred.

Current generations define success differently than those before them. Today we see a young generation confused and desperately trying to fit in while simultaneously searching for a unique identity and purpose. What results is an internal tug-o-war between a desire for individuality and a constant search for acceptance. What ensues, therefore, is a generation that is desperate to lead, yet instinctively and counterproductively following the loudest voice around them. They do so because of a culturally learned inability to discover and celebrate their own personal identity. We are desperately in need of those who will model another way; we are in need of those who will step up, demonstrate, and perpetuate *Higher Living Leadership*.

My generation of leaders led a revolution that has left our children and grandchildren searching for anything better than what they now know; they are searching for experiences that are higher, more meaningful, and healthier to the human soul. The emerging leaders of our society are desperate for a cause worthy of their time, effort, energy, and most importantly their heart. Rather than repeating a former model of revolution for revolution's sake, this time the goals will be to improve, advance, and produce positive change in the emerging generation's professional and private spheres of influence. This Cultural Revolution will be one of healthy internal leadership that influences our world and leaves it in a better condition than before.

On every level, from the family unit to the nation, a culture of justice will produce a breeding ground for H*igher Living Leadership* to flourish, reproduce, and have a sustainable impact upon the future. As *Higher Living Leaders,* our individual leadership is not about position or title, but the desire to make a significant difference in the lives of others, systems, and cultures. The internal motivation of justice—power used for good—is foundational to successful and impactful leadership. Justice will defend and honor. In the simplest terms, leaders who are motivated by justice will do what is right when confronted with the harsh opposing realities in their spheres of influence.

Every aspect of society is crying out for role models of higher thinking, higher responsibility, and a higher cause—a cause that makes life worth living and impacts society for good.

I very much appreciate the quality of leadership training that I have experienced. It has progressively influenced countless emerging and established leaders. I am now motivated to raise the bar even higher for our families, communities, and nations. Our world is searching for the fullness of intellectual expression, coupled with moral and ethical standards. It is by these terms that we will see a shift in the trajectory of our society by changing culture through acts of justice.

George W. Bush said, "...America's greatest economic need is higher ethical standards—standards enforced by strict laws and upheld by responsible business leaders."[1]

The manner in which we lead our families, organizations, and communities of today can shift culture through continual *Higher Living* that impacts others for good. It is our responsibility to *think* and *act* on a higher cognitive and emotional level to positively impact all of our relationships. I recognize that this is "easier said than done," but it is what will set us apart as H*igher Living Leaders.*

My hope is to provide both emerging and established leaders with relevant and applicable principles that can have a positive effect on every aspect of their lives.

I will freely tell you that I am not a neuroscientist or an expert in axiogenics. My goal, however, is that through my research and experience I can simplify some otherwise complex principles, making them accessible to you, and, as a result personally empowering. I hope to define for you the appropriate functions, in both intrinsic and extrinsic areas of life, to provide you with the ability to shift cultural paradigms through *Higher Living Leadership*.

Strategic reformers of culture are now actively integrated into our society. The question is, will you be one of them? I invite you to join a *higher* model of living and leading. These are the brave leaders who will redefine, for themselves and for future generations, power used for good that will establish and influence a new way—a way of *Higher Living Leadership*.

CHAPTER 1

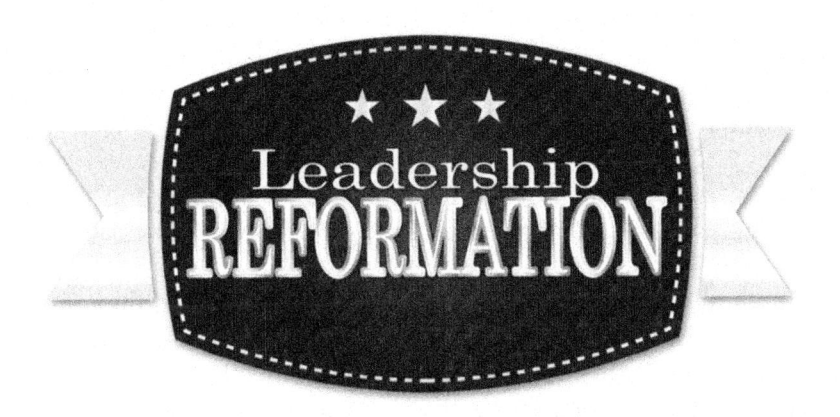

★★★ Leadership REFORMATION

The meaning of successful leadership is changing as rapidly as the society in which we live and function. Social trends and cultural values influence businesses, government, arts, media, and educational communities, thereby altering the way we live and lead. We can no longer passively stick our head in the proverbial sand. Instead, we must become a catalyst for positive change through personal leadership reformation.

The word "reformation" connotes rescue from error and a return to a rightful course. Courage is an attribute of one who rescues from error doing what is right for all. Our world needs *Higher Living Leaders* to step up to the plate and hit some home runs making our world a better place. We may not be able to change the whole world, but we can positively impact our personal spheres of influence for good.

Our lives can serve as "pictures of possibility" for others to follow, as we model the way through our words and deeds. Our attitudes teach what is right or wrong, good or bad, truth or lie, trust or mistrust, integrity or manipulation, love or hatred, celebration of or prejudice towards others, and so forth. With or without formal position or title, each one of us possesses the power to influence others positively.

Many people may consider me an idealist for believing that we can actually bring reformation to organizations, cultures, or even a nation. But, the truth is, we can! The truth is, YOU can!

"All that is necessary for the triumph of evil is that good men do nothing."[1]

Throughout history, good and bad leaders have shaped their world, influenced legislation, impacted lives, and shifted the course of cultures and nations. There are many un-sung heroes throughout history—those courageous individuals who stood up for a higher cause in order to combat the corruption surrounding them.

I HAVE A DREAM!

On August 28, 1963, Martin Luther King, Jr. delivered his famous "I Have a Dream" speech. His dream was to see an end to racism in the United States. While there is still work to be done to confront racism, we are living in a much better world "...where [man is] not judged by the color of [his] skin, but by the content of [his] character"—a cry of King's heart.[2]

I, too, have a dream! Begin to envision a multitude of *Higher Living Leaders* that sincerely believe they can bring positive change to their world! Imagine those same leaders embracing the responsibility for its implementation in their spheres of influence. Imagine a company of leaders worldwide who are committed to see families whole, organizations flourishing, communities prospering, and nations thriving.

James Kouzes and Barry Posner, authors of, *The Leadership Chal-*

lenge, said**,** "The domain of leaders is the future. The leader's unique legacy is the creation of valued institutions that survive over time. The most significant contribution leaders make is not simply to today's bottom line; it is to the long-term development of people and institutions so they can adapt, change, prosper, and grow."3

There is great power and responsibility associated with any form of leadership influence. Whether you are a school student influencing your peers, a friend, spouse, parent, teacher, actor, sports figure, business person, or political leader, you have a vital mandate for reformation. Wherever a platform of influence exists, there exists the opportunity for leaders to either bring positive change by building and empowering, or to harm, abuse, exploit, or control unjustly. We are either on one side of the fence or the other! Riding the fence is a fear-based reaction that positions the leader to live in a constant state of duplicity that results in internal conflict and external chaos.

Leadership is the source of life. It can be readily understood in examining the source of a river. When the source of a river is pure, clean, and healthy, it will supply the river with the same qualities and will benefit all who drink from it. Conversely, if the source of the river is contaminated, so too will the river be contaminated and it will harm anyone who drinks from it. The indisputable fact is that our decisions not only affect us, but also those with whom we share a relationship. Many people believe that they can compartmentalize their lives, living one way personally and another professionally. This way of living culminates in a tormented life, even in the face of high levels of influence or prosperity. A leader cannot simultaneously produce pure and contaminated "water" from the same source. When my freedom takes away another's it is morally and ethically wrong! Leadership, position, or authority by its very nature will have an impact on others—for good or harm; therefore, let us take what has already been entrusted to us and be a part of the solution.

DR. MELODYE HILTON

When we think about the profound responsibility that leadership brings, and the care that must be taken when one leverages a platform of influence, it is easy to believe that a world renowned humanitarian and Nobel Peace Prize winner could bring reformation. It is easy to believe that her platform to speak before the United States Congress, the United Nations, and governmental agencies worldwide would provide her with the necessary platforms to positively affect change. Yes! This individual's voice is still heard worldwide, even after her death, as her torch is passed to many who were influenced by her life and message. Even though she has passed away, her voice is still heard worldwide. With a heart to rescue many from error and return to a rightful course, she was one of the greatest reformers in history; she shifted mindsets, beliefs, values, and ultimately impacting culture for the good.

"People are unreasonable, illogical, and self-centered. Love them anyway.

If you do good, people will accuse you of selfish, ulterior motives. Do good anyway.

If you are successful, you win false friends and true enemies. Succeed anyway.

The good you do will be forgotten tomorrow. Do good anyway.

Honesty and frankness make you vulnerable. Be honest and frank anyway.

What you spend years building may be destroyed overnight. Build anyway.

People really need help but may attack you if you help them. Help people anyway.

Give the world the best you have and you'll get kicked in the teeth. Give the world the best you've got anyway."[4]

This quote was found on a sign on the wall in her Children's Home, Shishu Bhavan, in Calcutta, India. This leader was Mother Theresa and this well-known quotation represents her leadership approach. She knew that love, kindness, success, doing good, honesty, building, helping, and giving your best was the highest way to think, live, and lead.

Our ability to enact reformation that leads to good outcomes begins in the core of who we are—our heart, our character!

Leadership is not about position or title, but having the courage to make a significant difference in our sphere of influence.

In fact, the moment we lean upon our title or position rather than a heart of service, our influence will weaken.

Successful leadership validates and empowers others and the organizations with whom they connect. It enacts a heart of partnership, teamwork, and collaboration (aggressively working together with others to benefit the whole). It has the emotional fortitude required to be an instrument of justice.

LEADERS: INSTRUMENTS OF JUSTICE!

Justice has to do with the exercise and distribution of power, authority, influence, and wealth. This power is visible in the political and governmental arenas; in social, religious, cultural, family, and educational systems; and in the marketplace. When we use this power to do what is good we become an instrument of justice. But, when power is used to take from others what is rightfully theirs, injustice results. Today, we are witnessing blatant evil that saturates cultures with lies, hatred, and injustice and strategically plans to destroy anyone who believes differently.

It is also important to recognize that injustice is not the sole province of human beings. Many times we have encountered that life is simply not fair. Circumstances beyond our control—illness, accidents, loss, or disasters—can result in a battle of the mind, hindering our identity, purpose, and potential. *Higher Living Leadership* has the opportunity to be a voice expressed, hands extended, and an instrument of justice acting on behalf of hurting lives, struggling communities, and divided nations.

We cannot focus solely on ourselves, our business, or even the revitalization of our own towns and cities—even though that is a by-product when the people in those cities are impacted by justice. We must broaden our reach.

Years ago, I experienced a defining moment in my life while on a pilgrimage to Edinburgh, Scotland. I visited the castle there and saw the beautiful crown jewels of Scotland. I was confused when I saw a huge, ordinary-looking rock displayed next to the crown jewels. At face value, that rock looked out of place, but as I read the inscription beneath it, I discovered it was the "Stone of Destiny." The Kings and Queens would sit upon the Destiny Stone to be coroneted. At the moment of their coronation, their life was no longer simply "about them"—it about their kingdom, their people, and their very land. To the people of Scotland, the Destiny Stone's value far exceeded that of money or prosperity; it represents a people, a nation, and a mandate for their preservation and prosperity.

In the absence of understanding our leadership directive, we throw away that stone of destiny—our seat of leadership commissioning—for the more obvious beauty of the crown jewels—society's standard of success. We cannot ignore our most valuable inheritance and purpose, though appearing common, to exchange it for temporal wealth. Our highest and best leadership contribution rests in the ability to impact our society with wisdom, truth, and justice.

Tears began to trickle down my face when I recognized that to embrace my purpose—my leadership responsibility—I had to understand *in my heart* that it would no longer be "about me." I recognized that authentic commissioning as a leader calls and positions me to give of myself for the benefit of others and the land that I love.

In a world full of grey, where we are taught that truth is relative and one can even be one's own "god," people are desperate for a standard of right and wrong and trustworthy role-models. Injustice flourishes in the midst of moral uncertainty creating hot beds of fear, confusion, insecurity, and abuse.

"The human heart instinctively knows that it deserves justice. The human heart cries out for justice. However, our world is filled with injustice and suffering. The history of mankind is the history of injustice and abuse of our fellowman. It is the story of injustice, hostility, tyranny, brutality, anger, hatred, inhumanity, violence, and revenge..."[5]

The sad reality is that many people do not hold a justice worldview. A worldview is a mindset, idea, or a way of viewing things about our world and ourselves that determines how we will live. It is our ethos of moral conduct that we cannot violate regardless of external pressure. What we believe underlies all of our decisions and actions—even how we conduct ourselves in business. Whether deliberate or unintentional, our beliefs determine our personal level of success and how our decisions impact society.

Many say they desire to use their power and influence for good, but when in doing so affects their standard of living, they refrain because they do not want to be inconvenienced. "The sad reality is that man's nature desires justice for himself, yet he denies it to others."[6] This must change!

Teddy Roosevelt said, "We must diligently strive to make our young men decent, God-fearing, law-abiding, honor-loving, justice-doing, and also fearless and strong, able to hold their own in the hurly-burly of the world's work, able to strive mightily that the forces of right may be in the end triumphant. And we must be ever vigilant in so telling them."[7]

We have a responsibility to impact the world like no other generation has done before us. We are desperate to live for a cause greater than ourselves. Changing our model of leadership along with our image of success, and caring deeply for others is a revolutionary mindset in today's society. Picture what our world can become when a company of justice-motivated *Higher Living Leaders* take responsibility to invest into people and systems to bring positive change!

Justice defends, honors, and values. It connotes the generation of equality, truth, and fairness bringing peace to chaos. In simple terms, every time we do what is right, we demonstrate a heart of justice.

When we positively impact any aspect of culture, we are an instrument of justice. As previously stated, culture is a reproducible system of beliefs that shapes the actions of individuals. It communicates to others what are, and are not acceptable beliefs and actions. Culture tells you what is right or wrong and what you must do to "fit in." Therefore, every time I employ my leadership influence, my platform, or my power for good, I am modeling what is right and acceptable before my present cultural setting. Our leadership actions, in and of themselves, is an expectation placed upon others to follow.

My grandchildren love to come to my home every opportunity they are able. Even before they ask, we can already hear their heart-tugging words ring in our ears, "I want to come to YOUR house!"

Even though they are very young, they recognize that coming to our house means they are embracing our culture. The culture—the belief system—that we model and teach demonstrates to them what is or is not acceptable at our home. One aspect of our culture is that "we treat each other with respect." If they violate what is expected in our culture, they must go home. We do not become angry, nor do we punish. We simply teach and model the behaviors required to enjoy the benefits of our culture. If they honor this culture (belief system), they can stay, play, and enjoy their time with us. It is amazing how little ones are able to make good choices when the culture is clearly communicated and exemplified by leadership. What Abraham Lincoln once quoted is quite true, "When I do good, I feel good; when I do bad, I feel bad..."[8] Our culture is a living voice shaping moral and ethical behavior.

Not all culture is clearly communicated in homes, organizations, workgroups, or relationships leaving its members confused. Unjust or wounded leadership will create a "damned if I do and damned if I don't" culture to the detriment of others. Justice-minded leaders deliberately communicate what is or is not appropriate for the good of all. Leaders of justice use their power of influence to create a culture that will empower, build, and help each person to succeed.

Our society comprises a generation of emerging leaders that have experienced so much injustice (abuse of power). As such, there is burning passion inside of them both to receive justice and become instruments of justice. To do so, they are looking to follow *Higher Living Leaders* who have a heart to use their platforms and influence for good!

These emerging leaders are highly intelligent and have a keen awareness of what is relevant today. Their understanding of the rapidly changing culture may be leveraged as an effective weapon to destroy lies and limitations that once kept these potential-filled world-changers confined to fear-based choices, self-sabotage, and a vacuum of purpose.

The sad reality is that many relationships, organizations, systems, and structures are hotbeds of injustice (the misuse and abuse of power). This abuse of power is manipulative, deceptive, selfish, and corrupt. It takes advantage of others for the benefit of oneself. This is exploitation and is abusive! It creates a living and working environment of fear and intimidation, and it confuses the mind to believe lies over truth, shame over validation, and a non-existence of true fulfillment. It leaves a person feeling hopeless and without the ability to succeed. As such, injustice creates poverty. Poverty is more than the lack of money or resources; it is the absence of the ability to choose—believing, "I'm damned if I do and damned if I don't."

Any type of injustice fosters lies in the mind, corrupting an individual's belief system regarding themselves, others, and their specific sphere of influence. These lie-driven beliefs shape a person's functions, and in turn, convince him or her that actions taken are simply, "what I must do to survive" and "this is just the way it is." This thinking is what fuels a cycle of injustice (abuse of power) that then permeates the culture.

Remember, reformation means to rescue from error—from injustice and its lies—and return to a rightful course. Will we be leaders of justice who are willing to fight for what is right and true? Will we confront error with a courage and zeal that can impact individuals, systems, and structures? Moral, ethical, and unprejudiced leadership gives voice—a platform to ignite the passion of another's voice—ultimately freeing the very atmosphere, generating paradigm shifts, activating creativity and productivity, and bringing reformation! This is justice!

Error was not interwoven into our culture in a day and reformation will take time, effort, and many *Higher Living Leaders* positioned and leading in all the realms of society and culture. Can you imagine the influence for good that could be achieved if one by one we lived the mandate of *Higher Living Leadership*? Can you picture the impact that this would have on families, employees, clients, cities, communities, school systems, governments, and ultimately, a nation?

Though we are not exempt from fear, we can be courageously confident in the cause of justice. No longer will we be bound by a false identity or the injustices enacted against us. We know our purpose! Our willingness to turn from our selfish ambitions and embrace a leadership reformation of justice will position us to not only do what is right, but to become a trusted individual that will facilitate the full release of true success—internally and externally.

Helen Keller said, "...until the great mass of people shall be filled with the sense of responsibility for each other's welfare, social justice can never be attained."[9]

We are called to impact the world like no other generation of leaders has done before us. Reformation is stirring in our hearts and justice is its name!

The dawn of transformation arises when I surrender the familiarity of who I am today for the intrinsic potential of tomorrow.

Every organization requires competent individuals to develop strategic business plans and organizational structures that establish a strong corporate base. Though these leadership and management practices are absolutely necessary, my personal goal is to increase the intrinsic value of the leaders themselves. They are the organization's sources of life. They are the organization's foundation and, as such will determine its internal strength and external impact. When passion and compassion are ignited in the leaders, they will be contagious and it will spread throughout the organization.

Successful organizations are not solely defined by building the "bottom line," but through building their people, they build the bottom line.

"Cash flow problems are not simply financial problems; they are leadership problems, organizational problems—people problems."[10]

When an organization employs a team of: highly skilled theorists who see the greater vision, strategists who provide the blueprint for that vision, analyzers who see the potential pitfalls and the solutions to safeguard the vision, managers who lead the people in the vision's implementation, and finally, trusted task executors[11] who implement the vision, they are equipped to be successful. Subsequently, when these highly competent individuals build on a *Higher Living Leadership* aptitude, they will find the journey as fulfilling as meeting the objective of the organization itself, and those they serve.

CHAPTER 2

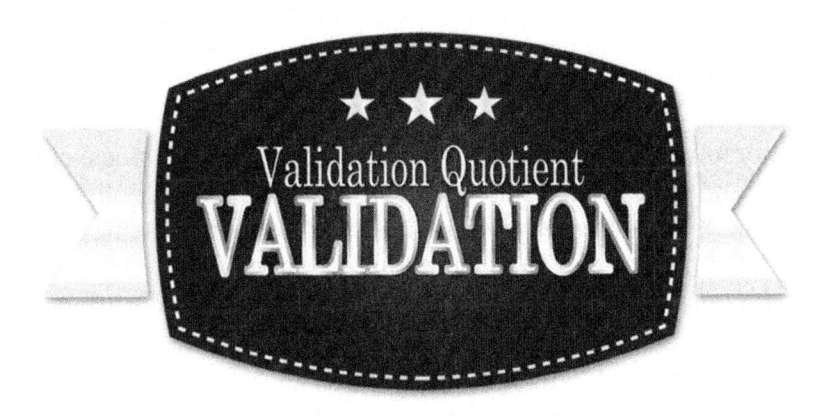

Validation Quotient
VALIDATION

My core purpose has always been to influence and train leaders to become instruments of justice no matter the type or size of their sphere of influence. My core value of justice has propelled me to invest into the individual in ways that inspire and motivate, as well as train and empower. I have learned that as individuals discover and release their leadership aptitude with purity of motives and for the good of another, the reward will unearth amazing treasures within them. Science supports the finding that the value we communicate to and in others is fed back into our own lives. This has the power to improve our lives—intellectually, psychologically, and even physically.

After years of studying, teaching, and providing coaching on leadership principles, I sought a foundational principle by which to simplify otherwise complex concepts, making them relevant, practical, and applicable to every sphere of life and influence. As a leadership enthusiast and life-long learner, I have always desired to apply my learning experience from world-class leaders, scientists, researchers, and entrepreneurs by authentically weaving them through my voice and purpose to unpack and define the passion, methodologies, ideals, and principles comprising what I refer to as *"Higher Living Leadership."*

When moral and ethical principles are the golden thread woven into the internal fabric of our character, then life becomes worth living and favor and external success will answer!

I explored various approaches by which to articulate values, ethics, contributions, attitudes and mindsets that could be applicable to personal and professional relationships, corporate achievement, moral character, and "over-the-top" competencies. One of the foundational principles that guided, by assessment of various approaches, is the idea that our success should exemplify holistic leadership that inspires up-and-coming leaders to arise and partner with us for societal reformation.

Albert Einstein best captured the essence of this principle when he said, "…one should guard against preaching to the young man success in the customary sense as the aim of life… The most important motive for work in school and in life is pleasure in work, pleasure in its results, and the knowledge of the value of the result to the community."[1]

I want my ceiling to be the floor for another. My desire is to build emerging leaders for platforms of influence. With this same passion, I also desire to partner together with them now. Emerging leaders of all ages are looking for established leaders to exemplify and impart healthy leadership from the inside out. They are not looking for those who will just tell them what to do; they want us to model the behavior as well. This produces an ecosystem where competence is built in alignment with what motivates their heart, and thereby, empowers them to discover personal purpose.

GIVING RISE TO EMERGING LEADERS

With this being said, it is important to understand that these emerging leaders must possess an intrinsic motivation; they must be willing to apply what they have been taught as they take personal responsibility for the knowledge and wisdom offered to them. I may see amazing potential within an up-and-coming leader, however I cannot work harder on their growth than they do. In other words, it is the emerging leader alone that has the power to make the most of the opportunity provided. *Change will be short-lived if not conceived from a person's own heart.*

While working with emerging leaders, I have witnessed the attributes and character traits that either enable or sabotage success both personally and professionally. One group seems to grab attention and instantly outshines those around them because of their noticeably visible talents, measurable abilities, intelligence, charismatic personality, or over-the-top potential. Others, at first glance, do not shine so brightly. They appear more reserved and their treasures hidden, yet to be unearthed. It is so easy to assume that the first group contains the most successful leaders on the planet, but that has not always been the case.

Through years of experience, I have discovered that the governing factor for accomplishment is not what was inherently given at birth, rather, it is the emotional maturity and character-based personal choices one makes.

The earmarks that separated the hungry go-getters were:

- Those who managed their private world while others lived for the moment.

- Those who daily and consistently gave their best, both internally and externally. They celebrated the journey while others were frustrated with the process.

- Those who refused to make excuses. They took personal responsibility for their growth despite negative circumstances while others were experts in half-truths looking for someone or something to blame.

- Those who were willing to do whatever it takes. They went above-and-beyond the call of duty while others gave the bare minimum and felt entitled because of their talent.

- Those who refused to quit and maintained an attitude of gratitude while others complained about how hard and unfair expectations were.

- Those who were team players working for something greater than themselves while others were focused on what was best for them.

- Those who valued themselves and others going the extra mile while others had to prove their worth through people-pleasing, self-promotion, and competitive criticism.

- Those who refused to allow their past to define them while others saw themselves as victims and demanded special treatment; and on and on it goes!

Each emerging leader or established leader who desires to become a *Higher Living Leader* has to ask him or herself the hard questions concerning his or her intrinsic motivation and whether he or she is willing to do whatever it takes, making the most of every opportunity given.

The military has an integrated system to develop and vet future generals in competencies, as well as core values; but who will be our future general managers, presidents, CEOs, executives, legislators, or educators? Most organizations are continually on the lookout for promising candidates that have the aptitude to be trained for these positions. However, often overlooked in the search for the qualified executive or leader are the softer skills of maturity, character, a justice worldview, and honorable internal motivations.

Most institutes of higher education and training programs focus on the development of skills and competencies, both of which are absolutely necessary. However, what is neglected (or only an occasional interjection) is the importance of the internal attributes and values of the up-and-coming leader's character-driven private world. We require accountability in task but often turn a blind eye to the emotional intelligence and internal order of our present or future leaders. Laying the foundational cornerstone of character-based leadership is absolutely essential if we want to see world-class leaders developed.

We have created a culture that values what a person can produce, but we are prohibited from speaking into the emerging leader's private life. The indisputable fact is, *my private life is what shapes my public performance.*

Throughout my developing years, as well as my initial introduction to climbing the corporate ladder, I learned that my internal state had a greater impact on my performance than merely the development of my competencies. This experience, along with my many years of working with potential leaders, has convinced me that the many saboteurs of success originate in the person's lack of personal identity. In other words, essentially, this is one's inability to see one's value. These individuals give away their power by allowing another's opinion to determine their worth. They are living their life searching for identity and purpose rather than living life FROM the security of knowing who they are.

When a person cannot see their internal worth they begin to search for ways to anesthetize themselves and look to external sources to meet an internal need. This may dull the pain and generate a temporary high, but reality always pushes them back to the source and thus continues to fuel the need to escape again and again. Where there is a lack of intrinsic control this leader will often become controlling of others or swing the pendulum to become dependent upon another's external management.

Lack of identity and self-devaluation will leave an individual:

- Struggling to follow-through to completion, afraid of failure but also afraid of success—"Am I able to maintain this level of success?"

- Judging themselves without mercy and seeing themselves as rarely able to measure up to their self-imposed expectations.

- Swinging like the pendulum from super-irresponsible to super-responsible or moving from driving themselves to success or giving up because of a belief that success is unattainable.

- Investing their emotional energies, time, and efforts into their professional lives leaving no room for committed relationships, or vice-versa.

- Never feeling good enough because of a controlling, deep-seated internal negative self-perception.

Our society is not aware of the concealed suffering of its citizenry—that narrows the eligible pool of capable emerging leaders. Yet, I have witnessed that *Higher Living Leaders* are able to see the diamond in the rough because their eyes see the value entombed in another. The more they are able to see, the more they can nurture another's intrinsic value and highest and best contribution.

My journey to develop a *Higher Living Leaders'* language that expresses a higher cause and heart motivations to serve justice has culminated with what I call the—*Validation Quotient*.[2]

WHAT IS VALIDATION QUOTIENT?

Validation Quotient is the attributes that unleash personal leadership value, generate it in others, and positively transform culture.[3] It is essential that a leader is able to see and celebrate who they are. Only then can they clearly define and walk in ownership of their unique purpose. This is what causes an individual to acknowledge and walk in the attributes that move them to positively impact their world.

Validation Quotient lays a foundation to validate and empower others, as well as bring valuable transformation to systems and cultures. It is able to authorize worth, place value upon the human soul, and produce the courage to fulfill individual purpose. Neuroscience affirms the importance of these concepts substantiating that our mind-brain is wired for love and validation. True value is expressed intrinsically and extrinsically as it acknowledges value in self and others.

Quotient deals with the magnitude of the characteristics and qualities represented and produced by an individual leader. The greater the level of validation established in and expressed by the emerging or established leader, the greater their ability to ultimately be a catalyst for positive change in the lives of people, systems, and the diverse areas of authority and responsibility entrusted to them.

As I move forward, you will see the threefold progression of Validation Quotient beginning with the attributes that unleash personal leadership value.

When a leader can begin to see their unique identity—their intrinsic value—an unshakable foundation is established empowering them to move forward with confidence. When a leader can appreciate, celebrate, and value their own uniqueness and abilities, the release of their personal purpose and unique voice is substantiated in their sphere of influence. These leaders convey humility and confidence in what they bring to the table because what they do extrinsically is a result of their intrinsic value, not vice-versa. Great questions to ask ourselves are, "Why is my team better off because I am a part of it?" "What do I add that makes the whole better?" "How does my leadership bring value to others and my organization?" "Am I trusted to give my best?"

When we can see our internal beauty and value, we naturally progress to recognize and celebrate the beauty and value in another. These leaders then see, communicate, and treat others as valuable confirming and **generating value** in them. These leaders are not in competition with but are builders of others. They are not trying to take from but to give to another. The private world of this leader is healthy and secure in his or her personal identity and value. This affects every corporate decision he or she makes.

Our external world is a product of our internal world. I cannot consistently manage my external world one way and my internal world another. I will subconsciously create an atmosphere that mirrors what is taking place on the inside of me—I can only conceal my private perspectives and perceptions for the short term. I can pretend I am wealthy, but when opportunity presents itself for my investment my proverbial check will bounce all the way down to bankruptcy court. I cannot bring to the table what I do not already internally possess.

Any internal perceptions will eventually leak out, especially when pressure is applied. We will "disturb the peace" externally if we do not possess internal peace. If I am consistently discontented with life, I will create crisis and drama externally. Anger, fear, frustration, negativity, and dissatisfaction will seep out, affecting the atmosphere and others.

If our eyes are blinded to our core value we cannot see clearly the worth and significance of another.

Conversely, the leader who is secure in his or her unique identity has an internal peace. Therefore, negative external circumstances will not cause him or her to stumble, back down, or become pessimistic. He or she will bounce back quickly when facing disappointments, or even betrayal, processing through the normal painful emotions. In fact, the internal stability brings external security when our world is shaken. A paradigm shift takes place when I begin to see my value, opening my eyes to the beauty within, and a sincere appreciation of those in my life.

Let's look through the life-giving lens of Validation Quotient! The conscious choices of Validation Quotient produce an internal support system where a love for life and hopefulness, a purpose-filled work ethic, and an optimistic attitude become contagious. This also conveys security to others in our sphere of influence! Deeper still, the plumb line to value others is found in our ability to see value in ourselves. If we can love, value, and celebrate our unique identity and purpose, we will equally see it in another and bring validation and empowerment to him or her.

When we recognize and express outwardly that others are worthy of our investment, we accept and welcome the potential of genuine collaboration and foster a shared vision and values. Without a doubt, possibilities become endless and our accomplishments honorable.

At this point we will recognize that we have the ability to lead valuable transformation to the very culture. Partnership with others will generate a morale, motivation, and momentum that will bring expansion making the existing culture better and improving the efficiency of current systems.

The momentum of Validation Quotient produces passionate team builders and, in turn, increase the effectiveness of the whole. The team begins to function together synergistically, as each person brings his or her best to the table. They are fulfilled by giving their best and are thrilled when their teammates give theirs. There is no desire to outshine one another, but to shine brighter as a cohesive team. In the same way, there is the necessity for our brain and heart to work in congruence. We recognize the heart cannot fulfill the brain's purpose or our brain the heart's purpose, but together they do an exceptional job!

The by-product of Validation Quotient is mutually beneficial partnerships that generate the ability to accomplish so much more together. This corporate validation releases individual uniqueness and builds cohesiveness in the corporate vision and an expectation for continued opportunity. We are actually better together than we are separately and we recognize the catalyst for this synergy is a celebration of value being fully actualized.

Our clients are not just money-generators for our success, but are our opportunity to bring about their success! We are partnering with their vision, mission, purpose, and values in the areas that have been entrusted to us. When our clients recognize our commitment to their success, trust will be established and will provide continued windows of opportunity.

There is so much power—the ability to affect change—when we intrinsically see value in ourselves, others, and the organizations we are serving. Genuine value motivates you to action that is evidenced by what you protect, invest into, sacrifice for, and treat as valuable.

Validation Quotient Confirms Value!

The higher the level of validation experienced and communicated, the higher degree of courage is given to the heart. The ability to take risks exponentially increases, because the capacity to determine what is really important is discernable. When the foundation of a risk is unquestionably valuable to our hearts, the risk is minimized despite the ultimate outcome. We know we are advancing because we are investing into what is greatly treasured.

When there is a confirmation of value, our words change the atmosphere around us as thoughts, mindsets, and attitudes are shifted in our spheres of influence. Our words plant seeds that influence the thoughts of those we lead and partner with. These thoughts are electro-magnetic light impulses that establish working memory in the mind-brain. This begins to bring a different perspective to the team, provides evidence to shift expectations, and ultimately brings a proper focus charting a course of action for the leader and their team.

Scientifically speaking, our words carry the power to create a culture of validation that positively affects physical and emotional health. It assists in the management of emotions and positive memory is affected. In actuality; our physical heart, brain, and body function better in a culture of validation, affirmation, and hope.

Our past experiences—personally or professionally—do not determine our or another's value. If I offered to give you a one hundred dollar bill, you would quickly welcome the gift knowing that it holds value. But before it is placed within your hand, I begin to scream depreciating, degrading, and devaluing things to it saying, "You are not worth the paper you are printed on!" "You are such a waste!" or "You'll never amount to anything!" While I am screaming shameful words, I am crumbling up the one hundred dollar bill. Then, in frustration and anger I throw it on the dirty ground, as I begin to stomp on it, rubbing it into the ground with the heel of my shoe.

Picture me picking up the dirty, crumbled, and harshly spoken-against money and ask you, "Do you still want this one hundred dollar bill?" You would quickly say, "Of course!" Why would you still want it after all that it has experienced? You recognize that in spite of the experience it still retains its VALUE!

Validation Key: You must recognize that no matter what degrading or shaming words were spoken over you, no matter how many times you were "thrown under the bus," treated unfairl, abandoned, rejected, cheated, betrayed, or lied to—no m type of injustice you have experienced—NOTHING TAKES AWAY YOUR VALUE!

Higher Living Leaders possess high levels of Validation Quotient that confirm the intrinsic value of those in their sphere of influence—no matter their past! *Higher Living Leaders* are celebrators, promoters, encouragers, and advocates of others! They recognize that where an individual was yesterday is not where he or she is today, nor where he or she is going to be tomorrow. His or her past does not define, nor determine his or her core identity or worth.

VALIDATION QUOTIENT PLACES VALUE ON THE HUMAN SOUL!

The Holocaust—the genocide, mass murder of six million Jews led by Adolf Hitler and the Nazi Party of Germany—[4] resulted in two-thirds of the Jewish population being murdered throughout Europe.[5] "A network of about 42,500 facilities in Germany and German-occupied territory were used to concentrate, hold, and kill Jews and other victims."[6] How could this atrocity take place? The leadership—influencers—first had to bring a dehumanizing devaluation to those they wanted to destroy.

There were messages preached that ultimately shifted the mindsets of the masses, making murder culturally acceptable. Hitler himself said, "By the skillful and sustained use of propaganda, one can make a people see even heaven as hell or an extremely wretched life as paradise." He also said, "How fortunate for government that the people they administer don't think." "Make a lie big, make it simple, and eventually they will believe it."[7]

The victims of the holocaust were hated and devalued to the point that they were not viewed as human. This same strategy took place in slave-states, giving slave owners the right to treat "their property" in any way they deemed beneficial for them. For the most part, the treatment of those of African descent in the United States was inhumane, cruel, and devaluing. "Slaves were punished by whipping, shackling, hanging, beating, burning, mutilation, branding and/or imprisonment...Pregnant women received the most horrendous lashings; slave masters came up with unique ways to lash them so that they could beat the mother without harming the baby. Slave masters would dig a hole big enough for the woman's stomach to lay in and proceed with the lashing."[8]

Once again, the only way this could have been woven into the very fabric of the culture was to propagate a message that devalued and dehumanized these extremely treasured human beings. Their absolute right to live, love, enjoy, and fulfill purpose was violently taken from them.

Gerrit Smith, a leading United States social reformer, abolitionist, politician, and philanthropist of the mid to late 1800's said, "We must continue to judge of slavery by what it is, and not by what you tell us it will, or may be." He refused to believe the depraved voices that were perverting the minds of the general population. Smith also said, "Truth and mercy require the exertion—never the suppression, of man's noble rights and powers." Smith saw the value in every human being! His political career championed social justice and he was unmistakably clear concerning governmental leadership when he said, "I believe that government is for the use of the people, and not the people for the use of the government."

I am sure it is obvious that I unequivocally loathe prejudice! *Prejudgment always gives license to abuse our fellowman in word, deed or attitude.*

The internet brings world news into our homes at record speed as we witness horrific human rights violations, present day slavery—numbers today exceed the combined number of the entire 400 year transatlantic slave trade—and innumerable reports of the abuse of power.

Today's generation watches on the news, internet, and social media videos of ISIS (Islamic State in Iraq and Syria) propagating hatred, fear, and threats through the beheading of children and genocide of Christians or anyone who does not align with their beliefs or resists their terroristic practices. "They are absolutely killing every Christian they see…This is absolutely genocide in every sense of the word. They want everyone to convert, and they want sharia law to be the law of the land."[9] ISIS's hatred is seeded into every aspect of their culture. Their children are being indoctrinated but also recruited to fight and even die for their unjust cause.

Spoken by a jihadist, "For us, we believe that this generation of children is the generation of the Caliphate.[10] This generation will fight infidels and apostates, the Americans and their allies, God willing. The right doctrine has been implanted in these children. All of them love to fight for the sake of building the Islamic State and for the sake of God…"[11]

I never dreamed in my lifetime that this type of injustice would take place on the world stage or the possibility of it evidenced within western culture. The laws of our land require punishment for such horrific outward displays of injustice, but all these things begin within the internal attitudes of a person's belief system, mindset, and worldview. These seeds of influence reproduce hatred, extreme prejudice, and dominance. Simply speaking, if we do not value the human soul we are positioned to be instruments of injustice and become influencers of a value system that is destructive to those we persuade as well as those we hate.

If we are going to make the most of our years upon this earth courageously preserving posterity, then value must be placed upon every human being! The application of Validation Quotient is a safeguard against any mindset that would devalue the human soul no matter their ethnicity, socio-economic status, sex, age, religion, etc.

The validation of the human soul cannot co-exist with prejudice, injustice or discrimination of any kind.

Our DNA provides a unique set of instructions that build us as individuals, however: **"All humans are 99.9 percent identical** [in their DNA sequence] and, of that tiny 0.1 per cent difference, 94 per cent of the variation is among individuals from the same populations and only 6 per cent between individuals from different populations."[12] Likely, your DNA is more similar to the DNA of someone you have never met living halfway around the world, than to your neighbor.

This is an amazing scientific fact that is profoundly revelatory to validation. When you think that 99.9 percent of humanity's 3 million base pairs of DNA are identical, it's absolutely mind-boggling. As I contemplate the estimated 37.2 trillion cells in the human body, each containing 3 million DNA base pairs forming 30 thousand genes, one resounding fact is that it is innumerable, demonstrating we are much more alike than we are different!

It is likened to an identical signature that makes us uniquely human possessing the same core needs physically, emotionally, relationally, and even spiritually. If "…there is mounting evidence that certain 'moral' Values may even be embedded in our DNA,"[13] we can begin to comprehend the significance of validation. Objectively speaking and scientifically proven, the physical brain and body need validation to be healthy, function properly, and develop full potential.

Leaders with high levels of Validation Quotient have the ability to generate and establish an atmosphere that is saturated in validation. They create a culture that communicates what is or is not acceptable in relationship for how people within the organization and those they serve are to be treated.

People will be drawn to us when we are carriers of hope, are trustworthy, and have the ability to see value in them! It is proven that proper neurological function produces healthy memory, emotions, and attitudinal responses that enable clear decision making ability. Isn't it safe to conclude that creativity, motivation, and production will also be a by-product, liberating individuals and empowering the recognized systems and organizational structures that are established?

Thomas Jefferson spoke from a governmental perspective, "The care of human life and happiness, and not their destruction, is the first and only objective of good government." Government is not just political but it is also leadership, legislation, administration, systems, and structures that are to serve with justice—power used for good. "Leadership is not about the next election, it's about the next generation."[14]

If people are merely a commodity to use to make the "man with his name on the door" look good and the organization fiscally sound, then the people will feel devalued, company loyalty will be weakened, leadership will be seen as unjust, and the culture will be injurious. We believe that it is wrong for a political leader to use people to gain a platform of power and then devalue the people who gave it to them. We call this injustice, corruption, and exploitation. If it is morally wrong—and it is—for a political leader, it is also wrong for any leader. *Devaluing those we are leading is cultural sabotage.*

There is value in every person and when that value is actualized we will see our greatest assets—the people—bring about corporate success where everyone benefits and all are fulfilled.

Validation Quotient Confirms Assignment and Purpose

Actualization carries the meaning of something manifested or the ability to bring to reality. I am thoroughly convinced the treasure within every person begins to be actualized when there is validation. When you see your intrinsic value and the good you add to a team, you can begin to activate latent creativity and unlock the depth of your potential. Simply put— Actualization entails taking the internal gift (one's contribution to society) and bringing it to an external reality.

When you begin to recognize why a relationship, team, community, or organization is better because of what you invest; the needed dedication, commitment, and loyalty to continue to give your best is activated. This releases the courage to be who you are and do what you do best! Actualization is experienced!

Validation helps to clearly define what is or is not your assignment and the platform where you make the greatest impact. Indecision and confusion is removed because you know your sphere of responsibility and are free to lead effectively and to benefit the whole. Living your life to the fullest fosters a sense of self-actualization and fulfillment. Validation gives an individual the confidence to make the most of every delegated responsibility, assignment, and window of opportunity presented. You are free to be uniquely you!

If we run from our assignment, we will be sabotaging our success because we are walking away from the purpose, the place, and the people that we were officially sanctioned to reach.

The skills and abilities within, and the motivation to release them is not the responsibility of another—it is our responsibility. We should sincerely appreciate and be legitimately encouraged when others see our value, but if we are not convinced beforehand we will struggle to believe their genuineness.

When you see your inherent value, you will make investments into your strengths, you will protect your intrinsic wealth, and you will make the most of every opportunity. Time is too valuable to waste, so now is the right time to throw off every excuse as to why you cannot be successful in leading reformation through building your Validation Quotient.

Now is your time to shine! When you impact a life for good, it will influence an entire family. In turn, that family will impact the community in which they live. Every sphere of influence has high level institutions and structures, but what makes up those structures? People that you have an opportunity to reach!

While traveling abroad, I had the opportunity to provide two hours of leadership training for one of my former students. There were approximately 150 leaders present whom I had never met. We had a great time, I loved every minute, and the feedback was encouraging. A few months later, I received an email from one participant who was impacted by the training. They requested that I return to their nation to provide training for an entire branch of government of which they governed. You never know who you may be demonstrating value to!

This one leader opened a door for me to touch a nation! However; if I was never invited to personally provide the training or if I had never talked to this governmental leader, I still would have had an impact in their life and those they lead—I had influenced an influencer. You do not always recognize the impact that you can make in a life. Make Validation Quotient a personal goal and you will **positively transform culture!**

CHAPTER 3

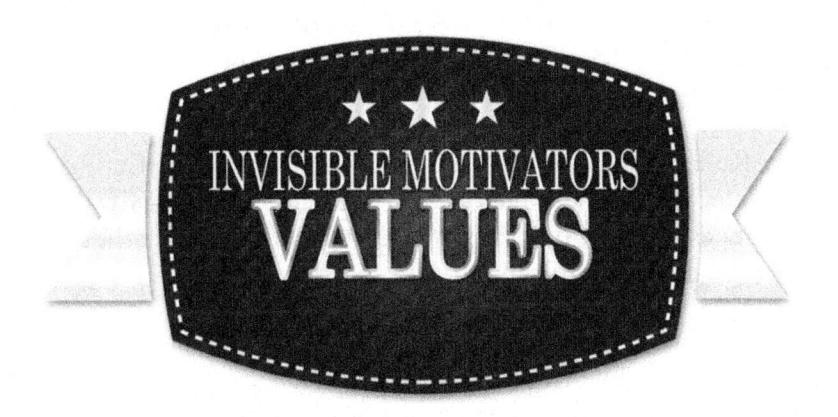

★ ★ ★ INVISIBLE MOTIVATORS
VALUES

Just as an artist places their signature upon their beautifully painted work of art, I am convinced that there is a "signature of value" written upon the very identity, purpose, and potential of every human being. Value is woven into the tapestry of our uniqueness, personality, skills, passions, and motivations. Every life is valuable and never a mistake!

After four boys, my mother was not looking to have another child. I was her surprise! Though my parents did not plan me, I was not an accident! In the same way, at the moment of your conception the "signature of value" was woven into your very being. This statement is not found in science, but I am convinced that science would not argue with this analogy.

Remember, Validation Quotient recognizes the value of every human soul. Indicative of the one hundred dollar illustration, our past experiences, injustices against us, or the challenges of the past or present do not diminish our value or determine our potential.

The greatest role models in history were not those who had a life of comfort without obstacles and pain, but those who chose to recognize their value, release their passions, and care for their fellow man in spite of their challenging journey. History causes us to recognize that someone actually increases their value to society when their pain has become an expression of their purpose and the injustices they faced develop a determination to become an instrument of justice on behalf of others.

Helen Keller, someone who was very familiar with suffering said, "Character cannot be developed in ease and quiet. Only through experiences of trial and suffering can the soul be strengthened, vision cleared, ambition inspired, and success achieved."

In present day, Malala Yousafzai, a Pakistani student who was targeted by the Taliban because of her educational activism at the young age of eleven amazingly survived a gunshot wound to the head. The Taliban boarded her school bus, asked for her by name, and shot her. Malala has become what many believe to be "the most famous teenager in the world."[1] Malala has taken her suffering and has become a voice of justice on behalf of a generation of girls who have been denied education because of unjust prejudicial beliefs. She has taken the injustice against her and has become an instrument of justice of behalf of others.

Those things that have our attention become our direction! What we behold, we become! If we continually ruminate on the injustices of our past, we begin to believe lies perverting our self-worth. We begin to adopt self-sabotaging emotions, attitudes, and actions. Fear-based memory will be our kneejerk reaction when facing pressure. We can become embittered and begin to lead autocratically or through passive-aggressive manipulation lowering the morale, destroying trust, and hindering our ability to be truly successful. It is important to discover our core identity woven inside our very being rather than adopt a variation of it through the seeds of negative experience.

Axiogenics is the mind-brain science of values generation. Peter D. Demarest and Harvey J. Schoof, authors of *Answering the Central Question: How Science Reveals the Keys to Success in Life, Love, and Leadership,* explain that axiology is the study of how Value, values, and value judgments affect the subjective choices and motivations of the mind—both conscious and sub-conscious."[2] They write, "Neuroscience is the science of how the brain works. Axiology is the science of value and, as you know, value drives the processes of the mind-brain."[3] I will reference this must-read book as I connect the concepts of Axiogenics in reference to Validation Quotient and *Higher Living Leaders.*

I will share three of the four basic principles of Axiogenics which include:[4]

VALUES DRIVE SUCCESS IN ALL ENDEAVORS.[5]

What you value underlies all of your decisions and actions. It may or may not be a conscious choice, but it determines your future and how your life will impact society. Therefore, one of my favorite training topics is helping individuals discover their core values which I will expound upon in a future chapter.

When we look at a person's behaviors and attitudes we have a clear picture of what they truly value and what is a driving force in their decision-making. Remember, if I value something I will sacrifice for it, invest into it, protect it, and treat it as valuable. What we value is where we focus the majority of our attention catapulting us in its direction. What we pursue is what we achieve!

Procrastination is not a personality trait; it is simply the indicator of what I do not value. It's amazing how forgetful we are when our appraisal of the task is, in our opinion, inconsequential. Bottom line, we do not pursue what we do not value and we aggressively go after what we highly value. What we value, we achieve!

I have heard young people say they "can't" do something because they do not have the money, yet they were able to buy the designer jeans they wanted or the latest video game. The fact is their lack of value was the reason for their lack of money excuse. What you value, you will pay the price to obtain.

YOUR MIND-BRAIN IS ALREADY VALUE DRIVEN.[6]

We are not dogs; we are human beings! Within the mother's womb, human beings were conceived with values woven into the cellular structure of the mind-brain even to the very DNA within every cell. This very fact is what separates us from the animal kingdom.

Dogs have thoughts, feelings, and even emotions, but they do not possess moral values. We inherently know right from wrong and are very aware that lying, stealing, cheating, and abuse of our fellow man is unacceptable for a morally upright human being. You'll never find a dog—man's best friend and a valuable member of many families—thinking and making decisions based upon morality, ethics, integrity, and honor. You'll never find a male dog thinking of anything but their animal instincts in the presence of a female dog in heat. To say a man or woman cannot control their "animal instincts" is incongruent with science. Human beings not only have the power of deliberate choice, but morality is woven into our cellular structure. Enough said!

THERE IS AN OBJECTIVE UNIVERSAL HIERARCHY OF VALUE.[7]

I am thoroughly convinced that people are inherently good. George Pugh, an 1850's politician said, "The biology of the human brain is hard-wired to add value." Even before science affirmed it, it was good sense to acknowledge the value of every human being. "The human brain is amazingly adaptable and pre-wired for incalculable goodness."[8]

When we increase our Validation Quotient we can actually bring change to every DNA strand within our bodies and establish health to our literal mind-brain, strengthening our hearts and bringing wholeness to our physical body. The return rate on this investment of value is well-worth the effort of *Higher Living Leadership*!

Our brain is extremely relational and is a highly social organ. "Most [of the] processes operating in the background when your brain is at rest are involved in thinking about other people and yourself."[9] Since our brain holds a hierarchy of value, "above all else, our relationships with other people have the greatest value and are the greatest source of potential value generation."[10]

Sincere and genuine value originates intrinsically and is manifested extrinsically. Every word, action, or decision we make will build up or tear down, add value or bring shame, seed hope or fear, and encourage or discourage ourselves and others. The old adage of doing unto others as we would have them do until us still holds true generation after generation.

It has been my personal experience when faced with the possibility of physical death that those I deeply loved consumed my thoughts. I didn't think about how much money I had, the house I lived in, the car I drove, or if I was having a good or bad hair day. My thoughts were upon my husband, my children, and those I valued.

True success is the intrinsic motivation to celebrate, honor, and validate every relationship in our life. Is it really important if we are the most successful businessperson or the most influential political leader if we stand alone on the proverbial mountain top? I might climb to the top of the corporate ladder, but if I stand there alone what fulfillment is there? We can't take anything with us when we leave this life, but we can be one loved, valued, and celebrated for the life we have lived, the investments we made, and the people we touched. Maya Angelo said, "I will write upon the pages of history what I want them to say."

We must recognize that, *without the desire and ability to communicate value to others, genuine relationships and doors of opportunity will gradually disappear.*

I'll not hire—a second time—a contractor to remodel my home, a mechanic to fix my car, or plumber to fix my toilet if they did not value what I entrusted to them. Customer service 101 is simply displaying the attitudes and actions that demonstrate that you genuinely value what is important to your customer or client—this is a huge builder of trust!

Higher Living Leaders are the greatest influencers on the planet because they win the hearts and minds of those with whom they lead—personally or professionally—planting and reaping true success internally and externally in their sphere of influence.

Hope-filled thoughts, expressed validation, extravagant generosity and purposeful choices are deliberate steps to a healthy mind and true prosperity.

Axiology's' Universal Hierarchy of Value[11]

"*The Universal Hierarchy of Value*...transcends subjective morals and ethics and provides a logical, mathematical foundation for both maximizing and optimizing goodness in the world."[12] As we choose to align our thoughts and choices to this universal hierarchy, we will experience the fullness of emotional health. Peter D. Demarest and Harvey J. Schoof's writing simply encapsulates, "People first, productivity second, and policy third."[13]

The highest and most important value **is intrinsic value** (people). This is the ability to see value in self and to value others. "Intrinsic 'things' are unique, incomparable, and irreplaceable...The intrinsic dimension is the dimension of being."[14] Though we are 99.9 percent identical within our DNA, that little .1 percent makes us so exceptional! Henry Ward Beecher said, "The human soul is God's treasury, out of which he coins unspeakable riches."[15]

The standard that enables a leader to value, celebrate, honor, and love others begins with celebrating, valuing, and loving ourselves. This is not a place of pride, but of awareness of, and confidence in your personal value. During the course of life's journey, the valuing of oneself unearths the amazing treasure within—value is actualized. From this solid foundation of self-value you can unreservedly and authentically communicate value to others. You can risk giving, serving, and empowering others to lead when you have this unwavering assurance of your own worth.

Conversely, if our intrinsic value is obscured through lies or shame, we will build self-constructed walls around us, causing us to feel powerless and unable to connect in heart. Fortified walls are erected that not only keep others out, but lock us in. We then live frustrated and angry lives, wanting the walls to fall, but afraid of being left defenseless and dangerously vulnerable.

Shame is a false identity that screams lies to us about our value.[16] From the roots of shame, pride, and self-devaluation, our leadership potential may be stunted by people-pleasing and performance-oriented driven behaviors. Withdrawal and isolation separates workgroups and relationships. This detachment becomes a hindrance to effective leadership and teambuilding. Defensiveness and victim mentalities rise to the surface, where the venting or suppressing of emotions become the response to stressful situations.

Anger or criticism leaks through those proverbial bricks in those self-constructed walls, demanding perfection of self and others, controlling or manipulative leadership, and a host of other fruits from the seeds of shame.

Internal value and worth is foundational for all motivation. It shifts perspectives and opens doors for us to begin to see who we are and what we can accomplish. *When you walk with a sense of intrinsic value, the by-product will be the valuing of others.*

You cannot honorably and rightly lead someone that you do not value. The heart to value others as you value yourself is the catalyst to heartfelt partnerships of purpose. Every government, business, educational system, even arts and media serve people. Without genuine value for others your service becomes obligatory, often mediocre, and self-serving.

Whether in personal relations or the tasks we need to accomplish, we position ourselves for failure when we do not value others. Then again, *when your service to others originates from a heart to generate value you not only have met their need but impacted their life.* Now this is *Higher Living Leadership*!

Subsequent in importance in Axiology's Hierarchy of Value is that of **extrinsic value** (productivity). This encompasses the valuing of our and others' gifts, talents, and abilities; those things that are quantifiable. Valuing the gifts within gives us the tools to unpack the inner-treasure in order to discern and develop our competencies. We love what we can offer our team and celebrate what others bring to the table. We acknowledge that we are a valuable resource, as those with whom we partner. The ability to personally produce and increase the team's productivity becomes a by-product of mutual validation and the ability to properly manage every resource to bring purpose to fulfillment.

For every leader, and within every organization human resources remain the most prized resource. Therefore, investing into the team's strengths will yield superior capability to accomplish the goals, objectives, vision, values, and mission of any organization. The more we treasure the proficiencies of our staff, the more we will experience a greater motivation to provide them with the tools they need to augment their abilities. This is a win-win scenario since the individual, the team, and the organization are strengthened and increased.

People are drawn to carriers of hope and will excel in an atmosphere of affirmation.

Yet, if a person's extrinsic value is not celebrated he or she will pull back from his or her roles and responsibilities and contribute only minimal effort. *The greatest violation of relationship—personally and professionally—is when the heart grows cold, vision dies, and we no longer care how our actions affect another.*

It becomes very evident that intrinsic motivation is absent and the desire to excel, produce, and partner are frustrated. This type of devaluation is often subtle but contagious within a workgroup and reduces the morale of the whole.

We should never place more importance on production than on the person, but it is imperative to value this second tier of the hierarchy of value. It is essential for an employee to bring the essential competencies to the table or there is no reason for his or her employment. The song lyrics "You don't know what you've got 'till it's gone"[17] is a mistake we do not want to make! *Looking through the 'wow' factor lens activates potential and builds relationship.*

During my former and present leadership roles, I have come to know that you can recognize the internal motivation of someone by observing their outward actions. I have discovered that if I have to extrinsically micro-manage production, the employee's heart is not present and he or she does not genuinely value what he or she was hired for. If I cannot connect to his or her heart—what he or she values—his or her intellect will not hear, nor will he or she respond as anticipated. Without the extrinsic value firmly in place he or she will be looking for a better job, the greener grass somewhere else, or his or her manager will purposefully leave the classifieds in clear sight wishing they will take the bait, "It's time to leave!"

The least importance element in the values' hierarchy is **systemic value** (policy). Systemic Value includes the systems and structures necessary to administrate the advancement of vision. Administration must always serve the purpose or it will be counter-productive. "A systemic thing exists only as part of a larger system."[18] Without the ability to value this area, we will find a division building as we fight, argue, and confront the "how" and lose focus on the "why" of the vision. Systems are very important and must work synergistically within the corporate purpose connecting individuals' skillsets, available resources, and structures that will bring the vision to completion.

As a behavioral analysis consultant I have seen the battle of relationally focused and task driven personality preferences or the struggle between the emotive and the cognitive. I have witnessed the arguments between the banner-waving of the aggressive verses the passive tendencies. The war of perceptions and perspectives has divided many relationships and workgroups. The fact is we need them all. We need the synchronization of every type of individual, personality expression, and team preference. When we all celebrate each other and work together beautiful things happen—personally and professionally.

We know that we place value upon systemic value, "…as the desire to do the right thing because it adds the most value to the larger system, not just because it is 'right.' The systemic mind is a primary source of motivation, creativity, and vision for a greater possibility."[19]

This hierarchy of values is listed in order of importance from the most important of intrinsic, to the lesser of extrinsic, to the least of systemic. If this hierarchy is not evidenced or is out of order it will cause emotional suffering, discontentment, fear, anxiety, and alienation within the team.

"We optimize value only when all choices, actions, and reactions are congruent with the Universal Hierarchy of Value."[20] The more we align our personal values with Axiology's hierarchy of value, the happier, healthier, and more productive we will be. We will celebrate the principles of Validation Quotient and manifest the qualities of a *Higher Living Leaders* that values the people, their skills, and the processes to benefit the whole.

"A man who works with his hands is a laborer; a man who works with his hands and his brain is a craftsman; but a man who works with his hand and his brain and his heart is an artist." [21]

Begin to think about how you feel when you are in relationship—work or personal—with those who genuinely value and celebrate you and your contributions. When the proper structures, systems, and strategies are in place to advance and benefit the whole there is a sense of safety. You have good feelings, positive emotions, and enjoy life but you also have a buy-in team mindset that stimulates a good work ethic and agreement of the delegated responsibility entrusted. A valued person outworks others and goes above and beyond the call of duty.

If science is discovering and supporting the fact that our human brains are imprinted with a hierarchy of value and we are wired for love and validation, we must also challenge our personal values to align with that "signature of value."

When your leadership motivation originates from a heart to generate value, you have not only met needs but impacted lives.

CHAPTER 4

**HIGHER LIVING LEADERSHIP
Head-Hand-Heart**

The dawn of transformation arises when I surrender the familiarity of who I am today for the intrinsic potential of tomorrow.

Following the foundation laying of reformation, justice, and Validation Quotient, let's delve into what it means to be a *Higher Living Leader*.

THE HEAD: HIGHER THINKING

Higher thinking exemplifies the deliberate choices to know and develop ourselves. *Higher Living Leadership* embodies a focused determination to advance and mature in our intellect, thoughts, mind, emotions, attitude, actions and reactions. Included in the continual development of a healthy mind is its self-governance of positive choice and life-giving internal management. Higher Thinking embraces the balance of a strong internal conviction of loving life today while possessing a healthy dissatisfaction of simply maintaining or stagnation. Our character typifies an internally-motivated agenda and daily lifestyle to advance, improve, and cultivate my personhood and competencies.

We are not looking for perfection—doing everything without fault, flaw, or error—but living life with an excellence—being, doing, and giving our very best! It is impossible to live in perfection, but we can daily choose to live a life of excellence. This process is not one of flawlessness, but of the ability to remain steadfast and refusing to move away from our deliberate purpose. We have keen awareness that the choices of today set the stage for our tomorrow.

Where you are today is a product of your past choices, and your future will be a result of today's choices.

We must acknowledge that what we understand today pales in comparison to what we are able to learn, develop, and experience. I've enjoyed reading the following quotes and perspectives from influential leaders of their day:

Ken Olson, President, Chairman and Founder of Digital Equipment Corp. said in 1977, "There is no reason anyone would want a computer in their home."[1]

Robert Metcalfe, inventor of Ethernet, in 1995 said, "I predict the internet will soon go spectacularly supernova and in 1996 catastrophically collapse."[2]

The president of the Michigan Saving's Bank said in 1903, "The horse is here to stay but the automobile is only a novelty – a fad." [3]

William Orton, President of Western Union, in 1876 said, "The 'telephone' has too many shortcomings to be seriously considered as a means of communication."[4]

Mary Somerville, pioneer of radio broadcasting said in 1948, "Television won't last. It's a flash in the pan."[5]

I can't be critical of these highly intelligent and competent individuals who made educated statements for their day. Nonetheless, this must be a lesson learned for all of us because our present knowledge, limited experience, and state-of-the-art education have caused us to think, believe, and communicate from what is, in actuality, a developing perspective.

We are all a work in progress and where we are at today has only scratched the surface of our potential. Let's not only knock down some of the walls on the proverbial box of limitation, but destroy the box completely! We are thankful for what we know today but we still recognize it is partial knowledge.

Intelligence Quotient

Intelligence Quotient (IQ) is the inherent propensity woven into your very DNA that enables you to develop specific skills and competencies. Throughout history many types of testing and determining factors were present to predict a person's propensity academically, the acquisition of information, or their job performance. There are still many theories as research continues along with many debates on the subject of intelligence.

My challenge is that many individuals have limited themselves to an IQ score, their school grades, and comparison next to the skills and ability of others. I hate labels and the lies that accompany them. The theory of multiple intelligences speaks volumes. Just search the internet and discover a world that breaks off the barriers that have been self-imposed through incomplete education.

There are nine different types of intelligences. Every person has them all in varying degrees but the key is to determine your dominate intelligences so that you can position yourself in ways and areas that are uniquely you! The central understanding to be aware of is that you possess the capability to increase your intelligence throughout your entire lifetime.

As you research the theory of multiple intelligences you can see the logical mathematical thinker. This individual develops intellect in areas of logic, reasoning, numbers, and systematic ways of thinking. Can't you picture the analyst, the bookkeepers, and scientists holding high levels of logical mathematical thinking?

Visual spatial intelligence deals with the ability to see in your mind's eye. Albert Einstein was determined to have possessed this intelligence. The ability to see before it is actualized is an intelligence that leads to great creativity, inventions, and the aptitude to provide solutions.

Linguistic thinkers have the proficiency with words and language. They love to read, write, and are effective communicators. How we love to listen to these highly motivational and inspiring communicators! They have the skill to paint pictures with their words and artfully articulate stories that cause you to see, feel, and connect emotionally.

Kinesthetic thinkers include those who learn through the practice of physical movement by means of their hands and body. Just imagine those who craft objects using their hands to create, repair, and build. When you investigate a vocation where the use of their hands is necessary you are able to recognize there is certain levels of kinesthetic intelligence engaged.

The musical intelligence involves sensitivity and ability to learn through music, tones, rhythm, as they possess a strong audio passage. I love music but I cannot think, study, and learn with music playing, so it is obvious I do not have elevated levels of musical intelligence. One day I entered the business office where my staff was playing music—rather loudly— while working. I didn't like what I heard and asked them to turn off the music so they could work more efficiently. They complied but commented, "We work better with music playing." I obviously disagreed with that statement until I learned about the theory of multiple intelligences. I realized that those who were working in my office fit into this category as music empowered them to produce, excel, learn, and think more clearly. I went into the office and apologized allowing them to have their music playing, however, not as loudly.

Interpersonal learners are fantastic in interaction with others. Their propensity for sensitivity to another's feelings, emotions, and internal motivations empowers them to be wonderful team members. They will actually learn and develop intelligence in the midst of team interaction. These individuals are capable to communicate competently and have genuine empathy for others. These individuals are great leaders in the aspects of influential communication like teachers, managers, politicians, counselors, sales persons, etc.

Intrapersonal learners are those who learn when they are alone. They are contemplators who have great ability to be introspective and value self-assessment. These individuals see both the strengths and weaknesses while processing thought in systemic order to determine a course of action! This is me! Because I must have absolute silence and isolation from the interruptions and noise around me to learn, I could not understand that my office staff needed music to be more productive. As I learned about multiple intelligences I then understood why I wanted my office in my home to be a refuge of quiet and minimized interruptions. There was a time I was critical of myself because my values are woven in validation and love for people, yet I longed to be alone to regroup emotionally, learn, and grow. When I discovered that in aloneness I was able to focus more effectively and increase my intelligence, I realized that the place of solitude was the necessary positioning in order for me to accomplish my core values when I left my classroom of introspection.

Have you ever met anyone who said, "I think better and clearer when I walk on the beach or hike the mountain?" That is the naturalistic thinker. They actually relate and connect to their natural surroundings empowering them to think more clearly. Can't you see the park ranger, farmer, or botanist having naturalistic intelligence? Picture the person who recovers emotionally when they take their boat out on the lake or sit on its shore to fish.

Lastly, many multiple intelligent theorists have added the existential thinker-- those who are highly spiritual and are very aware of thinking beyond the natural realm. They are "infinite thinkers" and often are drawn to pastoral roles or the field of physiology.

The importance of understanding your dominant intelligence/intelligences is to know how to position yourself to learn, grow, and increase your skills, abilities, and continue to be that lifelong learner. Making choices to increase your intelligence quotient (IQ) is a key component to Higher Thinking.

EMOTIONAL INTELLIGENCE

Higher Thinking also encompasses our ability to make healthy positive life-giving choices, as well as the ability to properly manage our thoughts, attitudes, and emotions. In future chapters, I will cover the neuroscience aspects of these to substantiate our intrinsic capacity to self-manage our capability to think higher. We must recognize that *we cannot minimize the power of the mind and our ability to choose for by it we can activate the whole of who we are.*

Higher Thinking deals with Emotional Intelligence (EQ or EI). EQ is a topic that I have taught for many years through the grid of my leadership methodologies and has proven to empower leaders in every sphere of society. It became very popular in the corporate arena by Daniel Goleman[6]. EQ is an aspect of intelligence demonstrating our ability to manage ourselves internally—personal competencies—as well as our interaction specific to relationship with others—social competencies. These individuals are said to be set apart from the ordinary because EQ is said to be the single most important factor in job performance and advancement.

Daniel Goleman says, "...we have found that, indeed, the higher the level of the job, the less important technical skills and cognitive ability were, and the more important competence in emotional intelligence becomes."[7]

One aspect of the highly emotionally intelligent is their commitment to continued growth in both their personal and professional lives through a series of mature choices. From the simple basic attributes to the highly detailed assessments, EQ originates from the same source...your choice. In actuality where you are today is a result of your past choices and your future is dependent upon the choices you make today. I so appreciate the five attributes of Emotional Intelligence but I would like to raise the bar even higher...*Higher Living Leaders.*

"Human beings, by changing the inner attitudes of their minds, can change the outer aspect of their lives."[8]

HAND: HIGHER RESPONSIBILITY

Higher Living Leadership embraces the Higher Responsibility necessary to provide the systemic investment into the people, the system, the organization, and the culture.

Higher responsibility moves beyond the power of execution which is the ability to execute a task and follow-through to speedy completion. We recognize the necessity to become that person and surround ourselves with those who are committed to the execution of tasks. However, Higher Responsibility is seeded by a loyalty of heart to the purpose of the task and the fulfillment of the vision from which the task was created.

My definition of responsibility is a mature "response-to-my-ability." They are the choices I make to act independently without extrinsic motivation or supervision. *Building a strong spirit is not built by past experience, but by taking responsibility for my future.*

Higher Living Leaders embrace the moral obligation to act appropriately in respect towards others as well as the task. *No matter our opinion or the daunting tasks that need completed, protecting the hearts of others is our moral responsibility. The only one who said "I am not my brother's keeper"*[9] *murdered his brother.* This leader is one who sees value in others and the task whether they are executing the task or delegating it to another.

Higher Responsibility deals with the application of what I know to partner with the high levels of Validation Quotient I acquire. You see, *unless we move beyond information to application we remain unchanged!* It is painless to be skilled but not employ, hear without understanding, or to ignore expectations and responsibilities; but it is extremely painful to face the consequences of our irresponsibility.

"What is magnificent about your mind is that you have the power, in any moment, to make conscious choices, independent of your habits."[10] The time for the blame game has ended if we desire to increase as *Higher Living Leadership*. No longer can we lead or live our lives blaming others or circumstances but grow, learn, and advance ourselves in spite of the challenges that we face. *When you push through the 'I can't' of life you discover hidden treasures of value-potential!*

No more excuses! Benjamin Franklin said, "He that is good for making excuses is seldom good for anything else." Ouch! So many times our excuse is merely covering for something we didn't desire to do in the first place. Synonyms of excuse are to gloss over, shrug off, whitewash, wink at, or disregard. Excuses carry the meaning of removing from you the blame or to be granted exemption or release of a responsibility. Simply, it is disregarded as trivial, unimportant, or a non-value so much so that it removes the importance or the obligation of following through to completion or taking responsibility. *Our choice will always be: excuses or results!*

A specific destructive consequence of adopting a lifestyle of exemptions, excuses, and entitlement—belief of deserving privileges of something not worked for or invested into—is that it stunts our growth in the area in which we shirk responsibility. Often when we become aware of an incompetency our human propensity is to withdrawal in fear of failure or make excuses rather than pushing through and developing the competencies needed to advance in that area.

In the late 1990's I was given the opportunity to speak on a very large platform with business and governmental leaders. This experience opened my eyes to see that I lacked the necessary competencies to address this level of international governance. I was emotionally shaken as I was faced with the realization of my undeveloped passion. At this point I had two choices: I could make excuses and run in fear, or rise up and take responsibility to develop the competencies needed. Actually, what I felt like "knocked me backwards" was a huge opportunity challenging me to "launch forward!" I locked myself in my "intrapersonal intelligence" room and invested hundreds of hours into studying through books and audio trainings from some of the nation's greatest leaders. I began to apply the lessons learned by making them authentic to my personal message and purpose.

Then, on a much smaller scale I invested into those in my current sphere of influence, as I gained practical application and experience. Refusing to give up or back down, doors began to open one by one providing opportunities beyond my wildest dreams—and I've only just begun! Instead of excuses protecting me from fear of failure, I took a superior road of Higher Responsibility.

If you believe you can't, you won't try! If you know you can, you won't quit even when you fail!

Higher Responsibility is absolutely imperative when it comes to relationships. We must recognize that our words, attitudes, and subsequent actions are constantly communicating to others a message—my hopes are that your message runs through the grid of Validation Quotient. We must take responsibility to properly connect in both tasks and heart motivations. We can increase our ability to generate value in others by the way we communicate—life-filled words, attitudes; and the culture of respect, honor, and validation we cultivate.

The quality decision to live a life of Higher Responsibility emboldens me to take the emotional risk to deal with my personal blind spots. How can we deal with a blind spot if we are blind to it? Good question! The answer is to present ourselves to sincere feedback from those we trust to speak with candor and integrity! One of the scariest and most beneficial things we can do for our own leadership development is to obtain straightforward and responsible advice, counsel, or mentorship from those who have achieved these levels of expertise.

Following a consulting job or training seminar I send a request for feedback asking questions on my presentation, application, and communication, along with what I could have done better to accomplish their goals and objectives.

This practice makes you vulnerable, but if we can recognize that if our blind spots are exposed we can take the responsibility to develop, improve, and progress. If our blind spots stay hidden we will encounter emotional conflicts as to what may be sabotaging success or hindering our ability to build trust. If we want to be skillful we must follow the words of Winston Churchill, "The price of greatness is responsibility."[11]

Do not live your life today based upon where you are at now but where you want to be! True success and fulfillment comes when I am able to overcome the saboteurs that once kept me locked in small places without leadership impact and influence. It is personally fulfilling and self-empowering to break through the personal limitations that once held you back. There is no longer a legitimate justification for excuses! We are not in competition with others but on a journey of becoming the best we can be!

Henry Ward Beecher said, "Hold yourself responsible for a higher standard than anyone else expects of you." That is not legalism or perfection but freedom to unwrap yourself from the grave clothes of constraint. Dream again! Just because previous events were met with disappointment, failure, or less than what I know I can be, doesn't mean that we'll not succeed now!

When the blinders are removed and the saboteurs exposed, we are positioned to walk out our innermost dreams. *When purpose and preparation meet, doors of opportunity open.* Higher Responsibility is not being a workaholic or having a "work will set you free" mindset but it is taking the responsibility to release the voice, the message, the purpose, and the beauty on the inside of you! The world needs what you have to offer!

A *Higher Living Leader* demonstrates his or her value by taking responsibility internally (for themselves), externally (task and responsibility—competencies), and interpersonally (creating value in the team).

HEART: HIGHER CAUSE

We've talked about the Head: Higher Thinking, the Hand: Higher Responsibility, but the groundwork for both is a Higher Cause. A Higher Cause exemplifies a sincere, pure, and genuine purpose-driven motivation for a cause greater than self. When we function from a Higher Cause there is a heart-driving force that enables every task to be executed in excellence. It endows us with a healthy perspective and inner sustenance in the midst of every external contradiction to the worthwhile cause. Why? *The success of our cause supersedes personal success.*

My core value, personal purpose, passion, personal belief system, and worldview seed a "higher call" to a Higher Cause. This impetus moves us from a place of personal validation to bring validation to others, organizations, and the culture. Money is a necessary compensation to manage the external, but laboring for a heartfelt cause makes life worth living.

I have heard people attack a not-for-profit leader, pastor, or organization saying they are just trying to get money for themselves at the expense of others. Would that be wrong? Of course! But, what difference is it for a political leader to use people to get a platform of influence to legislate decisions that benefit government or themselves at the expense of the people they are commissioned to serve? What difference is it if the business person focused all their attention on the bottom line, not caring for the people that business has promised to serve? What difference is it when a school teacher works only for a paycheck and doesn't really care about the students that they are there to teach, train, and develop? You've got the point!

It is time for our leadership to model a way that leaves our world a better place! *Higher Living Leaders* are duty-bound to serve a Higher Cause increasing their influence as lives, systems, and cultures are revolutionized.

In today's society, so many are demanding more and giving less! They want big paychecks, but get angry when expected to produce, accomplish, and empower those they are hired to serve.

What is problematic in today's society is many highly competent and even character-driven leaders have lost a Higher Cause. They are requiring more financial compensation because money is their only reward for their labor. Money becomes an idol worshipped in every decision they make rather than wealth being a necessary instrument to serve a Higher Cause.

If leaders operated from a Higher Cause, their hearts would be invested in a purpose that quenches the thirst of their soul. When they work for a cause greater than themselves they are overflowing with a sense of accomplishment and fulfillment. Financial compensation is needed and appreciated but it is not the core reason for their investment. Because we are hard-wired for validation, by the act of determining value in what we are doing and within those we are serving, life becomes exceptionally good!

The internal always trumps the external! Many call me a motivational speaker and that would be satisfying only when I am able to witness the inspiration activating in others a sustaining force amidst opposition and adversity. Motivation must move beyond temporarily touching the emotions for a day or two, to a heart-driven Higher Cause that produces an intrinsic motivation that brings transformation—internally and externally.

I must make a conscious choice to determine my course of action and not stop until it is accomplished no matter my fears, limitation, or the obstacles I face. Thus the process itself matures me.

This sustained motivation matures, guarding us continually in order to serve a Higher Cause. My competencies alone will not sustain me because I will always come face-to-face with something I cannot overcome without help. Serving a Higher Cause allows me to reach beyond my limitations into a reservoir of purposefulness. The conflict we face actually becomes the fuel to spark the fires of change if I respond from the core reason, purpose, and objectives of the cause. It pulls me out of merely cooperating to a deep-seated collaboration with those with whom I partner.

A sustained intrinsic motivation helps us to make appropriate adjustments to continually advance self, others, and our organization. Developing a culture of intrinsic motivation empowers personal achievement, recognition, a celebration of the work itself, and an embracing of responsibility for advancement and growth. We take pleasure in the depth of interpersonal relationships, partnering together for the shared cause. The Higher Cause increases motivation because it engages the core of who we are—the heart—not just the head or the hand. This internal satisfaction cannot be obtained any other way.

The end-goal and obsession of many is happiness. The emotions of happiness are wonderful but we cannot sacrifice *Higher Living* on the altar of pleasure. As we unpack the difference between happiness and joy, we can learn that true self-satisfaction originates from joy.

Happiness is short-lived because it is subjected to life's external circumstances. For example, I am compelled to do a "happy dance" after purchasing a high end product at a bargain basement price. That dance, however, quickly comes to a halt when I receive a text from a friend warning me of the charlatan in town selling knock-offs. Because of external circumstances and the information I received, I have emotionally shifted from a wild happy dance to anger and frustration.

On the flipside, I could be facing a horrific day in the office as my "to do list" redoubles backlogging productivity, leaving me feeling irritated and discouraged. The phone rings and I answer to a cheerful and appreciative client heralding exactly how their personal life and company have been transformed because of our investment. At this very moment, as I hang up the phone, an overflowing sense of happiness washes away the irritation from a fruitless day.

Happiness comes and goes as swiftly as a cheetah runs across the African plain! We all enjoy this blissful state of well-being and yearn for the pleasurable high it brings. We hope for those we love to live in a perpetual state of this ever-fleeting bliss.

Although we enjoy and hold closely these encouraging feelings and memories, we have to acknowledge happiness is not a permanent emotional state. If we try to stage-manage the episodes of our life story in order to continually experience the feelings of happiness, we are impairing our capacity to retain joy.

Joy is not a feeling but an internal character trait, a mindset and a belief that sources our ability to remain steady in the midst of the negative external disturbances to life's goals. Joy identifies that the negative existing feelings are momentary. Joy speaks through self-talk saying, "Everything is going to be okay. The sun is shining behind these threatening dark clouds." Because joy is not a feeling, it has become the inner source of happiness seeing beyond the ever changing scenes of our external circumstances. Joy does not fight against but empowers the valuable treasure of happiness. If there is an end-goal it must be the character-driven tree of joy that roots us deeply into the ground—the Higher Cause—sourcing the harvest seasons of happiness.

Higher Living Leaders recognize that true success is dependent upon intrinsic motivation, as much as it is dependent upon their individual talent and competencies. When we can inspire an emerging leader's intrinsic motivation, the fullness of his or her talents, abilities, and skills will be emancipated from a passionless prison. The Higher Cause will activate the creativity and treasure within, boosting morale and causing the team to move into an unhindered momentum.

A Higher Cause is the intrinsic motivation that allows me to see life from a healthy perspective. *If we focus on the disappointments of life we are blinded to the appointments right before our eyes.* Motivation signals the release of dopamine in the brain which increases neural functioning and the ability to progress. As *Higher Living Leaders* we can foster a culture of motivation that will empower personal achievement, recognition, enjoyment in the work itself, and a heart connection to those we influence.

Throughout the years some have approached me saying, "Dr. Melodye I want you to use me." In response to their request, I began to give them opportunities. As time passed, some returned to me complaining, "You are using me!" I gave them the opportunities they requested but their heart was not motivated by the Higher Cause they were commissioned to serve. The opposite has also proven true as others returned to me beaming with delight appreciative for the opportunities given. The difference was not the task itself but the heart connection to the Higher Cause. The ultimate cause was an expression of their heart's purpose—their intrinsic motivation.

If you are not aligned with the cause of the organization you are serving, you will feel abused by the opportunities given you.

The old proverb, "You can lead a horse to the water, but you can't make him drink" is evident when we try to lead people to a task that they are not thirsty for.

When an emerging leader is not able to clearly define their personal passion, purpose, and intrinsic motivation, we often find them drawn to our passion, not our cause. *Without clearly knowing our identity and purpose we will find ourselves echoing the loudest voice.* In order to properly serve the vision—the Higher Cause—it is imperative to discern those who want to use our cause for their agenda or need, rather than partner with joy serving the cause from a shared-passion and purpose.

Outward wealth without inner wealth, talent without character, or leadership without a higher cause is a recipe for destruction. The way to reach unadulterated joy in life and leadership is to discover your Higher Cause. When a Higher Cause shapes the culture of our homes and workplaces, when our words inspire its purpose, and when we model it without compromise it will attract those who share the cause—whether matured and competent, or hungry to mature.

Statues are not erected, accolades are not communicated, and dreams are not fulfilled for those who avoided great difficulties, but for those who overcame as they served a Higher Cause.

I think of Babe Ruth who struck out 1,330 times but is still considered by many as the greatest baseball player in history. He hit 714 home runs and famously stated, "Every strike brings me closer to the next home run."[12]

Can you imagine Thomas Edison's teachers saying he was "too stupid to learn anything?" This man with 17,000 inventions credited to his account—only one was his original idea—while making evident his intelligence, talent, skill, and intrinsic motivation to see his purpose actualized. He was inspired in heart and determined in task to take what others started— but didn't finish— and bring them to completion. He demonstrated an internal perspective of a Higher Cause when he walked among the ashes of his life's work after his laboratories in West Orange, New Jersey burned to the ground saying to his son, Charles Edison, "There is great value in disaster. All our mistakes are burned up. Thank God we can start anew."[13]

Albert Einstein, world famous German born theoretical physicist, also did not speak until he was four years old, didn't read until he was seven, leaving both his parents and teachers to believe that he was mentally handicapped. His name is known worldwide by every generation as a figure of genius. He demonstrated character and intrinsic motivation as he similarly served a Higher Cause. He said, "Try not to become a man of success, but rather to become a man of value."[14] You can see he was motivated for a cause, a value, a sense of worth and significance beyond outward success. Einstein also said, "The value of a man resides in what he gives and not in what he is capable of receiving."[15]

Walt Disney said, "All the adversity I've had in my life, all the trouble and obstacles have strengthened me…"[16] He was not moved from his intrinsic motivation even when he was fired by a newspaper for lacking imagination and not having any good ideas. Crazy! Walt Disney not having imagination? When we become aware of what is contained within us, we will not be unnerved by the external contradictory voices of man's opinions.

A Higher Cause that seeds a leader's intrinsic motivation is a key to enjoying the processes of life. The ability to stand strong whether experiencing defeat or victory, failure or success, loneliness or connection, devaluation or appreciation is the decisive factor of knowing we are furthering a Higher Cause if we do not quit! Validation Quotient is absolutely necessary in order to continue to celebrate and partner with our intrinsic value when our world is shaken. This security provides a culture that also creates value in others and the very cause we are working together to see accomplished.

"Life is a marathon, not a sprint. The race doesn't go to the swiftest, but to those who don't give up."[17]

"...I firmly believe that any man's finest hour—his greatest fulfillment to all he holds dear—is that moment when he has worked his heart out in a good cause and lies exhausted on the field of battle- victorious."[18]

UPROOTING SEEDS OF DISAPPOINTMENT

Disappointments can be the little steps on the road to frustration and failure or the building blocks of inner strength and triumph.

A Higher Cause seeds a harvest of courage. Every leader understands the emotions and challenges of fear but also knows that their decisions cannot be generated from fear. The vision, purpose, and cause must always be served to insure that our decision-making is not emotion-driven but cause-driven. If we respond in fear when the pressure is on, we will find ourselves compromising our individual and corporate purpose. We must recognize that any worthy cause or valuable endeavor is rarely obtained without obstacles and opportunities for disappointment.

When we constructively play against the disappointments, we are converted into an instrument that builds, matures, and empowers us. As our perspective on these "missed-appointments" can be shifted, it will translate a message of increased opportunity, rather than a foreboding sense of discouragement. Is it possible to see a disappointment or rejection as a protection from something or someone that could sabotage our future? Recognize when you're rejected, though painful for the present, your destiny steps are safeguarded.

Disappointments will teach us so much about ourselves if we accurately assess our emotions and reactions. As I previously wrote about the emotionally charged event where I realized my incompetence to address the group of prominent international leaders, I felt a deep-rooted disappointment in myself. Even though I was made for that opportunity I could not measure up to my own expectations or obtain the desired results I had envisioned. That disappointment presented a window of opportunity to evaluate where I was and where I wanted to be. That disappointment allowed me to strategically determine my course of action to construct an internal edifice from which to lead. That painful disappointment actually helped me to set a course for success not failure.

Every disappointment carries with it the ability to discover strategies and creativity. These strategies are preparatory to new and better ways of functioning, relating, structuring, or marketing the Higher Cause.

Training, mentoring, empowering—loving deeply from the heart—has been an expression of my leadership methodologies. Sadly, however, in the midst of that heart motivation I have faced some substantial disappointments that devastated my heart. The emotional pain of betrayal attempted to hijack the Higher Cause within me. I was emotionally used and injured and didn't want to ascend the difficult road required of *Higher Living Leaders*. My emotions pleaded my withdrawal to a position of isolation and self-protection. These walls of inaccessibility felt like they would protect me from future abuse, but in actuality they would have barricaded me inside their illusive shelter. We can never move forward through retreat or stagnation!

No matter how much my emotion, hurt, and fear pressured me to pull back, the Higher Cause and my personal purpose compelled me to make the most of my painful appointments. I had to set peace as my daily goal structuring my thoughts, emotions, attitudes, beliefs, motivations, decisions, and relationships around it. *Internal peace is simply found in giving today my very best.* I had to continue to give my best regardless of the heartache.

Throughout this book you will read many of my quotes which were "ah ha" defining moments in the middle of my challenges, experiences, and disappointments. These internal encouraging messages helped to carry me through and provided a means to help others. It's a fact that there is nothing new under the sun and every disappointment we face and defining moment we experience can be a support for others as they walk out their Higher Cause.

In one specific season of betrayal, I heard the following message originate from my broken heart: "If I am not close enough to be hurt, I am not close enough to make a difference." What did I value the most? Did I want to live my life protecting myself from hurt or making a difference by serving a Higher Cause? In a moment I knew I could never violate my core values, my purpose, and my reason for living in spite of my present or future disappointments. *Higher Living Leaders* will embrace personal risk—even the risk of the heart—for a Higher Cause.

Ralph Waldo Emerson said, "What lies behind us and what lies before us are tiny matters compared to what lies within us." The external aspects of life cannot trump the internal. Trump carries the meaning of outranking or holding higher value than. When we can accurately measure, judging every disappointment against the Higher Cause, the Higher Cause will always win!

When facing the relationally challenging and hurtful situations, I learned much about myself and actually increased in my tenacity to hold steady the course, not change directions or make life-altering decisions in the midst of a storm, nor focus on the threats of failure. I also discovered how to recognize if an individual was only echoing the cause I was championing to meet their own need or if the cause was truly who they were and what they valued. I gained a greater discernment on how to determine the core values of another so that I would know the depth in which I can lead and partner.

Robert Kiyosaki says, "The size of your success is measured by the strength of your desire; the size of your dream; and how you handle disappointment along the way."[19]

HIGHER LIVING LEADERSHIP

To summarize, *Higher Living Leaders* operate from an internal culture—a belief system that governs actions—where they Think Higher, take Higher Responsibility, and function from a Higher Cause.

Validation Quotient is woven into the tapestry of *Higher Living Leaders,* making them powerful for impact and cultural change, while inspiring and giving power to all they lead.

These principles produce an organic change in the leader's perspective of himself or herself and of others. I appreciate many of the self-help resources because they demonstrate the authors' desire to assist others and the reader's desire for growth. However, we have often substituted self-help courses to convince our minds of our value and the steps to success. In actuality, internal value and worth do not come through self-proclamation and external achievement, but through understanding the "signature of value" and taking personal responsibility as quality human beings and leaders of justice.

As we transition to unpacking the aspects of Higher Thinking, my hope is that you truly begin to discover the uniqueness of who you are, your personal purpose, and the amazing ability you have to demonstrate *Higher Living Leadership.*

CHAPTER 5

INTRA-LEADERSHIP

What in the world is Intra-Leadership? Intra is a Latin word meaning inner, inside, within. When I speak of Intra-Leadership I am conveying the ability that the *Higher Living Leader* develops to understand, value, and steward his or her ability to influence, impact, and bring positive change to the world. This concept is the central component of Higher Thinking.

"Human beings, by changing the inner attitudes of their minds, can change the outer aspects of their lives."[1]

Our thoughts, emotions, attitudes, beliefs, perceptions, and perspectives are the prophets of our future. Who we become is a direct result of our thinking. *We cannot minimize the power of the mind and our ability to choose, for by it we can activate the whole of who we are.*

World-changing leaders are not trying to be "nice" but, instead, are trying to do the right and the kind thing. They are proficient in the proper management of their thoughts and communicate them appropriately. *One of the greatest things you can do for others is to enjoy a well-ordered and healthy personal life.*

So often we want to deal with the actions of others, but their actions will not, nor cannot, change until they undergo a paradigm shift. When thoughts change, actions change! So often we become angry with ourselves because of what we've done, how we've opened our mouth and inserted our foot, or when we've responded to someone in a way that is inconsistent to empowering leadership. We focus on what we are doing, rather than what we are thinking and believing. The actions and attitudes we portray are a mirror of our intra-leadership. Our actions replicate our beliefs.

Proper self-assessment entails having an accurate knowledge of our inner self, while possessing the heart motivation to learn, grow, change, and steward the amazing treasure within. We must unearth our uniqueness, our purpose, and our passions in order to have a clear understanding of who we are and our core values. It is also important to discover the hindrances to, and the saboteurs of our growth, success, and our ability to establish healthy relationships and partnerships. *To understand is the beginning of personal discovery, growth, and change.*

Is it possible for us to have the ability to manage our thoughts and emotions in order to deal with conflict, pressure, and the stress-filled challenges of life more successfully? Yes!

Is it possible for us to develop a healthy intra-leadership lifestyle that makes it possible for us to assess our personal belief system, values, and automatic thought processes, brought about by past experiences, in order to redirect our present decisions in a healthy way? Yes!

SELF-ASSESSMENT, AN ACTUAL STRUCTURE OF THE BRAIN[2]

Every person houses a place of self-assessment in the frontal cortex of their mind-brain. It is the executive portion of the brain that gives us the ability to choose what thoughts we will think upon, as well as the choices we will make. It is the place of decision-making as we bring into effect our free will.

I am not a scientist by any stretch of the imagination, but I have gained knowledge about intra-leadership and the internal self-governance we possess. This understanding holds the ability to empower others through gaining understanding of the human brain. Our brain is astounding in its capacity to hold three million years' worth of memory. Our brain also houses approximately one trillion neural connections.[3] We hear one trillion and do not grasp the magnitude of how immeasurable that is. A second of time seems so miniscule, but it would take almost 32,000 years to contain one trillion seconds. It's astounding to think that is the number of neural connections within the human brain!

A neuron can be pictured like the trunk of a tree and upon that neuron approximately seventy thousand branches (dendrites) can grow. They will grow and connect to other branches building an elaborate network of working memory. Scientists call these the *magic trees of the brain.* "A typical neuron makes about ten thousand connections to neighboring neurons. Given the billions of neurons, this means there are as many connections in a single cubic centimeter of brain tissue as there are stars in the Milky Way galaxy."[4]

Every person can increase in his or her intelligence. We have the ability to cause our mind-brains to build healthy working memory that is abounding and beneficial in relationship to intra-leadership.

It is not what happens *to us*, but what happens *in us* that sculpts our mindsets, actions, reactions, and worldview. Many allow their past experiences to define who they are, their view of today, and their potential for the future.

I am not insensitive to the pain of an individual's past. I've had my share of injustice—those chapters in my life's book that were potentially devastating—I was sexually abused from the age of two to nine years old. However, I have learned that it is not the event itself that shapes us but the subsequent lies—harmful fear-based belief systems—that we embrace that negatively affect us. Dr. Daniel G. Amen says, "Your brain creates your reality. It is not what happens to you in life that determines how you feel; it's how your brain perceives reality that makes it so."[5]

"Growing dendrites [branches] is a normal healing process of the brain. It is also part of the normal learning process. When you learn a new complex behavior, the brain actually grows dendrites to make nerve connections more elaborate."[6] Simply speaking, what we think upon we believe, what we believe we do, what we do becomes habitual as intricate memory is developed shaping our beliefs, attitudes, emotions, behaviors, and reactions.

We face a daily battle to align our thoughts with information that will generate health-giving intra-leadership, as well as the ability to bring validation and empowerment to our external culture. According to neuroscientists, every thought that we have is either fear or faith-based, destructive or building, toxic or healthy. Because of the intense emotional component of negative thoughts, they become at least three times more forceful than the positive thoughts.[7]

"Scientists have learned that you can grow your brain at will, and you can change the structure of your brain by the way that you think."[8]

Our thought-life has such power to shape our internal world for good or harm, which in turn, affects every external aspect of life—personally and professionally. Once again, the *magic trees of the brain* within the cerebral cortex amass all your memory. From our very conception all the information, words we hear or speak, experiences, emotions, thoughts, imaginations, and actions build those amazing branches (dendrites). Every thought that I allow to remain and choose to meditate upon will build those branches on the trees (neurons) in my mind-brain. "Every time you have a thought, it is actively changing your brain and your body—for better or for worse."[9]

HEALTHY OR HAUNTED MEMORY

Our healthy life-giving thoughts construct branches that cultivate positive memory (the healthy oak tree image).

The negative, toxic, fear-based thoughts also form branches/memory. These unhealthy thoughts develop thorns on the branches which distort the memory (the haunted tree image). Because this distorted memory is fear-based and fear produces an emotional torment, I've equated or described these thorn-filled dendrites (branches) as "haunted" trees. These "haunted" trees carry the meaning of words, experiences, and thoughts that misrepresent, twist, and mislead us away from objective and healthy leadership. My thoughts become unreliable, therefore my source for my decision-making is defective and untrustworthy.

We must remember that just leadership is about influencing and empowering others for good. Therefore, I have a moral obligation—to myself and to those I lead—to safeguard my mind and move my thoughts away from the haunted, tormenting, twisted, thorn-filled branches towards the thoughts that build a healthy memory. These branches, healthy or haunted, will not only affect my mind, thoughts, attitudes, and actions but also my physical health. The holistic quality of life is in direct correlation to the health of our memory—the magic trees of the brain.

THE SIMPLIFIED PROCESS OF THOUGHT

Understanding the brain's process of thought facilitates our ability to become consciously aware of our capacity to develop the type of memory—healthy or haunted—that will be established within our mind-brain. Comprehending our authority to choose is liberating, as we guard our thoughts defending the intrinsic integrity of our emotional health and well-being.

We've unpacked the concept of reformation which embodies the meaning of rescuing from error and returning to a rightful course. This is the ability we have to insure that our intra-leadership, the internal management of our lives, is stewarded towards *Higher Living Leadership*. We have the mental capacity to be rescued from the error of the negative, abusive, or traumatic experiences of our lives—past or present. We possess the ability to facilitate and insure our mind-brain's return to a rightful healthy course through the continued practice of wholesome deliberate choice. This habit will progressively influence every aspect of your life, your interaction with others, and the leadership aptitude to positively impact your culture.

We've learned that the thoughts we choose to think upon build memory. The *magic trees of the brain* respond millisecond by millisecond to the messages we choose to send, activating and stimulating the intricate wiring of the brain.

It is difficult to presume that science will ever understand in entirety our remarkable brains, but what neuroscientists have discovered concerning the process of thought can influence the way we live and lead. Neuroscientists understand the many complexities of the process of thought, but I want to connect in simplicity what is complex in order to provide relevancy to our everyday lives.[10] My goal is to confirm our intrinsic ability to change our world by the way they think—it's very applicable and practical. When we know the power we have to change internally, we can become leaders of external change.

INFORMATION ENTERS

Information is flooding our minds in rapid fire through everything we see, hear, feel, touch, taste, intuit, and experience. Even our past—previous memories—provides information affecting our present. "The past speaks to us in a thousand voices, warning and comforting, animating and stirring to action."[11]

This sensory information enters our minds and passes through the thalamus—a structure in the central part of the brain that relays sensory signals to the cerebral cortex where memories are accessed.

INFORMATION BREEZES THROUGH THE *MAGIC TREES OF THE BRAIN*

Every intricate detail of the incoming information breezes through the trees/branches of your existing memories and consciousness. The information will attach itself or relate with either the healthy branches/memory or the thorny "haunted" branches in milliseconds exciting, stimulating and connecting in the neural memory base.

For example: When we face a disappointment, we not only contend with the present event but also the established memories of past disappointments with which it connects. It could be compared to a magnet drawing the current situation to a similar or related event from the past.

Information Returns to the Central Part of the Brain Where Biochemicals are Generated by the Body to Regulate the Body.

After the information connects to the memory/branches—healthy or haunted—it enters the hypothalamus where chemicals are released throughout the entire body. It is essential to understand this function of the thought process because what happens here affects our physical body as well as our thoughts, attitudes, emotions, and the type of memories that are formed.

One of two things will happen:

If the present information breezed through a healthy memory then, in response, beneficial chemicals in the correct portion are released into every cell of the body. Serotonin, for example, is a healthy chemical that supports the ability to focus, solve problems, enhance learning, and display a healthy disposition or personality. Serotonin is key to managing stress, which influences many other actions and reactions in the body including supporting immune and heart health. It basically makes me feel good. When serotonin levels are low, I will feel fear, anxiety, self-pity, stress, or depression.

Having a healthy memory helps you assimilate new information from a perspective that generates the right type of chemicals to reinforce positive life-giving memory, attitudes, and emotions.

Remember present information is like a magnet drawn to a past similar or related memory. There were many Sundays that my family would take a forty-five minute road trip to visit my Uncle Mike and Aunt Caroline. Even though I was so excited to see my cousins, forty-five minutes felt like an eternity so I would conveniently fall asleep on my mother's lap. I repeatedly remember being roused through a cold sensation on my cheek—it was a soft vanilla ice cream cone! Not only was the ice cream a highlight but I knew we were close to our destination! What a beautiful childhood memory!

Ice cream, especially soft ice cream, always brought back the feelings and the emotions attached to those beautiful memories. My first and only job throughout high school was to work at a Dairy Queen where we could eat all the ice cream we wanted for free!

Can you see why my comfort food of choice was always ice cream? Eating ice cream would connect to a happy and healthy memory releasing feel-good chemicals.

On the flipside; if the present information breezed through that thorny fear-based "haunted" memory then a distorted portion or type of neurochemical is released into every cell of my body. One type of chemical, for example, would be cortisol. "Cortisol is a potent chemical that surges when you slip into stress, and is now recognized as a drug that can literally shrink human brains."[12]

Have you ever relentlessly studied for an exam yielding all the information to memory? Do you recall how you could recite the material verbatim and were confident to face the test the following day? Do you also remember the times when the test was placed on your desk and you suddenly fell into stress as fear, intimidation, and anxiety flooded your consciousness? Suddenly your mind went blank? Do you remember that even though you knew the answer the night before, you were unable to recall the information? That was the result of fear-based cortisol surges!

Though cortisol can help us in the short term, it carries harmful consequences to our emotional and physical health—especially heart health. "Researchers have known for some time, for instance, that cortisol shuts down learning, creates anxiety attacks and can cause depression."[13]

We have all faced extended periods where fear was the dominate emotion and stress saturated every aspect of our lives. I was only 11 years old when my 46 year old father died of a heart attack. When he was six years old his mother died giving birth to twins and at eight his step-mother sent him to live with an uncle. His hard work was the payment for his room and board which was to sleep in the barn and feast on mush. He was treated harshly without love, care, or protection. It is safe to conclude that the harshness of his life had a direct impact on his physical heart.

Remember, when we face a painful, negative, or fearful event we not only contend with the present event but the established memories with which it connects releasing fear-based, stress-related chemicals.

THIS CHEMICALLY-CHARGED INFORMATION MOVES TO THE MEMORY OF EMOTIONAL REACTION

After the chemicals are released, this information will journey to the amygdala, a structure that provides **the memory of emotional reaction**. It is "Shown in research to perform a primary role in the processing and memory of emotional reactions..."[14]

Have you ever said or heard someone say, "That pushed my button!" or "That was an emotional trigger!"? What takes place is that present information connected to past experience produces similar feelings and reactions mirroring the past. In other words, the information that enters the amygdala, where the memory of emotional response is housed, causes a person to feel or want to react in a similar fashion much like they felt or responded during past experiences.

Because of the repeated abuse I experienced as a child I began to develop mindsets, beliefs, and lies about others—especially men. I also believed lies about myself and constantly fought the fear of being powerless. Therefore, as I grew older, men were an enemy along with anyone or anything that would hinder my ability to climb the corporate ladder.

I refused to be powerless!!! I was angry, forceful, and opinionated, believing that was the only way to demonstrate my power. It masked the deep feelings and beliefs of how defenseless I felt in a dog-eat-dog world. Karate became a god to me as I gave myself fully to what I thought would protect me from being victimized ever again. It is obvious to recognize that so many of my life choices were a direct result of the memory of emotional, fear-based reaction from the amygdala.

My external performance was displayed in a way that portrayed a young woman of superior work ethic, determination, and dedication to my career. However in the secret place of my thought-life and internal management I was consumed with shame and fear. The magic trees of my brain were filled with haunted memories—consciously and subconsciously—that created a cycle that reinforced and expanded those thorny fear-based memories. The amygdala continued to store all the old and newly added information just waiting for circumstances to push the proverbial button…again…and again…and again!

Any external information that was remotely similar to those haunted trees triggered a reaction that was sabotaging my ability to be successful—personally or professionally. What was destructive and caused me to hide behind a mask of "I am woman hear me roar!" was the foreboding sense that I was actually powerless. I believed that all my actions and reactions were who I really was as a person—my personality. But in reality, it was the amygdala triggering a habitual response based upon the years of writing instructions in the *magic trees of the brain* through the thoughts that flooded my mind.

All the steps in this process are in automatic rapid-fire succession; however, this next step is our place of emancipation through self-governance as we take every thought captive.

The Choice to Submit Those Thoughts to the *Seat of Judgment*

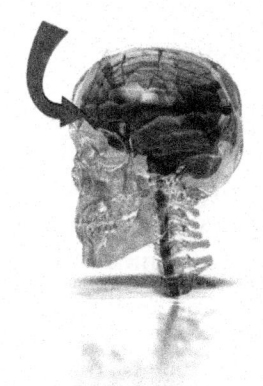

As we understand the process to this point it may feel like we have no choice—but that belief is what truly leaves us powerless. It is very important to understand that when the information moves to the amygdala that we must immediately acknowledge what is happening, deal with the emotion, the attitude, the feeling, and submit it to what scientists call the **seat of judgment** in the prefrontal cortex of our brain.

The *seat of judgment* is the executive portion of our brain, the amazingly powerful place of self-assessment. It is the place of free will, the place where I take the intensity of the emotion—the activation of the trigger—and submit it to wisdom. Here is the place of power, self-control, and intra-leadership.

We have the power to choose to accept or reject the thought. If we accept the thought and continue to rehearse its message, we will build a more established memory. If I reject the thought, it will halt the growth of those branches (dendrites). When we choose to embrace the healthy thoughts, rejecting the fear-based thought, we can change the very wiring of our brains for good. How liberating to understand and how life-changing when applied.

CHAPTER 6

WHAT WAS I THINKING?

Before I complete the process of thought, I want to interject alongside the necessary neurological function of the amygdala, the potential drawbacks to its memory of emotional reaction. As we understand the amygdala's role more clearly it will provide for us the insight to properly respond and literally alter the magic trees of our brain for good.

Emotional hijacking is the condition that occurs when a person's emotions take over his or her cognitive ability. This "taking over" occurs when the reward center of the brain, coupled with the memory of emotional response from the amygdala, overrides the executive portion of the brain.

It is important to distrust the negative emotions experienced when facing a stressful or fearful situation. Instead, one should invoke free will and submit his or her emotions to wisdom.

Actions and speech conceived from inflated emotion will result in actions and speech that you'll undoubtedly regret. Following a very stressful or emotional situation, have you ever said aloud, "What was I thinking?" The answer is, "You weren't!" The old adage of "hindsight is clearer than foresight" gives us a more accurate perspective when we recognize that our response was stemmed from fear, rather than wisdom.

As leaders, with greater levels of responsibility, we often face stressful circumstances that have the potential to positively or negatively affect the lives of many. It is never wise to make decisions or react out of fear on any level of leadership.

Emotional reaction overriding wisdom manifest on many levels and at varying degrees of intensity. For example, emotional reaction may manifest in horrific crimes of passion, road rage, and fights or screaming, as well as through shopping, eating, or isolation.

We all know that eating high fat foods, such as french fries or highly refined sugary foods, like cakes or donuts, is physically unhealthy for us. Wisdom tells us to partake only in moderation, yet many times we find ourselves running to comfort foods to escape emotionally stressful situations. We know this is not wise, but do we care at the moment? No! When we eat out of emotional reaction, we are programming our amygdala in the manner by which we choose to be emotionally hijacked. By creating this negative feedback loop, it is even easier to go astray the next time we experience an emotional reaction.

Emotional hijacking can be characterized as those moments when you want to grab a sledge hammer and smash your computer because it is either slow, frozen, or you have lost files and a day's work! Simply put, you're experiencing unhealthy, inflated emotions due to the stress or fear from the amygdala. We are not thinking about how much a new computer will cost us or the greater problems we will face if it is smashed into a million pieces.

Emotional hijacking is often known as the "freeze, fight, or flight" response. When you face stress or fear, you are paralyzed, rise up to aggressively fight, or run to escape as quickly as possible. It is a self-protective reaction responding to the fear from the amygdala. This self-protective response hijacks or overrides the thinking, reasoning, and the *seat of judgment* response.

Dr. Joseph Ledoux, professor at The Center for Neural Science of New York University discovered a "low road" pathway that "nerve impulses may be sent much faster from the thalamus directly to the amygdala" before it reaches the prefrontal cortex, "the area of the brain most responsible for planning and reasoning."[1]

I loathe snakes! I hate to admit it but if I saw a snake in our yard I would emotionally hijack…completely flip out! I don't care if it is little non-venomous garden snake or a dangerous copperhead found in Pennsylvania—fear grips me. Just thinking about this now is painting pictures in my mind that are not pleasant! I better finish this topic, fast!

Many years ago, when my children were very young, we lived in a little house that was surrounded by woods and a creek, and we often saw snakes. One day, as I drove into our driveway and walked toward our front door, all curled up on a decorative chair was a rather large snake with his head perfectly positioned looking straight at me.

I was seized by fear, now understood as emotional hijacking. I don't even remember getting back into the car. I found myself blasting the horn and screaming at the top of my lungs in panic. I then turned to see my wonderful husband and two precious children standing at the front door rolling in unrestrained laughter.

The backside of the story was my husband found a dead snake in our yard in picture-perfect condition. Knowing my fear and hatred of snakes he found himself in the ideal position for a practical joke. He told the kids, "Hey, let's see what Mom does when she gets home."

He carefully curled the snake up on the chair pointing his head in the precise direction. As my "adoring" husband and children lay in wait for Mom to get home they witnessed the perfect example of an emotional hijack. The only thing good about this story is the illustration for this book! All I will say concerning this is that my husband never did that again!

What I saw with my eyes sent information to the center of my brain transmitting it directly to the amygdala through that "neural back alley" and I reacted without thinking. I didn't take time to think or to process what I had seen. I didn't say to myself, "Let me check through the encyclopedia to see if this is poisonous. What color, what type of markings, what shape are its eyes and then I will determine if I am in danger or not." No! I immediately reacted.

You see this is a necessary neurological function that helps us when we face danger. The information enters through the senses as it reaches the amygdala-emotional response-before the cerebral cortex. It is a subconscious response to protect you from danger, rather than wait for the conscious brain to react. Chemicals such as adrenaline and epinephrine are released triggering a faster heart rate and quicker muscle response.

I took three young people with me on one of my many trips to Kenya, East Africa. As was my custom, we enjoyed a beautiful safari that took us through the Lake Nakuru National Park renowned for its vast flocks of pink flamingos and diverse population of wildlife including the lion, leopard, white rhino, and water buffalos. We were the ones "caged" in a little matatu (van) as we enjoyed the beauty of the African plain and the many wild animals in their natural habitat.

The matatu driver and guide, as they always do, communicate detailed information on the different animals, their temperaments, and how they function, feed, take shelter and interact with other wildlife. He focused on the water buffalo explaining that it was the most volatile of all the animals and therefore, very dangerous. He began to illustrate that if you became an irritant to the water buffalo, you would see him stomp his foot. If you did not back away, he would swing his head as a second warning. If you did not pull away, all 1,100 to 2,000 pounds of him would charge to remove a clear and present threat. Yeah right...little ole' us were a threat to a huge water buffalo—that'll never happen! We all know, however, that perspective is everything!

We trekked through the bush in the middle of the rainy season with many waterholes to circumnavigate or drive through if not too deep. We approached a lone water buffalo and sat quietly about six feet from him. While observing the huge creature, I saw him stomp his foot and then shake his head. This all happened in milliseconds, but I clearly remember thinking, "Hmmmm, this is what the guide said a water buffalo would do when they want you to get away." Within seconds that water buffalo began to charge our little matatu. The driver experienced an amygdala hijack as he put the pedal to the metal and we raced rapidly through the water filled holes fleeing for our lives—literally. What an adrenaline rush!

When we finally came to a stop knowing that we were now safe, we were astonished as one of the young girls sitting in the very back seat of the matatu was now hunkered down between the driver and the passenger seat. How did she do that? How did she leap over the three rows of seats, and not even remember doing so? She experienced an emotional hijack—a necessary neurological function that released large amounts of adrenaline and epinephrine to save her from danger.

Problem: Emotional Threats

What an essential benefit when faced with a physical threat! The problem, however, is when we emotionally hijack when facing threats of emotional pain. "...the amygdala will react similarly to the threat of being eaten by a tiger (physical threat) and the threat of an ego attack (emotional threat) by bringing on the fight or flight reaction."[2]

How many times do we find ourselves slamming on the breaks when someone stops quickly in front of us as our right arm reaches out to protect the one in the passenger seat? It's been many years since my children were little but this automatic response continues, yet protects no one.

When this takes place, "Adrenaline is released and will be present and effective for 18 minutes, and other [stress-related] hormones are released into the bloodstream that will take 3-4 hours to clear."[3]

Emotional hijacking is highly beneficial and can be a life-saver when facing physical threats but our amygdala wants to react in the same way when we are confronted with emotional threats. This can result in actions or speech that we may often regret as our emotions, frustrations, and fears explode through our words, attitudes, and reactions. However, when we recognize the fear-based emotion, this is the time when we must acknowledge what is happening and submit the emotions and information to the *seat of judgment*, the place of self-assessment, wisdom, and healthy choice.

When we face stress—the body's automatic reaction to fear—we must be aware of the propensity to hijack emotionally. If we continue to ruminate on those negative fear-based thoughts, we will continue to build fear-based memory and will experience the prolonged release of fear-related chemicals. That progression will keep us in that freeze, flight, or flight mode. This will accelerate the emotional stress, anger, and irritation which can sabotage our ability to make wise choices. You see, the amygdala is still trying to protect us from danger as reasoning and ability to think clearly is impeded.

My husband is a veteran who served in the United States Navy as a boiler operator. He explained to me that there was a pressure gauge that showed zero to one thousand degrees of pressure. When the hand of the gauge would move into the red they needed to cut back on the fuel—the fire—so the pressure would come to a safe level. If that didn't take place, there was a pressure valve that would automatically allow the steam to be released from the boiler into the atmosphere outside of the ship. If the pressure was not released automatically, or manually, the boiler could blow up and kill everyone in the boiler room. It could also kill those above the boiler room because of the heat's intensity.

When we enter into stress and are inundated with fear-based information, we need to recognize that the pressure must be released or we could "blow up" injuring ourselves and those in our sphere of influence. "Replay painful incidents mentally, or dwell on hurtful events, and negative feelings begin to crowd out possibilities and you may drown in a sense of [injustice]... The brain's basal ganglia stores every reaction to severe disappointments. And if negative or bitter—those reactions limit your chances for finding well-being in a similar situation."[4]

We can, in the same way, slip into emotional hijacking simply from perceived or anticipated threats. We can lose our sense of well-being as fear grips us as we anxiously think about the possibility of an emotional threat. Our amygdala is on high alert as we project ourselves into what could be an emotionally challenging, fearful, stressful or hurtful situation. We can travel to places in our minds and even experience the emotions associated with something that has not happened, nor may it ever happen.

Have you ever experienced the butterflies in your stomach before a job interview? This nervous and anxious sensation is experienced because the stomach or gut-brain—which houses its own neural connections—is connected directly to your mind-brain.

Have you ever experienced your heart race just thinking about facing a relational confrontation? The heart—which houses its own neural connections—is also connected to your brain as you think about a remark someone expressed, the hurt you experienced, or the nervous anticipation when you need to deal with a conflict.

Have you ever been upset over an assumption, which is the lowest form of knowledge, where you mentally construct a scenario that develops its own, unfounded emotional agitation? Has your mind replayed the many defensive conversational scenarios while your well-planned putdowns and comebacks were strategized? Then, after all the emotionally charged war-arming preparations, you find yourself gaining understanding when communicating to that person? You discovered that all your mental gymnastics only seeded your mind and body with stress related chemicals. Without your conscious awareness, many haunted branches were formed and are negatively affecting your emotional health and giving power to potentially divide valuable personal and work-based relationships.

We must recognize that what we think about and meditate upon, whether it is fabricated or factual, establishes memory. Have you ever met someone who rehearsed details that you knew were engineered only in his or her imagination? Nonetheless, though imaginary, he or she believed them to be true. The fact is, to him or her it was true because he or she meditated on that perception, perspective, or imagination so much that those things had become a literal memory-base reality in the mind that was established through these false thoughts.

Help? What Can We Do?

Science acknowledges that when a person immediately recognizes the emotional hijack, he or she is more able to submit it to reason. The recognition of what is occurring engages the seat of judgment.

Have you ever heard anyone say, "just breathe"? Good advice! When you choose to breathe calmly it engages your frontal cortex that is directly connected to your heart.

Tell yourself to think rationally and submit your emotions and thoughts to truth. Begin to reject worry, fear, and anxiety and think on the things that will generate peace, safety, and good reports. This is where we can begin to replace the toxic thoughts with healthy ones. Begin to think about what you're thinking about, which once again, engages the frontal cortex in the battlefield of the mind.

It is very difficult to have two emotional responses at the exact same time. Either it is going to haunted or healthy, fear or hope, anger or peace, etc. An attitude of gratitude is one of the most powerful ways to overcome an emotional hijack. When you start looking at what you have, rather than what you do not have; what is good rather than evil; what is beneficial rather than harmful; what is a celebrated and valued rather than demeaned and devalued; you will be able to stop the hijack rescuing your mind from error. Now that is intra-leadership!

Remember, it may take up to three to four hours for the fear-based chemicals to leave your system. It is essential to give you mind and body time to emotionally and physically recover. Have you ever had too much caffeine? The caffeine buzz did not feel good but you recognized why you felt the way you did. You stopped drinking caffeine, drank water, and allowed your body to recover. The same approach should be taken with the chemical surges you feel from the emotional hijacking. Stop feeding your mind those stress-filled thoughts, submit those thoughts to their healthy contradiction and give your mind and body time to recover. Recognize that you may have the healthy intra-leadership practices through Higher Thinking, but it will take time for those chemicals to dissipate from your body.

AFTER THE EMOTIONAL HIJACK

After you've returned to a healthy frame of mind, avoid self-defense, self-justification, and blame. Now is the opportunity to walk in Higher Responsibility and, in doing so, earn great respect and trust.

Think about what happened and how you responded, while determining how you will respond differently in the future. Think about the source of the hijack and what could have triggered your reaction. Take time to understand yourself and others through the grid of validation.

Our minds, understanding, thoughts, feelings, purposes, and desires, along with the power to consider and judge can truly be restructured. We can, by an act of our will, raise the bar and, in doing so, continue to mature our intra-leadership.

A humbling, but highly mature and responsible act is to convey sincere apologies to others, even if they were also at fault. Ask for forgiveness and extend forgiveness to others. "Okay, Melodye, now you have gone too far!" No, if we stop short of forgiveness we will retain the very neural-networking for future hijacking and self-sabotage. We must courageously commit ourselves to forgiveness because unforgiveness releases toxic thoughts that continue to build those haunted, thorny branches and the deadly stress chemicals are injected into every cell of the body, lowering our immune system.

Dr. Ellen Weber says, "Stress comes from hostility—and while it gets dubbed by many names, stress shrinks the brain and anxiety drains mental life. Simply stated, stress flips your brain into shutdown or shotgun mode... You may have defaulted to ruts or triggered further problems... [because] stress from unforgiveness masks as a savior, but strikes as a killer!"[5]

Why would I want to hold offense towards another when it ultimately sabotages my ability to be physically, emotionally, relationally, and even spiritually healthy? She continues, "Brainwaves slow to a grind and serotonin supplies diminish under excessive weights of a grudge."[6] We need high levels of serotonin and recognize that a healthy mind brings health to the body; therefore, it's time to "man-up" by asking for forgiveness and genuinely extending it to others.

It is important to understand that forgiveness does not excuse destructive behavior, nor does it mean you have to position yourself in harm's way again. However, forgiveness allows your mind to release another to his or her choices, while you choose those things that are beneficial to your emotional, physical, and spiritual health. It moves you internally from the sense of being powerless through the actions of another, to a place of inner strength no matter that attitude. Forgiveness does not mean you are to continue to trust the untrustworthy, but it removes their power to control your thoughts, mind, attitudes, actions, and reactions.

There are such amazing benefits to brain health when we forgive. "When we forgive we set a prisoner free and discover that the prisoner we set free was us."[7] Forgiveness literally cleans up the memory, allowing healthy memories to flourish. "When you forgive, the very chemical structure of the brain changes from the negative to the positive, affecting the entire thinking/memory building process."[8]

"Forgiveness literally alters the brain's wiring—away from distortions brought about by the past, and beyond fears that limit the future. It leads from misery of a broken promise, to wellness that builds new neuron pathways into physical, emotional and spiritual well-being."[9] Forgiveness transforms the haunted trees into healthy ones.

Scientifically speaking, our brains are wired to give and receive love. We learned through axiogenics that the most important aspect, the valuing of self and others, always leads to emotional health. Medical science clearly indicates that a large percentage of sickness and disease is psychosomatic. That doesn't mean the sickness is a figment of someone's imagination, it means that the source and/or severity of the disease is influenced by the biochemical state of the brain. Dr. Caroline Leaf shared in one of her thought-provoking blogs, Research shows healthy changes in the nervous, immune, and endocrine systems, to name a few, as well as the brain and the heart through genuine love.[10]

Whether we are the givers or the receivers of love, it releases a healing to our brain, as well as to our entire body.

Hope for Change!

"When you initially learn something, the pathway or connection is weak. The more frequently you think a specific thought and practice a particular behavior, the stronger the pathway becomes, forming an automatic habit of thinking."[11] This is our opportunity to begin to rewrite the instructions and literally change the neuro-networking of our brain.

As we deal with the automatic thought and emotional reaction that comes from the amygdala by submitting it to the frontal cortex—the seat of judgment—we can train our minds and build our intra-leadership. "When you become aware of what you are thinking and feeling, you can choose and practice using new thoughts and behaviors. With practice, your new thoughts will become your dominate thoughts replacing old patterns of thinking."[12]

"Neurons respond and are excited by receiving strong signals (thoughts) which makes them express signaling proteins. The stronger the signal (thought) the more signal is being released. These signaling proteins interact with the DNA in your neurons telling them to remodel their dendrites. This change in the structure of the neuron creates a new or stronger memory."[13]

Rewriting the Neurons' Instructions!

What a compelling scientific fact that articulates clearly the power of choice that gives us the ability to rewrite the previous instructions from negative fear-based memory and replace it with healthy life-giving memory.

A simple scientific fact is that our brains are constantly changing. This means that we have the ability to direct that change for good—through an act of our free will—our choice. Dr. Caroline

Leaf, neuro-researcher and author says, "Within four days of correcting the way you think, you can begin to start reversing the brain damage that you've done. Years of damage is reversible."[14]

Our choices will determine the type of memory that we build and the emotional health that we enjoy no matter what we experienced in our past, the emotional memory in our amygdala, or the disappointments stored in the basal ganglia. "The brain is constantly changing, unlearning and learning. YOU have the power to make it change the way you want it to change."[15]

Neuroscientist, Santiago Ramon y Cajal makes this magnificent statement, "Every man can, if he so desires, become the sculptor of his own brain." Can you see Higher Responsibility written all over this statement? It sure won't be easy, but it is possible to remove the power of a painful experience! We can begin to be who we are purposed to be and live a life of fulfillment that we are destined to experience. Dr. Leaf adds, "After 21 days you can change the whole circuitry of your brain."[16] We literally have the ability to rewrite the instructions to create new and stronger memories.[17]

"The world we have created is a product of our thinking; it cannot be changed without changing our thinking."[18]

We are not rewriting the instructions alone, inside the mind-brain are glial—or glia—cells. There are more glial cells than there are neurons. These cells surround the neuron and hold them in place, supply nutrients and oxygen to the neuron, and remove dead neurons. How does a neuron die? You stop feeding it!

I am the destroyer of many house plants simply because I forget to water them. Can you relate? What happens when you do not feed your plants? The leaves begin to wilt, dry up, and ultimately die falling to the floor. That is much like what happens to the branches that we stop feeding by changing the way we think.

I'll call these little glial cells "Pac Man" cells. When my children were small they would play an antiquated Pac Man video game. The Pac Man would eat up everything that got in his way! These glial cells move throughout your brain while you sleep, removing all those branches that are withered. This process not only supports the eviction of haunted branches; but through life-giving thoughts replaces and grows over the place they once inhabited with healthy life-giving branches!

I was providing three days of training for the administration, staff, and teachers within a public school in our nation's capital. There was a precious young man who provided feedback at the closing of the event. He began to communicate that he not only gained information, but began to apply these principles to his life immediately. He said that he made a decision he was going to do that "brain thing" refusing to allow destructive thorns to remain and replace them with healthy branches. In his own words he shared that at the end of the first day he felt lighter inside; at the end of the second day he felt a greater internal freedom and an increased lightness. Then with great enthusiasm, as the volume increased in his voice, he asserted that the final day that he felt more freedom and an increased lightness on the inside. He was so grateful! That young man did his part by an act of his will and those glial cells worked with him as memory began to be cleaned up.

As we reconstruct our thoughts, we will enjoy the benefits of living from a place of joy and expectation for good. Whether we are optimistic or pessimistic is not a matter of "biting-our-tongue" or just saying the right thing so we don't get scolded, but it is a direct by-product of our thought-life. It is not only what we say, but it is feelings, attitudes and subsequent actions originating from what we think and believe.

We often tell people to be optimistic, but that is putting the attitude before the thought. We can't get the cart before the horse, as it were. When the established memory is healthy, we will not only speak with optimism, but we will also live enthusiastically.

What we think and believe is the lens through which we see our lives, circumstances, and opportunities.

Looking through the lens of internal freedom empowers me to interpret my past with thankfulness, my present with courage, and my future with hope!

CHAPTER 7

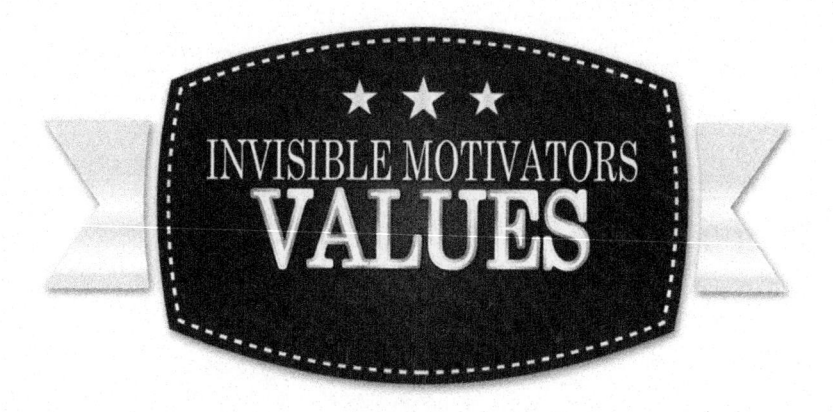

INVISIBLE MOTIVATORS: VALUES

It is important to properly assess your personal values-motivated behaviors.[1] Our core values are fundamental to the internal clarity and motivation of our Higher Cause. Our highest priority value system is the foundation for every decision that we make. Our decisions are the foundation of our behaviors. And, in turn, our behaviors are the foundation of the habits that we model. Our habits are the foundation of the results we achieve and the character that we develop.

I have been a certified behavioral analysis consultant since 1993 and have learned that there are many more conflicts relationally and within workgroups because of conflicting core values than because of personality differences. We recognize that we need different personality styles in order to complement one another's strengths, as well as to cover potential weaknesses or fear-based propensities. We can learn, understand, appreciate, and work through these differences when conflict arises. However, when there are conflicting values, we find it much harder to work through them to reach an understanding without focused effort and empathy.

"Concealed beneath the surface, your personal values are invisible, yet guide your attitudes, principles, integrity, and choices."[2]

When we discover that those with whom we are partnering with are going in different directions and holding conflicting or different agendas, motives, goals, objectives, and purposes, we can allow a seed of fear to invade our mind, causing us to see them as enemies to the cause rather than allies partnering for a unified purpose.

Contradictory values and motivations can become hotbeds for anger, division, and mistrust as emotions are escalated to hijacking levels. That teammate, client, employee, friend, or even a spouse can become—in our mind's eye—the adversary to what we truly desire. It is arduous to walk and work together with those that we cannot align our internal heart motivations with or move together towards a united cause.

Opposing values lead to a tendency to attack or be critical of another's decisions and character, filling the atmosphere with negativity and criticalness. Our leadership should be enjoying and fostering a culture of validation, but we can find ourselves leading mutiny on the proverbial bounty or throwing our crew overboard.

Why do we react so strongly to these conflicting internal motivations? Values are founded upon an internal system of beliefs. They are the belief-filter through which we base our life choices, what we believe is right or wrong, good or bad, acceptable or unacceptable. When we take personal responsibility for these beliefs we develop our character—what we are known for. This process establishes a firmly established memory through which all external information is processed. "Our value perceptions is the stimulus that causes changes in neuropathways of the brain."[3]

Our values shape our worldview—how we see, interpret, and think about the world—the friends we choose, how we spend our time, what we desire to do and pursue, and even the way we communicate, personally or professionally; all these originate from our values. Simply, the entire direction of our life comes from these invisible motivators.

It is important to recognize that the most challenging aspect of our values is within interpersonal relationships—whether the family unit or a corporate boardroom. *Higher Living Leaders* understand their own values but, most important, they learn to navigate the stormy waters of conflicting values without negative attitudes and critical, judgmental leadership.

Our staff has worked hard to clearly define our values in order to attract those of like-values and complementary motivations.

"In many respects, we do not 'see' with our eyes; we 'see' with our values, our minds."[4]

Through my experiential school of hard knocks, I have learned that I must hire, accept students, and embrace relationships based upon shared values and motivations. Many will sing your praises if their partnership with you helps them achieve their goals; but they are quick to attack you when they discover your purposes are in opposition to theirs.

Someone may be desperate to adopt leadership principles that build his or her success and produce results, but he or she will not partner and celebrate the values of other team members. *If you do not value the cause of the organization you are serving, you will feel abused by the opportunities given you.*

When the values and heart motivations are incompatible, the emotional energies of our leadership are invested into managing an opposing message rather than championing objectives. However, when values are shared, hearts and purposes connect. This connection creates an atmosphere that generates acceptance, ownership, partnership, and fulfillment.

Personal core values—the invisible motivators—will either build up or tear down, unite or divide, increase or derail the team.

"We've chosen not to live by needs alone but to have 'values' that govern our lives."[5] We all have desires, needs, and aspirations, but in the final analysis what dominates our decisions are our values. Our personal needs are important, but our core values hold greater meaning. Our needs are the things that work for US, the things that are most natural, comfortable, relaxing, easy, and stress free—the celebrated comfort zone. Our values, however, are the things that we are obliged to do—what is right, meaningful, important, consequential, necessary, or holds the greatest significance in our lives.

Without a doubt, no one has their needs met by changing dirty diapers or waking up in the middle of the night to feed or comfort a crying baby. It is a fact, however, that when a baby is in the home, our whole world revolves around its needs and not ours. Why? A higher motivation, cause, purpose, or love has become the primary value of our lives. We make decisions to meet the needs of our baby, rather than our own needs. We forgo the sleep that we desperately need, clean up messes we would rather avoid, spend enormous amounts of money to give our baby our best, and it continues for many years! Why? Because what we value far exceeds our personal needs-motivated propensities.

Values are based on a priority scale, helping us to determine what is most important to us and providing the intrinsic motivation to every choice we make. In my consulting practice, I have created a values assessment to help leaders determine their core values. There is a huge difference between things we value—aspired or adapted values—and our core values. Each person develops his or her own standard of what he or she deeply values or does not value, and what is or is not important. Each person has an internal gauge that shows what is or is not worth his or her investment. Let me reiterate from a previous chapter that your plumb line to what you value most is determined by what you protect, invest into, provide for, and treat as valuable.

We can look at our choices and see what we truly value, especially when pressure is applied—internally through negative fear-based thoughts or externally through challenging circumstances. When the "toothpaste tube gets squeezed" our highest priority value surfaces. *What we do trumps what we say, for our actions are a visible demonstration of what we truly value.* We fight to secure what we truly value because when we achieve, we experience fulfillment, freedom, and happiness. "Happiness is that state of consciousness which proceeds from the achievement of one's values."[6]

When our values are obstructed, we will experience a frustration that sends us a huge invitation to be angry, embittered, resentful and—looking for someone to blame for the blocking of what we want—our core values.

We must recognize that values need not to be identical—they rarely are—but they must be complementary and mutually empowering. Years ago I worked with a married couple that was experiencing constant relational conflict as they fought over every financial decision. We learned that the husband's number one core value was fun, while the wife's was sacrifice. His goal was to spend his hard earned money to vacation, provide entertainment, and purchase all the toys to simply love life today! Her goal was to sacrifice the pleasures of today to ensure their bills were paid, to purchase a home, to build a savings account for future needs and unexpected expenses, and to provide for their children's future education. Think of her frustration when he wanted to take an expensive vacation or buy a boat. Think of his irritation when she burst his "fun-bubble" because the rent and the car insurance were due. The battle of values ensued when he wanted to buy video games for the kids and she wanted to buy school clothes. They became a continual irritant to each other, creating an antagonistic, win-lose environment within the home. The person they valued most and vowed to love became the biggest obstacle to what was most important to them.[7]

We also find this scenario played out in organizations where people feel devalued and taken advantage of. Many look for a job simply to provide finances, but are not connected to the corporate values or the success of the organization. Many organizational leaders or managers have hired employees for skillsets, but are unable to connect to the values-motivations of those they hire.

When an organization/leader understands, values, and supports the core-motivation of others, trust will be established—producing partnership.

For this couple, the best solution was for them to come to a common ground where provision was made for both of their core values. They started a budget to divide their disposable income after taxes and other expenses. They divided the balance equally providing one half for fun and the other half for savings. The depth of this wisdom far exceeded financial management. It sent a message to the heart as validation was communicated to each one as finances were invested into what they both personally valued—fun and savings. The potential weaknesses associated with the win-lose equation came to an end, allowing win-win to create an atmosphere of love and validation.

HIGHER LIVING LEADERS RECOGNIZE WIN-WIN ALWAYS WINS!

First of all, it is important to clearly establish corporate values—the motivation for the organization's establishment. Provide these corporate values to every potential employee during the interview process, go over them in detail, make them a part of the employee manual, talk about them all the time, and process every corporate decision through them.

One of the greatest tools for conflict resolution is to "serve the vision and values" of the organization. We remove the emotion associated with the conflict, we separate the person from the problem, and we measure our decisions through the plumb line of purpose.

The best place to protect a marriage is in the dating process. Actions are the evidence of core values. As we witness the potential partner's actions, attitudes, and decisions, we assess whether they are congruent with our values. Choose wisely, because you do not marry someone to change him or her, but rather to partner with him or her.

In the same way, the best place to protect the morale and momentum of our organizations is during the hiring process. Most corporations wisely hire with a probationary period. They recognize that what is on the job application or is communicated in the interview may not be a clear picture of the core motivations of the potential employee. They also recognize what former employers cannot say when called for reference.

Accu-Screen, Inc., The Society of Human Resource Managers say that 53% of resumes and job applications contain falsifications, 78% of resumes are misleading, 21% reference fraudulent degrees, 33% include inaccurate job descriptions, etc.[8] With all this fraudulent activity, it is very clear that the applicant's core values may not align with your Higher Cause. Choose wisely because you rarely can change their values—invisible motivators—after you hire them.

After administering the values profiling and assessment instruments to both the leadership and staff, most often without foreknowledge, I can identity the conflicts in job performance, production, and team cohesiveness and collaboration. It's just difficult to experience support and partnership when there are conflicting heart motivations. This hinders the ability to trust the heart as well as to have confidence in the excellence of follow through.

I recognize I am speaking from a leadership training perspective, but executive teams, project managers, and supervisors throughout the organizational structure need continual investment. Sometimes the CEO or owner may feel he or she is wasting time and money to consistently invest reinforcement of vision and values, bring training, and provide personal empowerment for each of his or her key leadership; but it will not only be a catalyst for imparting the organizations values, but also to discover their personal values. There are many missed opportunities and untapped potential when we cannot discover the intrinsic motivation and proper placement of those to whom we have entrusted the success of our organizations.

CAN VALUES CHANGE?

Adapted values—personal invisible motivations—do not change easily or quickly. However, continued socialization frameworks can shift adapted values over time. We must recognize that bad company can corrupt good morals, just as positive influence impacts a person for good. Values are taught to us from the time we are born, as beliefs are modeled before us. Culture is a preacher of what is important—good or bad. The teaching, mentoring, and training we receive from influential leaders transform our mindsets. We all have childhood stories of those who believed in us, inspired us, and invested into us, swaying what was important to our hearts. We also have the stories of abuse and injustices that shifted our beliefs about ourselves, others, and our world.

More rapid value shifts can take place through highly significant and extreme emotional and/or traumatic events.

I grew up with a strong work ethic that is still evident in my life today. I am challenged when I see individuals who live a life of entitlement. I struggle when people want success, but do not demonstrate the willingness to work hard to accomplish it. I experience internal red flags when I do not witness a heart that desires to impact the lives of others for good. This sounds like my passion for justice which saturates every aspect of *Higher Living Leadership*! Justice carries the heart to sacrifice self for the common good.

Therefore, I have to guard myself from judgment towards those who demonstrate selfishness and a "look out for number one" mentality.

At a mere 18 years old, I did not have the language to articulate my values or the passion that I felt inside of me. However, with an adventurous spirit, I packed my bags and moved to Washington, DC where I worked in the laboratory division of the Federal Bureau of Investigation. I was determined to give my life unreservedly to do what was good! I saw myself as a world-changer! My first home in DC was a little room in a facility for young adults adjacent to the Capital Building. I loved it! I remember going to hurting areas of the city where I volunteered my time doing crafts with the underprivileged and just spent time with the children.

In those early days, my finances were limited, so I would walk to and from work. Every day, as I proudly promenaded down Pennsylvania Avenue, I would pass a derelict that staked his claim right outside a liquor store. He was horribly hunched over and could not straighten himself to stand erect. My heart just ached for him as compassion rose inside my heart as I passed him daily on my walk to work. We never spoke to one another, but we would acknowledge each other through a little nod of the head and a kind smile. I didn't have much money, but when I was able, I would buy him a cup of coffee and his eyes would light up. This is a perfect example of Validation Quotient! When you genuinely value others it seeds emotional health in the one giving and the one receiving.

I honestly looked forward to seeing him every morning and every evening. I know he also anticipated the humble acknowledgments daily affirming his value. I didn't understand at that time that our brains are wired for love and validation, but as I look back I can clearly see how my little gestures were a spark of life to a hurting man's soul.

One day, walking home during rush hour, the sidewalks packed with hundreds of people, I saw from a distance my *friend* lying on the sidewalk. My attention was drawn to this strange image because it was so unlike him. Normally he would crouch down against the liquor store keeping himself back away from crowds. As I moved closer I was shocked to see him surrounded in a pool of his own blood. Words cannot describe what my heart felt at that moment! It was a sense of powerlessness as well as a forceful compulsion to do something…anything!

I have no knowledge of what happened, but my assumption was he had been stabbed or shot. What I did know was that he was lying on that sidewalk dying. I witnessed how men in their fancy suits nonchalantly glanced down and just walked on by, not caring about this valuable life.

I began to yell for someone, anyone, to call the ambulance as one man replied, "He's just a dumb bum!" I won't go into the details of my reaction but needless to say I flipped out—emotionally hijacked! I ran into the liquor store and demanded they call an ambulance. Once again, the man's words were horribly demeaning! I was furious and terrified at the same time, as I jumped across the counter and said things I would never write in this book, but the store clerk responded, "Alright!" When the ambulance finally arrived my friend was pronounced dead.

My heart felt like it shattered into a million pieces as I grieved for a friend that I never spoke to and never knew his name. I could not believe that hundreds of people who passed by were not visibly shaken by what they saw, appeared not to care, nor showed any compassion. I cried and cried unable to find comfort, nor could I reconcile what I had just experienced. I realized that I didn't even have anyone to talk to—no one to trust. Disillusioned, I lie upon my bed that night with a pain so deep, anger so intense, and a profound disappointment in the people and the city that I came to serve.

In just a few short hours my adapted values shifted from justice—using my influence for the good of others—to "look out for number one"…me! What I hated before, I had now become. My thoughts were, "If the people of this city did not care about this man who lie dying on the sidewalk, they would not have looked twice if it was me in that pool of blood. Why should I care for others when no one would care for me?"

My healthy work ethic turned into an overachieving workaholic—I was now driven for success…MY success! This traumatic emotional event drastically shifted my values, purpose, and motivations. My heart turned polar opposite from that young vision-inspired instrument of justice. No longer did I care who I hurt as I climbed my personal ladder to success. If I had to step on someone else to get ahead then that is what I would do. I angrily lived my life behind self-protective walls, a guarded heart, and an inability to trust.

Remember, science is discovering our DNA and human brains are imprinted with a hierarchy of value. The more we can challenge our personal values to align with the "signature of value," the healthier and happier we will be.

My newly adopted value system appeared good on the outside as I outshined my counterparts, produced, and advanced appearing more and more successful. However, my value system was in total contradiction to the hierarchy of value—to value self and value others—leaving me suffering emotionally no matter how externally successful I became. I turned to socially acceptable substance abuse to anesthetize my internal pain.

About two and a half years later I faced another challenging and traumatic event in my life that, once again, shifted me back to my heart for justice. That three-year journey taught me volumes about success, leadership and the importance of the values that one holds.

I have scripted the internal motivation of adapted values and their influence upon decisions, interpersonal relationships, and corporate collaboration. It is important to understand, however, that every human being has an innate unchanging nature. These innate core values empower an individual to discover their highest and best contribution. It is an internal driver that propels him or her to impact society in ways instinctive to his or her uniqueness. This exists deeper than our personality—needs motivated behaviors—and the values we have adapted from environment, socialization framework, or significant emotional events.

"Abraham Maslow called this innate self the unchanging real self, which contains your natural dispensations; your preferred ways of perceiving, feeling, reasoning, deciding, and participating in your society. He proposed that your innate nature is unchanging from childhood until death. Maslow's central conclusion was that it is the unique self, this real you, that inscribes where in this world you fit best."[9]

When the voice of adapted values conflict with an individual's innate nature, he or she will experience a crisis of belief and an uncertainty of purpose. As an individual's innate nature aligns with the work that he or she does, high levels of *Validation Quotient* will emerge. When our innate contributions and roles come together, self-actualization takes place facilitating a continuous discovery of who we are and our unique purpose. The byproduct of this journey will be the celebration of the value an individual brings to the table and his or her ability to excel as a top performer. This will allow *every Higher Living Leader* to positively influence the organization's culture in which he or she partners.

If you are interested in learning more about your innate core values, I encourage you to take a free Core Values Index (CVI) assessment by connecting to a link on my website: www.DrMelodye.com/cvi. It is one of the simplest, most versatile tools you can find for improving self-awareness and the awareness of others. The CVI is highly reliable with greater than 97% repeat score reliability. This demonstrates its accuracy. And, if the CVI is this accurate, then what it is measuring, the innate nature of the person, must be essentially unchanging, as Maslow proposed.

CHAPTER 8

DISCOVERING PERSONAL PURPOSE

Intra-leadership is the ability to understand, value, and steward our aptitude to influence, impact, and bring positive change to our world. Woven into this is the proficiency to assess ourselves and know our core values as well as our personal purpose. All these are woven together to increase our Validation Quotient and to establish us as *Higher Living Leaders*.

Discovering, articulating, and walking out our purpose is absolutely imperative for personal success and effective leadership.

"Few people ever discover the work they love..."[1] The age old question is crying out, "Who am I and why am I here?" When that question can be answered we touch a source of energy that will not fade out or become obsolete.

We experience passion when we are doing what we value. Everyone has passion and purpose, but we may lack an avenue for its expression. When this occurs, it creates a disconnection among the head—higher thinking, the hand—higher responsibility, and the heart—higher cause. All areas of our lives suffer and we survive, rather than thrive. Our emotions, and subsequently our physical energy, are diminished as motivation dwindles.

When energy, passion, and motivation decrease, a psychological symptom of stress occurs. Stress is an unmanaged reaction, as the mind and body responds to any pressure that disrupts normal balance. Remembering back to those toxic thoughts, emotions, attitudes, actions, and possible emotional hijacking; we recognize this is not the way we want to live or lead.

I have found a wide range of percentages from 70% to 97% stating that illness is a direct result of our thought life. Even at the most modest percentage we see the impact of our thoughts on our physical health. If this is a fact for a negative thought life, it is safe to conclude that the opposite is true when we are walking in the joy of our unique purpose.

Let's picture a container that provides a specific amount of room to house our emotional energies. When we have limited space, we have to decide how we will spend our emotional energies. We do not want to fill the container with negative, fear-based thoughts, nor spend our lives on activities that are meaningless, purposeless, or fruitless.

We can exemplify loving life within our homes, workplaces, and spheres of influence. We can model a lifestyle of purpose and value-driven motivations that increase our ability to accomplish much. We can be a leader who empowers others and brings health to our organization. Finding our personal purpose, and helping others to discover theirs, is one of the greatest benefits we can offer. When our emotional energies container is filled with life-giving endeavors, it actually supports our physical health.

I have been honored to help many people worldwide to discover their personal purpose. I've witnessed their positive emotions as they begin to see their reason for being. When an individual touches the treasure within and sees his or her intrinsic value, his or her countenance changes.

When we can connect who we are and why we are here with what we are doing, we unleash our potential. *Walking in your purpose takes you from a life of success to a life of significance.*

I've worked with over-the-top intelligent, successful, and highly influential leaders. I stand in awe of what they are doing and how their lives impact multitudes of people worldwide. My heart leaps inside of me when I see tears fill their eyes or a huge smile appears with a "wow" on their lips, or a "Yes, this is me! I just never saw it like this before!"

"Deep within us is something we hold dear, and if it's ever violated we weep and wail. We'll fight to the death to secure it, grieve if we lose it, and shriek with joy when we achieve it."[2] We must understand that our experiences—good or bad—have the ability to shape our purpose, passions and values.

Our personal purpose is the WHY we do what we are doing, our vision is the WHAT we are doing, and our mission is HOW we are doing it. Identity is who we are and purpose is what we are graced to do. However, in my opinion, it is difficult to divide identity and purpose. I am not what I do, but I do what I do because of who I am. What I do is a reflection of my heart, my purpose, my values, my Higher Cause. That is why two people can have the same job description and both be highly successful at its implementation; but their work will carry their uniqueness, personal flair, and creativity. Your life is so valuable and the unique expression within you is needed in your sphere of influence.

"To wish you were someone else is to waste the person that you are!"[3]

Celebrate your personal identity, for it is the distinct uniqueness of who you are. It is a recognized set of characteristics that belong uniquely to you!

Identity releases a sense of self-acceptance and recognition that you are significantly important to others. When you embrace this awareness, you are able to open your heart to celebrate others. This process generates the ability to partner with others increasing the potential for societal impact.

Healthy and positive identity releases a sense of personal worth, validation, and enjoyment. The need for comparison and rivalry vanishes in light of being comfortable in our own skin. *When you are comfortable in your own skin you desire others to be comfortable in theirs.*

Identity releases courage! Even when taking risks, there is a bravery that rises up when we recognize that we will learn from failure, mistakes, and successes. When healthy identity is established there is a well-developed appreciation that you are internally successful. No one likes to fail or have less than the desired outcome of a project, task, or endeavor; but when there is internal strength through clear identity you continue to move forward just being you!

Identity releases self-trust! This self-trust is an absolute necessity, as it reveals to us that giving our utmost is sufficient. It is the knowledge that we have the heart and the ability to succeed and generate the confidence that we are trustworthy.

Identity releases optimism when we recognize that we are positively contagious in our sphere of influence. We recognize that our life-giving mindsets and actions empower and encourage everyone with whom we connect.

Identity releases purpose and we then recognize that we have a destiny that can be expressed wherever we go and in whatever we do. It brings a sense of significance to even the most menial task, an appreciation to the simplest conversation, and a heart to treasure the journey.

Personal Purpose Statement

The importance of a simple statement to articulate your core purpose is an effective combination of leadership influence and practical applications that meets a need. A purpose statement is much like a GPS mapping out the way to reach your destination. It empowers us to verbalize our core values enabling a level of proficiency directing us towards where and how we will focus our time and energy.

Without a destination any choice will do. When you know where you are going, structure will ensure an order to our steps with strategic single-mindedness. My journey is not just what I am doing, or where I am going, but a reflection of who I am.

A personal purpose statement helps to connect tasks to the heart, bringing discipline to our thinking. This disciplined thinking keeps us focused through all the external demands for our attention. We can focus on what WE want, which would be rather selfish. We can direct our attention to what ANOTHER wants, but that would be catering to their selfishness. Or, we could focus on the plumb line of our PURPOSE, which is both self-empowering, and caring for the needs of others. We must recognize that we will be chased by the urgent, running in many different directions if we do not keep our focus on our purpose.

Purpose lays the groundwork for what I should or should not do. What do I say "yes" to? When do I say, "no." Without clarity of purpose we'll say "yes" to almost anything feeling resentful for being taken advantage of, even though we said, "yes!" However, great freedom comes when we say "yes" to what we truly value!

Purpose helps us to answer "yes" or "no" to opportunities, requests, and the expectations of others through the plumb line of my core purpose—the center of who I am. This is an internal restraint showing us what is truly important to us.

When our personal purpose is our plumb line, it becomes much easier to align our actions to our decisions. We are motivated to follow-through to completion of a task, because every aspect of the process is intrinsically motivated. This helps us stay on course with a heart declaring, "I will not quit!" This is a manifestation of operating from a central heart of conviction. When we recognize we are purpose-minded, and not emotive-led, we have the staying power to drive toward our purpose, even in the midst of challenges.

In the same way, a map both shows us where we are going, as well as how far we have come. Purpose helps us to determine our progress—are we growing, advancing, and reaching our destination? Throughout the journey we discover the resources that are necessary for its successful completion or its succession. It helps us assess the areas we need to develop, as well as how to prepare. No one would invest money without a purpose for increase. Intra-leadership causes us to recognize how we need to invest to bring the purpose to fruition. Is there additional training, mentorship, or adjustments of mindsets?

When you have a personal purpose statement articulated and captured in written form, it can be seen and easily communicated to others. I was asked to join the president and vice-president of a division within a very large corporation to interview for a consulting job. The president told me their areas of need and the challenges they were facing. Quite a few times I simply said, "I do not have expertise in that." After a short season of time he graciously said, "What do you do?" This was easy to answer because I knew my purpose! I wasn't trying to get a job by selling what I am not, but by selling who I am and what I believe. I did not want to be a "cloud without rain"—selling without delivering, which would be bad business and would sabotage my credibility. However, I simply shared my purpose and my experience. I was hired!

Purpose helps you to communicate to others, and it also is a motivator to invest into others when you recognize they are in need of the passion that you possess. The last time I brought training to this corporation, the facilitator said they were not going to call me Dr. Melodye any longer because we were family! There was a partnership that began to form that was mutually beneficial and empowering.

I was invited to an international government for a full day of training for every employee in the department. The room was so large I could not see the faces of those sitting in the back of the room. I was speaking for a while and realized how much FUN I was having. I just stopped, laughed at myself, and said to everyone, "I'm having so much fun!" They all cheered because it was evident my passion accompanied my purpose! The overflow of my enjoyment spilled over to all those present—even the ones I could not see. "Choose a job you love, and you'll never have to work a day in your life."[4]

THREE BASICS OF A PURPOSE STATEMENT

Now let's look at how to develop our Personal Purpose Statement.

Keep it short! We are talking short—not a book, page or even a paragraph! The Purpose Statement is an abbreviated statement that just bubbles out of your heart when asked about it. This short little statement carries such depth of meaning and stirs passion-filled emotion in the words that you choose.

"One famous study from Yale in 1953 said that the 3% of Yale graduates who had written goals had more wealth years later than the other 97% of the class combined."[5]

What has your attention, will also have your direction. What you keep before your eyes and within your heart will chart your life's course.

Some of my clients went the extra mile to reinforce the amazing purposes of their staff:

A public school principal took all the purpose statements of her staff and framed them for their classroom. Every student, parent, fellow teacher, and administrator that entered their classroom could then see the teacher's purpose. The staff conversations surrounding purpose unified hearts and tore down walls of judgment, as many saw shared-values and shared-purpose.

A corporate level president took his executive's purpose statements and kept them before him. He began to give opportunities and positioned his staff around their purpose. This was not only empowering to them, personally and professionally, but it revealed the heart of their leader and led to high levels of trust.

Must be flexible! The fact is, our lives are constantly changing, evolving, and advancing. Our purpose is progressive, by its very nature. Though you'll probably always see a dominant theme or focus, the expression of your purpose statement may take different forms and may become more inclusive or exclusive. Seasons of life bring change, but we'll find that the core of our purpose is foundational throughout our entire life, vision, and methodologies. Simply put, as we progress, so does our purpose. At the same time, our purpose will continue to illuminate and stir our passion and core innate values.

Simple for understanding and application! Our purpose statement must be easily understood by others. We can't expect others to know the intricacies and the depths of what it means to us, but that is not needed. A fundamental aspect, however, is that it is simple for application. Wrapped up in this short statement are three basic components revealing the why, the how, and for whom my purpose is to support and empower.

Three Components within Purpose

Let us unpack the three components that weave the tapestry of our life's purpose. I encourage you to get a piece of paper and divide it into three parts. As you begin to go through each section, begin to write down your perspectives. Though this is an expression of your personal purpose, many people ask others who know them well to provide input. This is sometimes helpful because you may not always see what others witness through you.

What are Your Strengths, Talents, and Abilities?

These are the indicators of the tools that you use to fulfill your purpose. Begin to assess what you excel in right now. Think about what comes natural to you and what is easiest for you. Often we discover the tool we can feature in our tool belt by looking at what we absolutely love to do! It's not work, it is fun, empowering, and fulfilling! What do people tell you that are good at even though you may not see that in yourself?

Think about what you do that energizes you. Often people have said to me that I am a workaholic and I will get burned out from working long hours. The opposite is true, because I put long hours into the things that I absolutely love and I am actually motivated, energized, and empowered when I close up shop for the day. When I have tasks to accomplish that I am not gifted in nor that fit me, I am more mentally and physically exhausted from one hour of dreaded work, then I am from 12 hours of doing what I love.

Think about what you are doing when you feel those creative juices flowing. When you discover your place of creativity and self-expression, you'll find a treasure in your life's bedrock that will empower your purpose.

Does this mean that we never do what we do not like? Sadly, no. The fact is, we are all faced with tasks that while they may challenge us, they are nevertheless necessary to enable us to do what we love to do. I love strategy, but hate to do all the little details to implement the strategy. I must devote large blocks of time on details that I do not like, but, if I didn't complete these tasks, I would be hindered in doing what I really love.

I really do not like making presentation slides, but I devote many hours developing them because I love the results and the platform it builds for me to do what I love. It gives me opportunity to provide resources for others to be able to do and teach what I have taught them. I love to reproduce into others and these presentation slides are a great tool. If I am genuinely passionate about training, then I will celebrate the process, even though it is not my favorite task to accomplish. The difference in the less-appreciated task is the understanding of its importance to the ultimate objective, making it something you wholeheartedly embrace.

What task is required of you to do that you would rather not do, but you need to accept it in order for you to release what you really love to do?

What are your Passions and Core Values?

Passion is not emotion though it often stirs strong emotion; therefore, our focus is not found solely on feelings, but action. The Latin word for passion actually means suffering. When a person is passionate about something, they will enter into suffering for it or to obtain it. What are you willing to pay a price for? What will you sacrifice for? What are you extremely tolerant of? What are you willing to lose or give up in order to attain something greater?

A farmer might not like to till the ground and plant the seed, for what does that profit now? What he is very cognizant of, and passionate about, is the harvest. Without the labor of planting and caring for the seed, the harvest would never be manifested.

Think about what you love to learn about or research because you value the journey. The price of your willing preparation is a good indication of what you are passionate about.

Think about your interaction with others, whether in personal or professional settings. What are you very opinionated about? Think about the things that are difficult for you to compromise when in the mix of conflicting thoughts, ideas, and judgments. It can feel like you are violating yourself to agree—even if it is just mentally ascending to avoid conflict.

When do you feel judgment or criticalness towards others? Remember, when someone does not value what you value, you may feel judgmental or become overcritical. Why? You are fighting for what you are personally passionate about. On the heels of this statement, think about what makes you angry, irritates you, or frustrates you. A source of anger is when our convictions—values or passions—are being violated.

You already know my passion for justice—power used for good. When I see any type of injustice, prejudice, or abuse I feel such anger. I have to properly manage that because I do not want my anger to be displayed through inappropriate means. I hate injustice, so I do not want to become an instrument of injustice while I am raising my voice or action against it.

What stirs emotion—positive or negative—on the inside of you when you talk to someone? Certain topics are avoided if you do not want heated discussions, like politics or religion. Why? These are topics where opinions and passions are so strong that many will throw wisdom out the door and just allow themselves to emotionally hijack.

On a positive note, we find this when those of like passion, purpose, vision, and values meet together. All the positive reinforcement and celebration creates a heightened atmosphere where people are so excited that they talk over one another, raise their voice in excitement, and release a river of ideas, dreams, and aspirations. There is such energy released in the midst of this emotionally-charged, purpose-driven environment.

Passion supersedes your position, title, or job description. Passion is imposed upon and displaces your personality, personal preferences, and personal needs. Our passion cannot be compromised and it must be expressed. That internal GPS of passion is constantly directing us toward certain goals and objectives that we will continually sacrifice for.

Passion drives us to influence others to adopt what we are passionate about. That is why we have motivational speakers, speeches, human rights activists, social justice organizations, YouTube clips, and people who write books about the importance of being a *Higher Living Leader!*

WHO IS IN NEED OF THE PASSION I POSSESS?

When you are made aware of a need that is a reflection of who you are, your passion and values, you are intrinsically motivated to action. Are you drawn to meet the need of a particular race, age group, nation, sphere of society, or drawn to meet a specific need? At the time of this writing, my mother is a healthy, active 90-plus year old woman who has such a heart for those shut-in or in nursing homes. She is a motivated individual who is moved by compassion. She goes two to three times a week to visit many who have no one and are facing loneliness, illness, and a knowledge they do not have long to live. She is welcomed by the administration of these facilities and loved by many because she continually sacrifices to demonstrate value to others. That's purpose!

Her passion was evident throughout her entire lifetime, even though it was demonstrated in different ways as the seasons of her life changed. She was a nurse and when her age hindered her ability to work, she became a chaplain at the hospital. When she was 82, she was uprooted from her home and the community she served for many years as she came to live with my husband and myself. What was she to do? She found those who were in need of the passion she possessed and the values she held dear to her heart.

Who is in need of the passion you possess?

Bringing the Three Components Together

To develop your personal purpose statement you bring the three components together. I've been patiently waiting to get to this point so I could share my personal purpose, but you probably have me pegged by this point.

The three components are: skills—what we love to do, our passion and values, and who needs the passion we possess.

My personal purpose statement: Influencing and training leaders to be instruments of justice.

My skill set: Influencing and Training

My passion and core values: Justice

Those in need of the passion I possess: Established and Emerging Leaders

Justice is just one word, but for me there is tremendous meaning behind this one word. **Leaders** is just one word, but once again for me, it encompasses every age, from babies through the oldest citizen on the planet. The most important years of a person's life are the first three years—the foundational years—where trust begins to be established around six months old and builds throughout the third year. Identity is established from the foundation of trust and 75% of a child's personality is established by three years old. If we take the time to teach and train our babies at this most formidable age, we are building the very core of a potential world-changer. This process prepares the soil of the child's heart to release their innate contribution.

Woven into the fabric of every human being is the making of a *Higher Living Leader,* and we have an opportunity to nurture that seed. My granddaughter at four years old wanted to show a group of visitors her pretty pink bedroom. As we all were heading toward the steps to ascend to her little princess room, she aggressively ran in front of everyone shouting, "I want to be the leader, I want to be the leader!"

I realized all my skill sets summed up in the two keys words of influence and training. If I use my influence for the good of another and I invest into the seed of another's greatness through training, equipping, empowering, and activating; my life is not only successful but extremely significant.

This purpose motivates me to work hard, love deeply, sit in airports for hours, drive long distances, spend hours on the phone, and use my platforms of influence for the good of others. This is who I am, this is what I do, and this is my purpose!

Once you formulate your purpose and keep it before you, it will have your attention as well as your direction!

What you value underlies all your decisions and actions. It may or may not be a conscious choice, but it determines your life and how your future will impact society.

CHAPTER 9

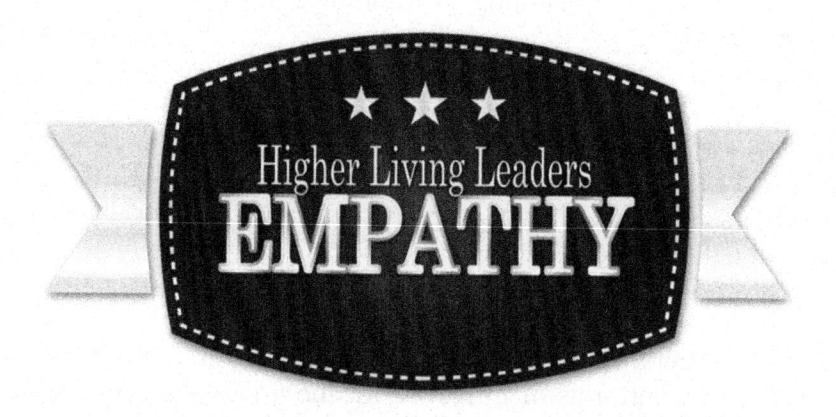

Higher Living Leaders
EMPATHY

Maya Angelo said, "I've learned that people will forget what you said, people will forget what you did, but people will never forget how you made them feel."[1]

What we say is important, because when we speak life-giving words, we create thoughts that produce electromagnetic light impulses that build healthy memory. Leaders need to speak words that empower. However, words are interpreted through the perceptions and perspectives of the hearer.

What we do is extremely important, especially with regard to those we lead. However, my personal accomplishments and the accolades of men really do not touch another's heart. Though another's accomplishments may stir the waters of purpose, they do not ultimately empower another unless, of course, what we have done brings justice on his or her behalf.

What I believe Maya Angelo is communicating is that when we

truly touch the heart—the core of the person—and what is important to them, they will never forget how we made them feel. When a leader reaches out with compassion and understanding, he or she transmits value to the recipient.

Empathy is the ability to connect and relate with what another feels and how he or she perceives a particular situation. When there is heartfelt responsiveness to see from another's perspective, it brings identification with what they are experiencing or communicating. This builds trust, breeds loyalty, and creates a culture of validation.

I use the aid of optical illusions in my presentations where one picture or animation can be seen from multiple perspectives. Through automatic thought we usually see it, at first, from one perspective. When we are challenged with conflicting and contradictory thoughts, we have to make a conscious choice and a determined effort to try to see from another's perspective. Often this takes time and you hear a revelatory "ah ha," when participants finally see the other point of view.

This is a fun training activity, but in real life situations, especially where the heart is involved, many times we do not *want* to see from another's perspective. We want to hold to our viewpoint, thinking it is the only correct way to interpret a situation. Without the power of empathy, we lock ourselves into a box with guarded walls. We feel as though another's viewpoint is a personal attack and a disapproval of who we are. We believe that their critique is belittling and degrading.

Empathy's final destination is to touch the heart of a person. It, however, is not just about comforting them in loss or sadness, but hearing their perspective in practical areas. In a self-centered, "look out for number one" world, we see independence rather than interdependence and validation. This creates emotional walls, legalism and perfectionism in interpersonal relationships; it produces entitlement mindsets—expecting more while committing less, and self-focused decision-making.

There are times when executive decisions are necessary. For the most part, however, and in most situations, the autocratic leader may conquer but concurrently divide and drive the people away that they have hired to build and support the purpose of the organization. To be very honest, the day of domineering and overbearing leaders is over!

Successful leaders and cohesive teams give honor, respect, and validation to one another. They take the time to understand and see from different perspectives—they demonstrate empathy. "Some people think only intellect counts: knowing how to solve problems, knowing how to get by, knowing how to identify an advantage and seize it. But the function of intellect is insufficient without courage, love, friendship, compassion, and empathy."[2]

Another poignant quote from Dr. Maya Angelou communicates the wisdom of empathetic leadership, "The desire to reach the stars is ambitious. The desire to reach hearts is wise..."[3]

Every person has chapters in his or her life's story of injustice, abuse, rejection, and loss. We learned how negative memory appears as *thorn branches* in the brain and can literally cause physical pain from emotional triggers. Leaders who have high levels of Validation Quotient display an empathy that builds those they lead. *Higher Living Leadership* practices will send messages that encourage the heart of those they influence. The more emotionally healthy our team is, the greater the creativity, productivity, and partnership for purpose we will experience.

The human brain is a highly social organ. Remember, "Most [of the] processes operating in the background when your brain is at rest are involved in thinking about other people and yourself."[4] I am not saying that we are to have parties and play all the time. In fact, unless it is in response to a celebration of a person or reward for great accomplishments I believe that this can be counterproductive. Parties are fun but they rarely create an atmosphere for heart connection and empathy. Neither is it about giving people gifts, bonuses, and rewards. These are great and can demonstrate value for a job well done, however, many give in order to try to win the team and breed loyalty. Have you ever heard a young person say, "My parents gave me everything but themselves"? All the "stuff" did not fill the void where Mom and Dad needed to be. Parties and tangible rewards are great as long as they are not a substitute for heartfelt validation and empathy.

At the end of the day, what builds faithfulness to task, productivity, loyalty of heart for collaboration, and partnership for united purpose is this: the confidence that I am understood and appreciated.

When empathy and validation are not expressed, we have the potential to lose what we truly value. *When we focus on what someone is not doing—task or relationship—we will get offended and stop celebrating their value.* "…if you can't have empathy and have effective relationship, then no matter how smart you are, you are not going to get very far."[5]

Respect is warranted when we, as leaders, are able to partner validation, empathy, and genuine concern for the person, while confronting personal and relational saboteurs. I have worked with many young people throughout the years having witnessed habits, behaviors, attitudes, and actions that would keep them from their full potential. I had to address how their actions were negatively affecting our ability to accomplish our goals and how it was hurting the morale and momentum of the team. It was essential, however, that genuine care for them was conveyed. I spoke into their obvious potential as I rehearsed to them the hopes and dreams they had previously shared. In dealing with the character flaws, negative attitudes, laziness, and many other thieves of their personal purpose, I reminded them that it was with concern for them as well as the team that we confront head-on these saboteurs.

I wish I could say that everyone was changed, matured, and is walking out their full potential and demonstrating justice in their sphere of influence. I cannot. However, there were many who possessed the intrinsic motivation to push through the mountain of negative emotion and rise to confront the self-imposed encumbrances to be the best they can be.

Empathy is a key to motivate. Those who know that they are valued, understood, and have their potential activated will work harder and better than those who simply want a paycheck. "Lovers will always outwork workers..."![6] Obligatory service does not exist in one who loves. They are not quitters and they are willing to do the small and menial things, as well as the great things. Even the obstacles become opportunities to fulfill purpose. This type of partner, team member, teacher, political leader, or business person holds onto empathy as a key leadership practice.

EMPATHY IS A NATURAL NEUROLOGICAL RESPONSE

Empathy is not something we have to force ourselves to do; it is natural to healthy neurological functioning. There are different neurological pathways of empathy.[7] As you research empathy you see the importance of **modeling empathy.** When you see a behavior displayed, an emotion expressed, a tone of voice, or even seeing someone in pain you discover that these are contagious. Have you ever found yourself yawing when seeing another yawn? Have you ever wanted to cry when another cried? Have you ever echoed whispering by whispering in response asking, "Why are we whispering?" Have you ever heard a story of abuse and you imagined and felt the hurt?

As you model it in your brain you begin to relate, and even begin to understand, how someone feels. "How would I feel if that was happening to me?" The Anterior Temporal Lobe is the part of the brain that models emotions. "The temporal [lobe is] involved in the retention of visual memories, processing sensory input, comprehending language, storing new memories, emotion, and deriving meaning."[8]

Ralph Waldo Emerson said, "Let us treat men and woman well,

treat them as if they were real. Perhaps they are."

EMPATHY IS ALSO EVIDENT THROUGH PROJECTION.[9]

This is empathy that is demonstrated by projecting yourself to see another person's point of view from a different perspective. Have you ever thought about how you would view life if another's experience had happened to you? Have you ever thought about how your worldview would be affected from another's perspective? "How many times have you acted or reacted in a specific way, only to later realize that you had erred in your judgment? Clearly, our conclusions about the 'right' thing are not always right."[10]

Dr. Thomas Lewis explains projection as the imagination of an intentional action that is projected to a future time to gain a perspective of what you would experience.[11] This is cognitively purposeful and deliberate action. Have you ever thought about how you would feel if prejudice was displayed against you or your emotional reaction to an imagined failure; could you actually sense the emotions as if they were a real?

In my opinion, this final neurological pathway is the most important for leadership. It is the **adjusted balance of empathy in relationship to self and others**.[12] This is the ability to properly adjust and bring balance as you model another's emotions. There is a portion of our brains that is used to properly manage and suppress our pain in response to the pain and experience of others. Can you imagine a counselor weeping as they agonize over another's pain and, as such, are unable to help them move past their traumatic experience? We must recognize as leaders that we must develop the ability to adjust our empathy in order do what is best for the whole, the vision, and the individual.

Every strength, purpose, and passion must be properly managed in order to avoid the potential back-sided weakness. Let me use myself as an example; by now you are very much aware of my passion for justice. When I hear people's stories of injustice my heart breaks and I feel compelled to do something! Throughout the years I was convinced that if I followed all the practices of *Higher Living Leadership* I would see lives change, potential fulfilled, and purposes actualized in the life of those who had suffered injustice and neglect—and I have! However, I have had to learn to balance my empathy for the good of others, myself, and the corporate vision.

My core focus is the development and empowerment of emerging and established leaders. I established a training center for emerging leaders, but I found myself attracting those who needed to be reformed, but who were not necessarily interested in being leaders of reformation. Many were looking to be rescued out from their situations, but they were not willing to pay a price to overcome. Entitlement—expecting more and committing less—was the mindset of so many. I found that my heart of mercy and empathy left unchecked began to sabotage the very purpose of raising up *Higher Living Leaders*. I placed a demand upon myself to pay a huge price for their growth and required of my staff to do the same. Sounds noble, but it was not wisdom. I learned a painful lesson that you cannot work harder on another's growth than he or she does. You cannot legislate the heart, establish intrinsic motivation in someone, nor administrate and activate another's purpose.

I so wanted to make a difference and empower the lives of those disenfranchised, knowing their pain could become their purpose, the mess of their lives become a message, and their shame became a place of true identity. I came to realize I am not that powerful!

I have now learned to balance my empathy—still so very hard—in order to serve the vision, purpose, mission, and values of the our organization. My staff is always there to speak into my life and help me to see clearly—yes, the leader desires feedback from the staff because the staff is serving the vision!

You see, without the ability to balance empathy, I made decisions out of love for people rather than the purpose we were serving. In the process, I was hindered in reaching those who were intrinsically motivated, willing to do whatever it takes, making the most of every opportunity, and were desperately hungry to be *Higher Living Leaders*!

Those years were good years, many lives were impacted, many are now established leaders, and lifelong relationships were forged. Though I celebrate those years and the seeds planted, I recognized that change was necessary (the balance of empathy) to transition us to our core purpose.

Your purpose holds a passion—which creates such emotion—that balance must be applied to release the full potential of purpose. When empathy is properly managed, we are empowered to properly—in a healthy way—connect to how another feels. Validation Quotient is demonstrated by true empathy, because you set your eyes on the value in those you lead.

I love the movie *42*, a 2013 biographical film written and directed by Brian Helgeland about the life of baseball player Jackie Robinson.[13] Jackie Robinson was the first African American to play major league baseball. He had the honor to break through the color barrier, paving a way for many others. However, he also faced the pain and prejudice of pioneering that journey.

One scene in the movie that so impacted me was seeing a Dodger's (Jackie Robinson's team) fan, a father, talk about how great Pee Wee Reese was and attack Jackie Robinson because of his race. The son echoed his father prejudicial remarks, spewing hate speech from the stands. Jackie Robinson committed an error, he stood on second base feeling shamed not only by his error but also by the taunting mockery of the "fans." Pee Wee Reese stood by him and put his arm around Jackie Robinson and faced the crowd.

Pee Wee Reese operated in an empathy that motivated him to action. He felt the pain of Jackie Robinson and his quiet but deliberate action brought inaudible reprimand to the voice of discrimination and intolerance. The fans were silenced that day! Jackie Robinson later said that, "Reese's arm around his shoulder saved his career."[14]

Wisdom applied to the power of empathy is like the rain that waters the seed of potential allowing fruit to grow and be harvested to benefit many.

A great way to demonstrate empathy is through our words. Words are a creative force that gives rise to thoughts that release the fireworks of electro-magnetic light impulses into the physical brain. The wave forms fire differently based upon whether they are a negative or positive, developing memory.

Our destructive words, or the destructive words of others, can develop the thorn trees that establish lies. Lies can be perceived as truth when we speak them long enough, shaping our memory and emotional perceptions. As previously communicated, have you ever met an individual who talked about something so much that he or she actually believed it? What took place is that they continually fed that imagination over a long period of time and it developed into a fabricated memory—we know it is not true, but we are thoroughly convinced of its validity.

Whatever we say to ourselves, or others, feeds back into our memory—those magic trees—reinforcing and strengthening the memory they came from.[15]

One day while addressing bullying before a classroom of high school students, I began to share this concept. I told them that a person being verbally bullied can choose to reject those words and not allow the thoughts or lies to take root in his or her mind. When we reject a thought, it does not have the ability to grow a branch and the very choice to throw a thought out empowers healthy memory to form. But, the words the bully says actually feedback into his or her own brain, reinforcing the memory it came from. A young man caught the concept and recognized the implications of his actions and he said out loud, "I ain't gonna do that anymore!" He realized that his bullying hurt him and, though he was not empathetic towards others, my hope is that his reign as a bully had ended that day.

Leadership is a platform of influence and opportunity to use our words to partner with the recipient, thereby generating and establishing a healthy thought life that releases potential. The electrical impulses cause a dense networking of memory that can rewrite or reprogram former ways of thinking, feeling, and acting. *Every thought I entertain is a seed of destiny—for good or harm.*

CHAPTER 10

★ ★ ★ BUILDERS OF TRUST

An automatic by-product of the attributes of *Higher Living Leadership* and high levels of Validation Quotient is that trust is fostered! When our motives are for personal gain (especially at the expense of others) trust will be destroyed and we will become an instrument of injustice. However, if we invest into others with pure motives, trust will be established and we will become instruments of justice.

Having the position or title of leader, does not automatically mean that we will be trusted, followed, or valued. Also, we cannot expect the loyalty of those who serve us. Trust is a valuable commodity that is earned through making deposits and avoiding withdrawals from the invisible trust account. It takes time to see the harvest of trust seeds sown and we must choose daily to water and protect the field where the seeds were planted. Trust is a choice that we extend to others and build with others.[1] Trust is the power to become credible in both tasks and heart.

Stephen M.R. Covey and Rebecca R. Merrill in their must-read book, *The Speed of Trust: The One Thing that Changes Everything,* share the two domains of trust, "character and competence."[2] I will build upon these domains throughout this chapter.

Competence is developed through Higher Thinking and Higher Responsibility. It is an excellence in what I do along with the ability to follow through to completion. It is the evidence of the skills, talents, and abilities that empower personal purpose. When I am committed to increasing my abilities to expand the influence of my core values and purpose, I will bring credibility to my competence.

Character is developed from the Higher Cause for which we live and lead. It is demonstrated by the purity of our motives, aligning our actions to our values, and being true to our purpose and honest in principle and practice.

It is possible for us to build trust in one area, yet neglect to develop it in another. To build trust, we must have more deposits into the trust bowl than withdrawals.

Pictured are two bowls. The first is full of both white and multi-colored poker chips—representing trust deposits. The white chips represent character and the multi-colored represent competence. It is obvious that many conscious daily choices have been made to deposit into the trust bowl. This is an aspect of Higher Responsibility as I embrace the commission to lead.

The second picture shows the trust bowl with few deposits. We might tell people to trust us but if their experience has been withdrawals or refusals to deposit, they will not have the experiential foundation to trust us because of our demonstration of untrustworthiness. Trust is a lifestyle, not an attribute you can vacation from because it takes time to build.

Filling our trust bowl with deposits of competence and character is a *Higher Living Leader's* commission and moral obligation.

COMPETENCE

Competence is the ability to do something extremely well, especially when there has been the investment of training, education, and experience supporting ability.

When our talent and skills are supported by education and experience, we cultivate confidence in what we bring to the table. When we demonstrate that we have the ability to repeatedly produce, advance, and get results, we make deposits and gain a reputation of getting things done.

Whether we are the set leader or a serving one, having a track record is crucial to building credibility in our competence. "A good leader is probably no different in any culture in the sense that a good leader must have credibility. That is something one establishes…based on the way one handles himself and by his established track record."[3]

"Somebody who knows what they're doing, who has a good track record, they come across as very articulate, bright and looking for a challenge— that's absolutely my kind of hire."[4]

Results not only produce credibility with others, but they also build self-trust and increase our courage, determination, and single-minded focus.

Let's look at some attributes of competence recognizing that faithful execution establishes the ability to trust ourselves and be trusted by others.

DISCIPLINE

This is a habit of self-control and internal management. The need for extrinsic control and pressure from authority is not needed to motivate. It is the capacity to order our private world and steward external responsibilities.

"Discipline is the refining fire by which talent becomes ability."[5] "Discipline is the bridge between goals and accomplishment."[6]

Work Ethic: People need to see us working hard. It is hypocritical to expect others to work harder than you—that carries the impression of an entitlement. When a member of a team does not do his or her part, the morale of the team will diminish, hindering forward momentum.

Many miss out on amazing opportunities because it involves a lot of work! Work with purpose and doors will open!

Run from purpose-filled work and you'll face closed doors, stunted growth, and live a boring frustrated life...so, roll up those sleeves and enjoy the adventure!

RELIABILITY AND DEPENDABILITY

We are faithful to accomplish the task delegated to us but also loyal to the heart of the task. This individual will not just produce but show up and deliver with constancy and excellence. You know they will give their best day-in-and-day-out. I've had employees that I had to constantly manage to ensure they would complete a task. When corrected they would dig in and produce amazing work at an amazing speed, but it was short lived. Though there was great ability I could not trust their competence because of their inconsistency. I've also been overjoyed to have ones that I know they are giving their best all the time! Who would you trust?

"The secret of success is constancy of purpose."[7]

EXPERTISE

We will not be good at everything, but we can develop proficiency in our field of study, service, or leadership responsibilities. Just as important is our commitment to develop, improve, and advance our present skill level. This life-long development will build us from the inside out.

"Never become so much of an expert that you stop gaining expertise."[8]

Value improvement over approval, advancement over change, and internal growth over the external pleasures.

CHARACTER

"Good character is more to be praised than outstanding talent. Most talents are to some extent a gift. Good character, by contrast, is not given to us. We have to build it piece by piece by thought, choice, courage and determination."[9]

Character needs to be woven into every aspect of leadership if we want to be builders of trust. Dwight David Eisenhower said, "A people that values its privileges above its principles soon loses both."[10] As leaders we model before many the ways to live, lead, learn, and love. What we do in moderation those who follow will do in excess, so we have a Higher Responsibility to choose the great over the good and courage over compromise.

Higher Living Leadership raises the bar in order for up-and-coming leaders to build upon the foundation that we have established. I need employees with the competencies to take us places I never could. I need to surround myself with people who are so much better than me; however, if their heart and the character do not surpass their competencies, I will have wished I had never hired them. Let's look at some character trust builders.

INTEGRITY

A person of integrity is one who has the courage to align actions with values—core invisible motivators—whether they are their personal values or that of the organization. When a person's actions align with the values of the organization, there is an acceleration of opportunities for advancement. When their actions contradict the values of the organization, everyone will feel stress, irritation, and loss of passion and enthusiasm in the team.

When we live contrary to present-day culture to be the one whose word is our bond, doing what we say we'll do, we will be filling up our trust bowl quickly. We don't need salesmen. Instead, we need those who deliver the goods! We don't need the good talkers but the faithful walkers!

"Don't worry so much about your self-esteem. Worry more about your character. Integrity is its own reward."[11]

"The most important persuasion tool you have in your entire arsenal is integrity."[12]

"Have the courage to say no. Have the courage to face the truth. Do the right thing because it is right. These are the magic keys to living your life with integrity."[13]

HIGHER AGENDA

When our motives, intents, and personal agendas are directed towards the good of others, we will not only build trust but enjoy a higher quality of life...daily! When we are genuine, transparent, honest, and willing to invest into what will benefit the whole we will be entrusted with what is most valuable and important to others.

Once again, justice—power used for good—is my higher agenda. Sacrificing for the common good does not always feel good; we will be taken advantage of and even hurt in the process. I've learned, however, that if I am not close enough to be hurt I am not close enough to make a difference. I had to decide if I cared more about justice or the protection of my heart—I chose justice. I am not trying to sound noble, but if I violate the Higher Cause than my life would be most miserable. One person you cannot run from is yourself and since you must live with yourself stay true to the Higher Cause!

When asked to provide behavioral consulting and leadership training to an influential corporation, I told them that I wanted to communicate my passion for justice before I started the training I was hired for. They agreed. This corporation and its leaders had great influence in their city and I wanted to utilize this platform for my purpose, "Influencing and Training Leaders to be Instruments of Justice."

I communicated to the executives surrounding the table that I wanted to be honest about my personal motivations before I begin my training. I began to share with them the value that I saw in them and the knowledge I had of their influence to positively impact the city. As I shared my heart for justice they all began to clap! I was in the right place doing the right thing not only fulfilling my purpose but empowering theirs. The fact that I was open and honest about my motives built an instant trust that opened their hearts. What a great time we had!

Right on the heels of purity of motives is **honesty**. Honesty is the whole truth! Partial truth can be more destructive than an outright lie because it is rife with deception. Choosing which parts to share that benefit you will destroy trust. I've had individuals come to me for my opinion and later found out that they used my name to authenticate their decision, but the information communicated to me was partial. They did not lie, but their behavior was still deceptive because they didn't tell the whole truth. Honesty validates, but is sincere. Flattery is a manipulator and it sets traps for the easily swayed. Friedrich Nietzche said, "What upsets me is not that you lied to me, but that I can no longer believe you."

"Whoever is careless with the truth in small matters cannot be trusted with important matters."[14]

"Honesty is the first chapter in the book of wisdom."[15]

AUTHENTICITY

This is a form of honesty that deals with who we are as an individual, more than our words and deeds. Oscar Wilde said, "Be yourself; everyone else is already taken."

There really is nothing new under the sun—everything has been seen before—as we experience learning curves and deal with the process of personal development. Our life's journey reveals values, purpose, and who we genuinely are. People trust real people, not those who try to be someone or something they are not. Authenticity grows in the seedbed of humility, inner honesty, self-discovery, and transparency.

It is liberating to cease from striving to be someone you are not, to try to be better than another, or live a people-pleasing mindset where you have to compromise your core passion and purpose. People-pleasing, in reality, is not a selfless act but an extremely selfish one. People-pleasers act in response to another in the way they assume others want them to respond in order to get their need met.

Investing into your development to be the best you that you can be is empowering but also authentic. When you are authentically you there is a freedom to get rid of masks and simply be transparent.

"Try to be transparent, clear and truthful. Even when it is difficult, and above all when it is difficult."[16]

"It is not our purpose to become each other; it is to recognize each other, to learn to see the other and honor him for what he is..."[17]

SHOW HONOR AND RESPECT

Respect is the ability to feel and desire to show regard and appreciation for another, to avoid all violation, and to esteem another highly. Validation Quotient is saturated in showing honor and respect consistently making deposits into the trust bowl. *Higher Living Leaders* are secure in their own value, thus it becomes the standard in which others are valued!

The author of the Declaration of Independence and the third president of the United States, Thomas Jefferson, said, "Nobody can require honor by doing what is wrong." When we live an honorable life and we do what is right by our fellowman, we will be a conduit of honor towards others.

George Bernard Shaw said, "The most tragic thing in the world is a man of genius who is not a man of honor." That right there is competence without character!

The very simple fact is every little thing that we do that is right, just, pure, and/or empowering to others is a deposit into the trust bowl. Simple things like keeping your word, demonstrating a loyal heart to your team and corporation, stewarding the resources of the corporation as if they were your own, going the extra mile to insure excellence or completion of a task, pitching in to help a co-worker, speaking positively, genuinely valuing others and the corporation, refusing to gossip and be critical of others, etc.

"Leaders must give something up in order to get something more significant...by sacrificing they demonstrate that they're not in it for themselves...the most admired are those...who have sacrificed the most... for the sake of a higher purpose... When leaders are selfless and humble, people are much more inclined to trust them. Putting others first—and meaning it—will earn you...credibility..."[18]

EXTEND TRUST

Extending trust is a bit frightening for leaders who have been hurt, been taken advantage of, cheated, or lied to. It is especially challenging when your heart is to be a *Higher Living Leader*. We've all been there and have experienced violations of trust. We've all faced individuals who have made so many withdrawals that the trust bowl breaks completely. However, it is extremely important to "extend trust."[19]

It is never wise to open the team to an individual without the ability to extend trust before they have had a chance to make deposits. Sometimes we can extend trust through their past experience, work history, or positive recommendations; but we must recognize that each person is an individual and it is unfair to judge a person through the emotional framework of your negative experience with others. At some point we must extend trust before it is proven.

This is not being gullible or trusting the untrustworthy, it is simply giving people the opportunity to prove that they are trustworthy. It is accepting the trust bowl and putting a couple chips—some character (white) and competencies (multi-colored) in the bowl. It's like opening a checking account and allowing them to make the deposits. "The best way to find out if you can trust somebody is to trust them."[20]

Abraham Lincoln said, "The people when rightly and fully trusted will return the trust." Though there is always the exception I truly believe people are inherently good. The signature of value written upon our DNA is proof of that value—to have and create in others. Therefore, I believe when people know you trust them they will arise to the occasion and give their all to prove you right!

"It is impossible to go through life without trust: that is to be imprisoned in the worst cell of all, oneself."[21]

TRUST WITHDRAWALS

We've talked a lot about making deposits, but what about the dreaded withdrawals? Withdrawals are larger than deposits because they carry greater emotional impact. Just as a negative thought is three times more powerful in establishing unhealthy memory, I believe withdrawals are similar in their impact upon the mind-brain and subsequent emotions, attitudes, and reactions. To protect the health of our thought-life we do not want to be those who make withdrawals. We also must choose proper management of our thought life when we experience withdrawals from those we trusted.

Validation Quotient is so important because without placing a high value on the person, project, or organization, actions will demonstrate that you cannot be trusted. We must also recognize that if another's actions do not place value on us or our shared projects, we cannot trust that they will come through for us. Remember, what we value we protect, invest into, sacrifice for, and treat as valuable. When withdrawals are made rather than deposits it is sending a message that the person or program is not valuable. This is not a good message to send and will destroy trust rapidly. What type of person do we want to be?

Warren Buffet said, "It takes twenty years to build a reputation and five minutes to ruin it."[22] This is a reason we must be trustworthy as well as partner with those who are.

LEADERSHIP WITHDRAWALS

When our hidden motives are for personal gain, especially at the expense of others, trust will be destroyed and we will become an instrument of injustice.

Leaders are to set the standard, model the way, and be the most trustworthy individuals in any team—family, political leader, teacher, business person, media personality, etc. If we are influencers we are leaders and our world needs those they can believe in and trust. There are certain blind spots, character flaws, or attitudes that leaders must avoid because they are trust withdrawals and will eventually destroy relationship and close every door of opportunity.

"It's all about me" leader: This leader is a self-focused, competitive, "my way is the only way," type of person. People are either friends or enemies as these types of leaders climb their personal ladder to success. They often think, "Don't get in my way or I'll roll right over you"! Leadership is not about conquering for self; it is about serving the whole. Every victory we gain together we can celebrate together; but if my accomplishments are for my gain alone I will celebrate alone.

"I'm the boss" leader: This leader seeks power and control for self-gain focusing solely on their personal self-benefiting self-promoting agenda. This is the one that demands respect but doesn't give it, expects to be served without willingness to be a servant themselves. Abraham Lincoln so eloquently stated, "Nearly all men can stand adversity, but if you want to test a man's character, give him power."

"Power intoxicates men. When a man is intoxicated by alcohol he can recover, but when intoxicated by power, he seldom recovers."[23]

"Can sell it, but can't deliver it" leader: This leader is a great salesman and has the ability to gather people because of their great vision. The challenge with this leader is they do not have the strategy for implementation. Not every leader has to be a strategist, but they need one! Vision without strategic structure and execution will quickly die.

This leader is unrealistic about what it will take to accomplish a job; he or she just wants the job done...NOW! This leader wakes up in the morning with a vision for a new website. They send out a memo to their entire client base celebrating that their new website will be available in three days—thinking they are being kind to the web designer giving them three days to complete the task. The web designer gets a call from their passionate leader with the wonderful news. The leader cannot understand why the web designer is frustrated, overwhelmed, and is not at all excited about this "one day" project. "Don't have unrealistic expectations and remember you are human too." [24]

Taking the time to gather the information to learn what it will take to accomplish a task is a great step to present a job with realistic expectations and time frames for completion. Leaders who solicit input and embrace the expertise of their team have not only gained knowledge but have fostered partnership. It never happens as fast as you want it but when it comes all will be winners!

"Want the return without the investment" leader: This is the leader who is quick to make a promise, but does not follow-through. These promises are soon viewed as manipulation because the promise stirred hope and the lack of follow-through leaves others feeling taken advantage of. This leader is left with earned disrespect and disloyalty of others. The most damaging result of this type of leader is they cannot trust themselves. The worst kind of mistrust is our inability to trust ourselves nor to believe what we say or do what we plan.

"Not the maker of plans and promises, but rather the one who offers faithful service in small matters. This is the person who is most likely to achieve what is good and lasting." [25]

"Work will set your free" leader: This is the propensity of the type "A" personality leader. This is the high task oriented individual who wants it done yesterday. I'm not picking on this awesome personality because I am one of them, but this area of weakness does not have to be "just the way I am, live with it!" This is where our core values can be a balance to this propensity. When you can take the work ethic of this leader and couple it with core values that benefit and empower those they serve, this individual can become a world-changer. Then their work will not be an expression of injustice—taking advantage of others for their own gain—but of justice—power and authority used for good.

The workaholic propensity requires self-governance to establish a balanced lifestyle to protect him or her from always striving, running on empty, or being in danger of burnout. It is unfair for the "alpha" leader to require others to follow their example of "all work and no play."

This leader can place all their trust in themselves and their own abilities driving others to sacrifice for the leader's agenda. Even if they serve a Higher Cause, if they drive their staff or volunteers to exhaustion, they have already defiled the noble cause they are serving.

This leader may neglect their intra-leadership as internal management of his or her private world is put on the back burner. His or her focus may be on external success hurling others to exhaustion.

On the tail of this individual may be the **"Crack the whip" leader:** These leaders will micromanage ushering in a culture of fear where their staff is afraid to make a decision or think independently. This leader is actually leading out of fear and mistrust towards others otherwise they would not need to micromanage.

Let me bring balance to micromanagement. Is this the best leadership model? Of course not! However, when you have repeatedly discovered that a staffer is constantly dropping the ball and the trust bowl has become bankrupt, the need for vigilant oversight is necessary. This individual is not earning their paycheck or the volunteer is interfering and damaging the corporation. Until these individuals are replaced allowing the leader to "trade up" with more trustworthy and competent individuals, micromanagement becomes the order of the day. However, barring this scenario, when you try to micromanage a competent and trustworthy staffer or volunteer they will feel your fear and mistrust exasperating them, wasting time, and hindering production. Not trusting the trustworthy is not wise.

The "crack the whip" leader will often communicate with insensitivity and abrasiveness, harming others by barking out orders, intimidating with their words, and condescending attitudes. In the movie *Braveheart*, William Wallace rebukes the nobles because they valued their platform more than the welfare of the people.[26] Though a commoner, he was more noble because he valued the people above his platform of influence.

The "Know-it-all" leader: This leader rejects feedback or constructive criticism and excuses him or herself by blaming others and not admitting mistakes or personal saboteurs. The 33rd President of the United States, Harry S. Truman, said, "The only things worth learning are the things you learn after you know it all."[27] The fact is the moment you reject feedback, ignore counsel, and discount the ideas and opinions of others your ability to advance is suffocated by your pride—a mindset of superiority.

It is important to understand that any idea that you are superior or better than another is a mask covering your own shame. The only way to exalt yourself is to demean another and the only way to feel powerful is to treat others as if they are insignificant. For example: if you feel shame because you lack a degree, you will feel superior to others when you get a degree.

"A proud man is always looking down on things and people; and, of course, as long as you're looking down, you can't see something that's above you."[28]

Humility is a display of strength, an indicator of security, a sign that you are teachable, and a positioning for true success.

"To become truly great, one has to stand with people, not above them."[29]

When we recognize we become better, smarter, and are positioned to advance through a consensus of minds, ideas, strategies, skills, and counsel. "Our best thoughts come from others."[30]

Lastly, let's deal with the **"I'm the superstar" leader:** This leader truly believes it is all about them and the gathering of those who will bow down in subservience to their platform, position, or influence. These are individuals who must look good at all costs and must be the center of attention. This type of leader lives for the public's accolades.

Once again, this type of leader uses people for their own gain as those who serve them must become subservient to the demands of the "star." On the flip side, individuals may work for a paycheck only or serve to use the platform one day for their own personal gain, but are never loyal in heart. If a bigger superstar comes along they will jump ship.

"You've got to give loyalty down, if you want loyalty up."[31] I have a cousin who is a very successful business man with international and national companies. He is a man who is loyal to his employees and demonstrates value for them in so many ways. One of his practices while at his home office is that he personally moves from work station to work station connecting and validating each of his employees one-by-one as he gathers their trash. This successful entrepreneur is building a culture of honor as the trash collector! Now that's Validation Quotient! He truly is a *Higher Living Leader*!

People are drawn to carriers of hope so use your leadership platform to inspire, empower, and serve. In today's dog-eat-dog society we will stand out in the crowd as we serve.

Often when traveling people picture you 'larger than life.' I joke saying that a consultant is just an ordinary person coming from a long distance. Everyone laughs but it is so true! In almost every training opportunity I have, I use the crumbed up, stepped upon money illustration. When I lift up the mangled money and tell them that no matter what they have experienced, no matter how many times they have been knocked down and stepped upon, nothing takes away their value; the superstar bubble is burst and their hearts are opened. It is in that place that seeds of value, courage, hope and confidence are planted. What a moment of humble awe we experience when the atmosphere is saturated in mutual validation and honor. That very moment makes *Higher Living Leadership* worth the price paid.

SELF-TRUST

It is two-faced to judge another by their actions and ourselves by our intentions.[32] We will inherently trust or mistrust others based upon our ability to trust ourselves. Do we trust ourselves in character and competence?

The worst kind of mistrust is our inability to trust ourselves—to not believe what we say or do what we plan. As I wrote of the leadership withdrawals, we can find how we treat others is the way we inwardly treat ourselves. If we expect others to be disloyal, is it because we struggle with being loyal? If we believe people are out to use us, could it be that we've had a tendency to take advantage of others?

When frustrated with another, take a breath...look inside...and you'll learn something about yourself. I do not have the power to change another! When there is no trust, there must be extrinsic control through rules. That's not the way I want to lead. If I can capture the heart through validation and practice the principles *of*

Higher Living Leadership, I will have a greater ability to lead out of love rather than law.

An avenue that has empowered my personal leadership is to always place myself in followership roles. Serving helps me lead! When I empower others to succeed it gives me courage to anticipate that others will want to partner with me for our shared success.

If I want my leaders to be real, open, authentic, and transparent with me, then that is what I want to give to those I lead. If I desire to be respected by my leaders I will, in turn, give that to those I lead. If I want my leaders to hear my ideas, opinions and thoughts for advancement, then I want to give that same courtesy to those I lead.

Humbling myself to serve, truly empowers me to lead. The more teachable I am, the more earned authority I have gained. When I position myself to be mentored, I am motivated to mentor. This encourages me to reproduce leaders that, in turn, reproduce leaders, rather than search for followers. I don't want "yes men", I want partnership. I don't want people to do it my way; I want to find the best way. I have learned if I can trust myself to follow, I can trust myself to lead!

REPAIR TRUST

We are all a work in progress. We will never arrive but we can give our best today, living a life of excellence. Excellence is doing our best—that's always possible! Perfectionism is doing without fault, flaw, or error—that's impossible! So as we walk out our *Higher Living Leadership* journey, we must learn how to repair trust when we have made withdrawals from the trust bowl.

It is important that when we break trust, we admit it and immediately take personal responsibility for our actions without defensiveness or blame. I have to decide whether I want to be right or have relationship. We do not want to win the battle and lose the war. It is amazing when we admit our failure and take responsibility for it, trust is built and respect for our leadership role increases!

The more we try to protect our reputation we lose it. When we humble ourselves we gain respect. We also model repairing trust so others can follow our lead. We start to create a relational culture that actually learns to work through to understanding!

Secondly, we face the consequences and pay the price to compensate for breaking trust or dropping the ball. When we are quick to make the wrongs right, the quicker we are able to start again. When we do right we feel right!

Approaching Others Who Have Made Trust Withdrawals

As much as we hate confrontation we can embrace this conflict positively and optimistically by using it to train ourselves and others for personal and corporate advancement.

It is important to separate the person from the problem. If we cannot see the separation we will see the person as the problem and the only way to get rid of the problem is to get rid of the person. As we can separate the two we can confront the severity of the problem while continuing to value the person.

When you look at the trust withdrawals, was it a breach of competency or character? Often we just throw out an attack, "I can't trust you," when in actuality you might not be able to trust their ability to accomplish the task in excellence, but you know their heart is right. Or vice versa, you see they are good at completing the task, but a character flaw is hindering the team. This is not a time to attack the whole of the person, but the specific area where trust has been violated.

I have had employees that were extremely competent, but their lack of character hindered their ability to fulfill their responsibilities in excellence—doing their best. I have also had employees that were so connected in heart and purpose, but they just did not possess the needed competencies to succeed in their position. We have to objectively determine the area of the trust withdrawals.

Yes, objectivity is an important key. We need to separate our emotions and subjective thinking from the problem. This is not a time to emotionally hijack but submit our thoughts, emotions, and attitudes to the seat of judgment.

Even before you meet with an individual the decision is already made to work through to understanding. This is the place where each communicates without attack or defensiveness in order to build trust and start again. As you work through it is important that you do not conclude without a strategy for repair and change.

I am friends with an amazingly competent and character-motivated corporate executive. I provided leadership training for his executive team where trust was taught. He liked my object lesson of the trust bowl and the poker chips and purchased a bowl and poker chips for his desk. He was honest as he dealt with the specific areas of trust withdrawal as he removed some of the chips from the bowl. He encouraged them that they could repair by making deposits of trust. They also discussed the strategy for practical ways to make deposits. His direct reports followed suit and slowly but surely *a Higher Living Leadership* culture impacted the bottom line.

The way in which violations of trust was addressed empowered the individual as well as confronted the breach of trust.

Building, extending, and protecting our trust deposits is worth the price we pay and the depth of relationships we enjoy.

CHAPTER 11

The Greatest Form of HONOR

Higher Living Leadership has focused on you, the leader. We can never expect someone to follow our lead if we refuse self-governance. However, it is important to recognize that we do not have the power to control others' choices or demand he or she receives our investment.

The true earmark of honor is evidenced through those who receive what we carry. In this chapter we will look at the practical realities of what we are able or unable to accomplish. Leadership is relationship-based, never one-sided, and requires both the giving and receiving so everyone is advancing.

The greatest act of honor is demonstrated through the desire and ability to receive from an individual. When those we lead receive our gift he or she communicates to our heart that what we hold is treasured by and beneficial to him or her.

"Anyone who teaches me deserves my respect, honor and attention."[1]

I have already communicated that our society is riddled with the disease of mistrust, self-absorbed autocratic leadership and influencers who selfishly manipulate for personal gain. Many speeches have been made, seminars attended and books written to address the destructive mindsets and methodologies of narcissistic leaders. These types of leaders do more harm than good as injustice intensifies.

On the other hand, it is important to recognize that a leader cannot give to those who do not receive. It's impossible to teach the unteachable, lead the defiant, or partner together with the disloyal if we desire success corporately and relationally! The reality that hearts cannot be legislated causes each of us to recognize that our influence, competencies, and investment can only be beneficial to the one that committedly receives and makes use of what has been given. Unless he or she moves beyond information to application he or she will remain unchanged.

Until the art of receiving is fostered inside the heart and mind of the recipient, genuine honor will not be experienced by the benefactor. If the giver's contribution is not received and applied, the window of opportunity will close making the valuable investment insignificant and ineffective to the intended recipient. You see, in the final analysis, our ability to receive from and invest into others is the true earmark of a successful life.

I have experienced the dichotomy where words of *"honor"* were accompanied by actions of devaluation as my contribution was rejected. I've observed how these lives, that I supposedly led, were unchanged because he or she really never wanted what I carried.

Anger towards and rebellion against the giver is the fruit propagated within the soil of latent dishonor.

On the magnificent flipside, the highest honor we can communicate to someone is to receive what they are giving! With a sense of great fulfillment, I have experienced the demonstration of honor from many recipients. This honor was felt deeply within my heart as their eyes would light up as I prepared and served a gourmet leadership-building meal. I was filled with energy as their hungry hearts couldn't get enough as they absorbed life-transforming principles. His or her honor was lavishly poured out toward me as he or she desired more! The greatest source of fulfillment was witnessing the exponential growth in competence and character as he or she applied what was received. Not only do I feel honored to have invested into quality emerging leaders, but I also receive and honor their contributions. Countless have grown into amazing influencers and their impact continues to bring justice worldwide.

" along others honoring without dreams your reach never will You way the."[2]

Embrace the greatest honor that can be given as others receive the treasure inside you! Give honor to others as you receive and welcome their gift! Choose alliances with those who give the greatest form of honor—receiving from you as you receive from them. It is from this hallowed place of mutual honor that true success stories are written!

Thomas Carlyle summarizes this so perfectly when he says, "Show me the man that you honor, and I will know what kind of man you are."

POWERLESS LOVE

Love can only be the solution for those who are hungry for its answer.

The word love is so common in our day to day vernacular. It holds such vast and varied meanings that it is far more complex than a simple four-letter expression.

Love frequents the languages of relationship, social justice, and faith, but is seldom voiced in reference to leadership. This void is misguided because love is, in fact, applicable to every sphere of leadership influence. After all, leadership is the business of people and love is our central need. Governments, businesses, educational systems, or any organizational structure for that matter cannot be instruments of justice—power used for good—without the love-motivated values of its leaders.

Many elude the word love because its attributes and expressions are vastly misunderstood. Counterfeit definitions have been constructed through the selfishness, manipulation, and needy perceptions of its participants. Just fill in the blank: "If you really loved me you would _____." These faulty expectations often create co-dependent relationships where the mentor sacrifices more and works harder than the beneficiary is willing to do for themselves.

In a world of entitlement, the recipient will wear the exterior mask of gratitude when they are getting what they want. Sadly, the heart is quickly revealed when the leader draws a boundary line and instead of gratitude for all that was invested the result is accusatory allegations of abusive control and lack of love.

Love is NOT defined by sentiment. Though sadly mistaken more often than not, love is NOT giving people whatever makes them feel good or causes them to be happy. It is not becoming the proverbial doormat or meeting their felt-needs so they love you in return. It is not about being the fixer, enabler, or the one who bails them out of their self-sabotaging behaviors. Love is not evidenced through clingy dependence. The end of that saga is estrangement not partnership. This often *feels* like love, but it is *powerless love!*

Love IS the most powerful force in the universe when welcomed, appreciated, and reciprocated. We have learned that neuroscience has proven that our brains are wired for the giving and receiving of genuine love and validation. This passion is intrinsically conceived from the courage to invest into another's growth, development, and success. Love is a genuine desire to nurture the seed of another's value, uniqueness, purpose, and gifting. As it develops and grows the result is full potential actualized as each one contributes their gift to the world. This love is a deliberate action not based upon emotions, sentiment, or obligatory service.

The giving and receiving of purposeful love originates from a place of mutuality. It stems from a life-giving exchange of integrity and wisdom in order to identify what and when to invest. Wisdom will empower the love-motivated leader to know if it is the season to give or hold back, to speak or remain silent, to be accessible or draw boundaries, or to provide assistance or step away.

Purposeful love will initially model and do for someone when they are learning to "walk." As the person matures, the leader partners with them in order to build their confidence, see their value, and support their passion. There must come a time, however, when the protégé must stand on his or her two feet and personally pay the price. Their healthy independence does not mean that the relationship or partnership is diminished, but rather maximized to its full potential.

When you've sown into someone's life and they then continue to work the field and reap the harvest, it is powerful! When you have invested and are able to witness the return from the mutually-empowering relationship, it is something to celebrate! When love is not forceful, but waits for the invitation and reciprocation of the beautiful gift being presented, it is life-giving and gratifying.

Remember that investing into someone will only benefit them if they are hungry. This can be exemplified through one of my simple life experiences. One day my husband received a call from a distraught father who said he did not have milk for his children. We were thrilled to meet this man's need, but when we presented our gift he began to complain that it was 2% milk and not whole milk. Our investment of love was met with a lack of value and criticism sending a clear message that it was not good enough. *Powerless love* cannot change a life without the recipient's commitment to celebrate, embrace, steward, and pay it forward.

Here are some considerations to help identify whether a potential investment is solid or shaky:

1. Avoid investment if there is dishonesty in the relationship. Half-truths are just as deceptive as a full-blown lie. Is he or she saying what he or she wants you to hear or being respectfully honest and authentic with his or her communication?

2. A wise investor looks at the track record. How responsible is the individual with opportunities previously given to him or her? Did he or she steward the investment in authenticity? Did he or she value the opportunity and the one who gave it to them? Was he or she lazy and irresponsible or vigilant making the most of his or her opportunity?

3. Does he or she play the "blame game" complaining about the unfairness of his or her life or where he or she was victimized by others or circumstances? Do you hear the "hard luck" stories in order to gain your sympathy? Or, contrariwise, in spite of life's challenges has he or she embraced the willingness to take personal responsibility for his or her growth?

4. Does he or she want investment but not accountability? Can you imagine a financial investor giving without accountability? Your life, time, emotional energies, and resources are more significant than money.

5. Is he or she a person who honors, values, and genuinely appreciates both the small and the great investments, even if it is a ten minute conversation on the phone?

No matter how great your love-motivated investments are, if the recipient does not treasure what you are offering, as genuine as your love is, it is powerless for them. No matter how grand your desire to build platforms of opportunity for someone, it is powerless if they do not make the most of that opportunity. No matter how pure your motives and authentic your love-motivated leadership, if it is belittled or unappreciated it is, to that person, powerless love.

Invest where you are celebrated, not tolerated. You will see your influential love impact lives, build mutually beneficial partnerships, and accomplish great things!

IDENTIFYING MANIPULATION

I'm not naïve to the fact that we live in a fear-driven world; you don't have to look far to see that it is sorely infected by an epidemic of mistrust that I have repeatedly addressed. With that being said, we cannot allow our highest and best to succumb under the weight of pessimism and cynicism. We must refuse to allow the minority to sculpt our worldview or frustrate our personal purpose. We must continue to live and lead believing that people are inherently good as we choose to extend trust and believe the best of others.

I do not have my *head in the sand* and I *do* have a "boatload" of experience with liars and manipulators. This *school of hard knocks* has become a springboard of understanding that has armed me with tools to recognize and confront these perpetrators of injustice.

Two types of manipulators:

1. The first are the *subconscious controllers* who feel powerless and, as a result, develop character traits of "taking and getting" rather than "contributing and giving." Almost every human being steps into these characteristics when motivated by fear. However, if these individuals are teachable, we have a great opportunity as leaders to help them recognize and overcome.

2. The second are the *conscious manipulators* who perfect their deceptive trade. They become skillful in their dishonesty and their practices are immoral and devious.

Whether a client, employee or employer, vendor, teacher or student or social relationship; here are some ways to help in identifying perps of injustice:

They make you feel that only they are the solution! This is the *worm on the hook* because at this point the lie is so hidden that you can't see that you're being baited.

Here's an example: My 92-year-old mother had a problem with her computer and she came to me for help—her first mistake! I was on the phone with tech support—or so I thought—as they assured me that they could solve the problem. Everything about the conversation was initially professional and I felt secure—this was the trap! As the conversation continued I began to see the *red flags* of a manipulative perpetrator. The *red flags* began to become more evident as he tried to silence my questioning and I observed his customer service protocols. It did not take long before I recognized that my mother was being targeted by a manipulator.

Red Flag #1: Quickly irritated. A manipulator has an objective to take something from you. The moment you question, challenge, or ask for authenticity they begin to display an edge of impatience. If a person is genuine, on the other hand, they welcome inquiry knowing they are able to substantiate their claims and validate their honorable motives.

Red Flag #2: Degrading demeanor. This individual will treat you in a way that portrays their superiority. If you require accountability, request proof for what is presented, or require explanations for actions their anxiety will begin to leak out through their subtle or overt lecture of how inept you are.

**Red Flag #3: Escalated emotional response or hardline reac-

tions. The manipulator is now losing their sense of power as you are becoming more aware of their identifying traits of manipulation. Their fear of exposure thrusts them into an aggressive posture.

Red Flag #4: Threats and intimidation. A few years ago one of my staff received a call that they owed a certain amount of money that needed to be paid immediately or the police were going to come and arrest them. Now, she did not owe money and it was an obvious scam artist, but she was so fearful by their threatening that she was ready to pay the money! A manipulator's last ditch effort is to create fear. Threats of loss, harm, failure, rejection, and a barrage of impending doom are thrown at you. The manipulator must keep you in a subservient position in order to remain in control and take from you what benefits them.

When you do not let a controller control they will be positioned to either mature or quickly leave you for someone they can manipulate.

As justice-minded leaders, we give ourselves to noble causes and business endeavors that can impact our society for good. You must protect your vision from the toxicity of manipulators and those who piggyback on your labor for their own gain at your expense.

You'll never lead perfectly and you won't always see the hidden agendas of practiced manipulators immediately. However, when the *red flags* become visible, you must confront them to protect the vision that has been entrusted to you. This process builds you so that you can face your future with optimism!

Powerful Positioning

Powerful individuals change what they can and choose internal peace in what they cannot.

I would love to be four inches taller! I mean, my grandson when only seven-years-old was almost as tall as me! I would be so happy to have the beauty and body I enjoyed when I was 21 so I wouldn't have to "spackle, prime and paint" my face and cover the gray in my chemically-dependent hair. Oh, how I would love to time-travel to my past with my present understanding, go through the doors that my shame and fears kept me from, and refuse to do the things that were seeded from the pressure of people.

Whether past events or present circumstances, let's face it, some things we are powerless to change for ourselves, others, or society. This, however, does NOT make us completely powerless. My internal response to unchangeable facts actually has the ability to empower me! It is through this that I can interpret my past with thankfulness, my present with courage, and my future with hope.

Daily we encounter what we cannot change, but that does not mean we are powerless. Circumstances may send fear-based invitations, but that does not mean we are fearful or insecure. We may be confronted with individuals who turn a deaf ear to our voice, but that does not mean we are silenced. The past or present events of our lives do not define who we are nor can they govern our contribution to the world. In actuality, what I believe to be true shapes my reality. Our internal responses to opposing messages accurately reveal to us how secure and powerful we are intrinsically.

To embrace the fullness of our powerful positioning we must recognize where we do not have power. As soon as we attempt to control what we cannot or should not, the results will be counterproductive and frustration will follow. We stand powerless when wanting to manipulate another's decisions, attitudes, actions, or perspectives. We cannot force the honor or the acceptance of our investments. Think about this: Is there ever authentic love, loyalty, partnership or validation from one who lives in intimidation from power-handed leadership?

We do not have the power to control the external or expect it to align perfectly with our desires, wants, or dreams. Actually, the challenges along life's journey do not destroy a vision, but build the visionary, which is a far greater achievement. True success is not built upon the quantity, but the quality of our contribution and is able to exponentially increase in the midst of adversity. A monument was never erected, a hero never recognized, nor a goal ever achieved without the courage to stand when our world is shaking.

Powerful positioning is an internal posturing. You are the only one that can truly determine the genuineness of your internal order. When there is a peaceful vigilance to your unique expression you'll witness the birthing of greater confidence. We must acknowledge that we are powerless to change the unchangeable while simultaneously possessing a quiet strength to persevere and grow. This internal dichotomy allows us to walk surefooted when confronted by the rocky terrains of life.

We equally share 24 hours in a day, as well as hold an account of emotional energies to steward each day. When our internal posturing refuses to waste emotional energies on critics, cynics or things we cannot change, we find increased motivation to influence society as an instrument of justice.

No one is designed to meet every need of everyone on the planet…thank God! We are only responsible to do our part from a heart that is able to discern what we can or cannot change. It is at that point that our external world begins to change; it is by this powerful positioning of being the best we can be, no more or no less.

This position is actualized when I choose to give my best every day. It is when I love despite the actions of another and spend my life for those who want my investment. When I choose to serve, give, and care just because it is right, because people are valuable, and because I want to leave the world a better place, life will be truly good because of who I've become and the cause that I serve.

Making a Difference

Every pure-hearted leader wants to make a difference and bring societal change. When your leadership is courageously sourced by a higher cause, your central core finds an unparalleled expression. When you are an eyewitness to positive change, small or large, you become aware that your life example and daily investments make an honest difference.

Though inevitable, no one wants to be hurt! Our humanity subconsciously tries to protect us from emotional pain. The dichotomy of our self-protective mechanisms is that the same walls we build to protect ourselves keep others out, which ultimately sabotages our ability to make a difference. I had to choose years ago where I was going to place my leadership attention. I had a choice to protect my heart from pain or take the gutsy leap to change my world for good. I chose the latter.

I'd love to say that my courageous and *noble* decision protected my heart from hurt pounding at its door. It did not. Hurts have come and gone, but they have not stopped me from making a difference. That decision didn't have the power to legislate another's heart or externally control their decisions, but it did have the capacity to solidify my internal response in spite of the pain.

If I am not close enough to be hurt I am not close enough to make a difference.

Let's look at some powerful benefits of managing pain's internal responses.

Protection from being controlled by fear-based strategies: Our initial innate response to disappointment, rejection, betrayal or devaluation is fear. Fear will act in response by emotionally spewing as *a piece of our mind* is regurgitated creating a huge mess to clean up. Or, in another potential fear-reaction, we may hide in internal avoidance devising embittered plans. Both are the results of emotional hijacking and are destructive!

Our internal compass persistently points "true north:" True north describes our life's direction. Hurts are like arrows hurled at the core of our ability to make a difference. As we understand healthy internal responses to pain we can choose to hold steady the course; we can disallow the pain to re-route us away from our true north. We will not relegate the control of our life's helm to the temporary storm of heartache.

Necessary emotional energies are protected for proper distribution: We are containers of unique contributions that will make the difference. As we employ an internal guard to conserve our emotional energies, we will recognize that wasting our energy on what we are powerless to control uses up the fuel that is needed to advance our journey.

Allow your internal courage to take you from a place of powerlessness and pain to a place of making a difference. Yes, you'll face unforeseen challenges. At times fear will scream, "you're not good enough!" The price you pay will be substantial, but when you see the difference you are making—small or great—it will be worth it all and you will be doing the happy dance!

You carry within you everything you need to be *a Higher Living Leader*! You possess the authority to choose Higher Thinking, Higher Responsibility, and serve a Higher Cause! You carry the ability to Influence Societal Design as an Instrument of Justice!

BIBLIOGRAPHY

Allen, Dr. Gary. "The Healing of Nations: Healing the Wounds Inflicted by Injustice." Speech, United Nations, June 11, 1998. Christian Mission for the United Nations Community. http://www.christianmission-un.org/resource-center/manuscripts/pdf/the-healing-of-nations-healing-the-wounds-inflicted-by-injustice.pdf .

Amen, Dr. Daniel G. *Making a Good Brain Great: The Amen Clinic Program for Achieving and Sustaining Optimal Mental Performance*. New York: Three Rivers Press, 2005.

"Amygdala." *Wikipedia*. Accessed on September 25, 2016. https://en.wikipedia.org/wiki/Amygdala#cite_note-amyg-cytoarchitecture-3 .

Angelou, Dr. Maya. "A Conversation with Dr. Maya Angelou." By Trisha LaNae. *Beautifully Said Magazine*. July 4, 2012. http://beautifullysmagazine.com/201207feature-of-the-month-3/.

"Anger: Managing the Amygdala Hijack." *Life at the Bar*. Last modified on May 11, 2007. https://lifeatthebar.wordpress.com/2007/05/11/anger-managing-the-amygdala-hijack/ .

Belludi, Nagesh. "The Best Inspirational Quotations by Maya Angelou." *Right Attitudes: Ideas for Impact*. Last modified April 4, 2015. http://www.rightattitudes.com/2015/04/04/inspirational-quotations-by-maya-angelou/.

Berman, James. "The Three Essential Warren Buffet Quotes to Live By." *Forbes*. Last modified on April 20, 2014. http://www.forbes.com/sites/jamesberman/2014/04/20/the-three-essential-warren-buffett-quotes-to-live-by/#765ed17732f5.

Bethune, Gordon M. "Remember to Share the Stage." By Adam Bryant. *The New York Times*, January 2, 2010, http://www.nytimes.com/2010/01/03/business/03corner.html.

"Big Lie," *Wikipedia*, accessed September 30, 2016, https://en.wikipedia.org/wiki/Big_lie

Boland, Barbara. "Leader: ISIS is 'Systematically Beheading Children' in 'Christian Genocide'." *CNSNews*. Last modified August 7, 2014. http://www.cnsnews.com/mrctv-blog/barbara-boland/leader-isis-systematically-beheading-children-christian-genocide.

Braveheart. Directed by Mel Gibson. Hollywood, CA: Paramount. 1995.

Bush, George W. "Remarks by the President on Corporate Responsibility." Speech, New York City, July 9, 2002. The White House George W. Bush Archives. https://georgewbush-whitehouse.archives.gov/news/releases/2002/07/20020709-4.html.

Churchill, Winston. "The Gift of a Common Tongue." Speech, Harvard, September 6, 1943. The Churchill Centre. http://www.winstonchurchill.org/resources/speeches/1941-1945-war-leader/420-the-price-of-greatness-is-responsibility.

Cinderella. "Don't Know What You Got (Till It's Gone)." In *Long Cold Winter*. Mercury Records, 1988. Album.

Covey, Sean . The 6 Most Important Decisions You'll Ever Make: a Guide for Teens. New York: Simon and Schuster, 2006.

Covey, Stephen R. *The 7 Habits of Highly Effective Families*. New York: Golden Books, 1997.

Covey, Stephen R. and Rebecca R. Merrill. *The Speed of Trust: The One Thing That Changes Everything*. New York: Free Press, 2006.

Demarest, Peter D. and Harvey J. Schoof, MS. *Answering the Central Question; How Science Reveals the Keys to Success in Life, Love, and Leadership*. Philadelphia: HeartLead Publishing, LLC, 2010.

"Dendrite." *New Word Encyclopedia*. Accessed on September 26, 2016. http://www.newworldencyclopedia.org/entry/Dendrite.

Deutschendorf, Harvey. *The Other Kind of Smart: Simple Ways to Boost Your Emotional Intelligence for Greater Personal Effectiveness and Success*. New York: AMACOM, 2009.

Drysdale, William. *Proverbs from Plymouth Pulpit*. New York: D. Appleton and Company, 1887.

Eagleman, David. *Incognito: The Secret Lives of the Brain*. 1st ed. New York: Vintage Books, 2012.

Einstein, Albert. "On Education." Address, State University of New York at Albany, October 15, 1931. TODAYINSCI, http://todayinsci.com/E/Einstein_Albert/EinsteinAlbert-Life-Quotations.htm.

Eisenhower, Dwight, D. "First Inaugural Address of Dwight D. Eisenhower." Speech, Washington D.C., January 20, 1953. Dwight D. Eishenhower Presidential Library, Mueseum, and Boyhood Home. https://www.eisenhower.archives.gov/all_about_ike/speeches/1953_inaugural_address.pdf.

Ephenus, Pius, "Goal Setting: The Power of Writing Down Your

Goals." *EzineArticles*. Last modified on July 22, 2007. http://ezinearticles.com/?Goal-Setting---The-Power-Of-Writing-Down-Your-Goal&id=655551.

Goble, Gordon. "The Top 10 Bad Tech Predictions." *Digital Trends*. Last modified on November 4, 2012. http://www.digitaltrends.com/features/top-10-bad-tech-predictions/7/.

Goleman, Daniel. *Working with Emotional Intelligence*. New York: Bantam Books, 1998. Graham, Morris and Kevin Baize. *Executive Thinking:From Brightness to Brilliance*. Bloomington: iUniverse, Inc., 2011.

Grant, Dr. George and Karen Grant. *Lost Causes: The Romantic Attraction of Defeated Yet Unvanquished Men and Movements*. Nashville: Cumberland House Publishing, Inc., 1999.

Greene, Graham. *The Ministry of Fear*. London: Penguin Group, 1943.

42. Directed by Brian Helgeland. 2013. Burbank, CA: Warner Bros. Home Video, 2013. DVD.

Hendrix, Mary Lynn. "The Emotional Brain: Lessons in Fear Conditioning." *NIH Record*. Accessed on September 26, 2016. https://nihrecord.nih.gov/newsletters/06_03_97/story04.htm.

Herndon, William H. and Jesse W. Weik. *Herndon's Life of Lincoln: The History and Personal Recollections of Abraham Lincoln as originally written by William H. Herndon and Jesse W. Weik*. Cleveland, Ohio: The World Publishing Company, 1949.

Hesse, Hermann. *Narcissus and Goldmund: A Novel*. Translated by Ursule Molinaro. New York: Picador, 1968.

Highfield, Roger. "DNA Survey Finds All Humans are 99.9pc the Same." *The Telegraph*. Last modified on Dec. 20, 2002.

http://www.telegraph.co.uk/news/worldnews/northamerica/usa/1416706/DNA-survey-finds-all-humans-are-99.9pc-the-same.html .

Hillman, Os. *TGIF: Today God is First*. Grand Rapids: Revel, 2014.

Hitler, Adolf. *Mein Kempf*. Translated by James Murphy. Archive Media Publishing, Inc., 2011.

Holton, Gerald and Yehuda Elkana, eds. *Albert Einstein: Historical and Cultural Perspectives*. Mineola, NY: Dover Publications, Inc., 1982.

Hopkins, Tom. Selling in Tough Times: Secrets to Selling When No One is Buying. New York: Business Plus, 2010.

"How the Brain Works." *Self Esteem Experts: Nurturing Vibrant Self Esteem*. Accessed September 27, 2016. http://www.self-esteem-experts.com/how-the-brain-works.html.

Howes, Lewis. "20 Lessons from Walt Disney on Entrepreneurship, Innovation and Chasing Your Dreams." *Forbes*. Last modified on July 17, 2012. http://www.forbes.com/sites/lewishowes/2012/07/17/20-business-quotes-and-lessons-from-walt-disney/#195f5e4d1f56.

Jobe, Anthony E. Sr. Discovering the Passion Thieves of Success and Unleashing the Real You. Bloomington, IN, Authorhouse, 2012.

"John Paul Warren Quotes." *Goodreads*. Accessed on September 29, 2016. https://www.goodreads.com/quotes/414326-you-will-never-reach-your-dreams-without-honoring-others-along.

Keith, Kent M. "Paradoxical Commandments." *Kent M. Keith. Accessed Sept. 15, 2016,* http://www.kentmkeith.com/mother_teresa.html.

Keller, Helen. *Helen Keller: Rebel Lives,* ed. John Davis. Melbourne New York: Ocean Press, 2003, 24.

King, Martin Luther, Jr. "I Have a Dream." Speech, Washington, D.C., August 28, 1963. National Archives. https://www.archives.gov/press/exhibits/dream-speech.pdf

Koch, Christoph. Biophysics of Computation: Information Processing in Single Neurons, 1st ed.. New York: Oxford University Press, 2004.

Kouzes, James M. and Barry Z. Posner, eds. *Christian Reflections on the Leadership Challenge.* San Francisco: The Leadership Challenge, 2004.

Kouzes, James and Barry Posner. *The Leadership Challenge.* 3rd ed. San Francisco: Jossey-Bass, 2002.

LaBar, Kevin S. and Roberto Cabeza. "Cognitive neuroscience of emotional memory." *Nature Reviews: Neuroscience* 7, no. 1 (Jan. 2006): 54-64.

Leaf, Dr. Caroline. "The Perfect You: About." *Dr. Leaf.* Accessed on October 26, 2016. drleaf.com/about/the-perfect-you/.

Leaf, Dr. Caroline. Who Switched off My Brain? Controlling Toxic Thoughts and Emotions. Nashville: Thomas Nelson Publishers, 2009.

Leaf, Dr. Caroline. "Who Switched Off My Brain." LoveLife Conference video. Youtube video, 1:00:54. Posted July 29, 2014. https://www.youtube.com/watch?v=1-goBWumIN4.

Leaf, Dr. Caroline. Who Switched off My Brain? Series # 1. DVD.

Leaf, Dr. Caroline. *Who Switched off My Brain?* Series #4, DVD.

"Learn How to Increase Self Esteem." *Self Esteem Experts: Nur-*

turing Vibrant Self Esteem. Accessed September 27, 2016. http://www.self-esteem-experts.com/how-to-increase-self-esteem.html.

Lewis, Dr. Thomas. "The Neuroscience of Empathy." Presentation at the Authors@Google Series, Google Headquarters Mountview, CA, December 5, 2007. Center for Building a Culture of Empathy, http://cultureofempathy.com/references/Experts/Thomas-Lewis.htm.

Lindsley, Dr. Art. "C.S. Lewis on Humility (and Pride) by Dr. Art Lindsley." *C.S. Lewis Institute*. Last modified on October 8, 2012. http://www.cslewisinstitute.org/C.S._Lewis_on_Humility_and_Pride .

Long, John F. "There are No Federal Aid Funds Except Those Taken From Your Pockets." *Eerie Railroad Magazine* 45, no. 6 (August 1949): 3. Accessed September 29, 2016. https://books.google.com/books?id=m4szAAAAIAAJ&pg=RA15-PA3&lpg=RA15-PA3&dq=When+a+man+is+intoxicated+by+alcohol+he+can+recover,+but+when+intoxicated+by+power,+he+seldom+recovers.&source=bl&ots=GNUGYo3mM-&sig=4tt_AyG-Xlc6BxvGbxjhBFa7wcc&hl=en&sa=X&ved=0ahUKEwjy7azj97XPAhXJaz4KHVHAArUQ6AEINDAF#v=onepage&q=When%20a%20man%20is%20intoxicated%20by%20alcohol%20he%20can%20recover%2C%20but%20when%20intoxicated%20by%20power%2C%20he%20seldom%20recovers.&f=false.

Maxwell, John C. and Jim Dornan. *How to Influence People: Make a Difference in Your World.* Nashville: Thomas Nelson, 2013.

Maxwell, John C. The Right to Lead: Learning Leadership Through Character and Courage. Nashville: J. Countryman, 2010.

McKinnon, Kyle. "Will Malala's Influence Stretch to Europe?" *Deutsche Welle.* Last modified on January 18, 2013.

http://www.dw.com/en/will-malalas-influence-stretch-to-europe/a-16532149.

Moore, Daniel T., Phd. "Six Ways to Help a Brain Heal." *Your Family Clinic*. Accessed on September 26, 2016. http://www.yourfamilyclinic.com/trauma/heal.htm.

Morgan, Robert J. *Real Stories for the Soul*. Nashville, TN: Thomas Nelson Inc., 2000.

Nizer, Louis. *Between You and Me*. New York: Beechhurst Press, 1948.

Pomeroy, Dr. Leon. *The New Science of Axiological Psychology*, Edited by Rem. E. Edwards. Amsterdam:Rodopi, 2005.

Oberbeck, Chris. "5 Ways a CEO Can Build a Culture of Trust." *Entrepreneur*. Last modified on May 17, 2016. https://www.entrepreneur.com/article/273457.

Palestini, Robert. *No Laughing Matter: The Value of Humor in Educational Leadership*. Lanham: Rowman and Littlefield Education, 2013.

"Persuasion Tool." *Ziglar, Inc*. Accessed on September 29. 2016, https://www.ziglar.com/quotes/persuasion-tool/.

Power, Rhett. "7 Qualities of People with High Emotional Intelligence." *Success*. Last modified on April 2, 2015. http://www.success.com/article/7-qualities-of-people-with-high-emotional-intelligence .

Rampton, John. "20 Quotes from Jim Rohn Putting Success and Life into Perspective." *Entrepreneur*. Last modified on March 4, 2016. https://www.entrepreneur.com/article/271873.

Rand, Ayn. *The Ayn Rand Lexicon: Objectivism from A to Z*, Edited by Harry Binswanger. New York: Meridian, 1988.

"Resume Falsification Statistics." *Statistic Brain*. Last modified October 1, 2015. http://www.statisticbrain.com/resume-falsification-statistics/.

"15 Ridiculous Predictions which didn't Come True!—Part 2." *History Rundown*. Last modified on January 7, 2014. http://www.historyrundown.com/15-ridiculous-predictions-which-didnt-come-true-part-2/.

Robert T. Kiyosaki's Facebook Page. May 10, 2012. Accessed on September 26, 2016. https://www.facebook.com/RobertKiyosaki/posts/10150958481151788.

Rock, David. "Managing With the Brain in Mind," *Strategy + Business*, last modified on August 27, 2009, http://www.strategy-business.com/article/09306?gko=5df7f.

Ruth, Babe. "Babe Ruth Quotes." *Babe Ruth*. Accessed September 24. 2016, http://www.baberuth.com/quotes/.

Secretan, Lance. *Inspirational Leadership: Destiny, Calling, and Cause*. Canada: The Secretan Center, Inc., 1999.

Shepherd, G.M. ed. *The Synaptic Organization of the Brain*. 5th ed. New York: Oxford University Press, Inc, 2004.

Shi, Yingchao, Weiming Zeng, Nizhuan Wang, Shujiang Wang, and Zhijian Huang. "Early warning for human mental sub-health based on fMRI data analysis: an example from a seafarers' resting-data study." *Frontiers in Psychology*. Last modified on July 23, 2015, http://dx.doi.org/10.3389/fpsyg.2015.01030.

Sinek, Simon O. "Simon Sinek, Creator of 'Discover Your Why' Course." *VerticalRising*. Accessed on Sept. 20, 2016. http://verticalrising.com/about/simon-sinek/.

Smedes, Lewis B. *The Art of Forgiving*. New York: Ballantine

Books, 1996.

"Sonia Rumzi Quotes." *Goodreads*. Accessed on September 29, 2016. http://www.goodreads.com/quotes/345671-anyone-who-teaches-me-deserves-my-respect-honoring-and-attention.

Sweeney, Michael S. Brain: The complete Mind: How it Develops, How it Works, and How to Keep it Sharp. National Geographic, 2009.

Taylor, Lynn Ellsworth. *The Core Values Handbook*, 3rd ed. Tukwila, WA: Elliott Bay Publishing, Inc., 2010.

"Teaching to Kill: The Islamic State's Jihad Camps for Kids." *The Clarion Project.* Last modified on August 28, 2014. http://www.clarionproject.org/news/teaching-kill-Islamic-states-jihad-camps-kids.

"Treatment of Slaves in the United States." *Wikipedia*. Accessed on Sept. 19, 2016. wikipedia.org/wiki/Treatment_of_slaves_in_the_United_States.

Trim, Dr. Cindy. *Reclaim Your Soul*. Shippensburg, PA: Destiny Image Publishers, Inc., 2014.

United States Holocaust Memorial Museum. "Documenting Numbers of Victims of the Holocaust and Nazi Persecution." *Holocaust Encyclopedia.* Last modified July 2, 2016. https://www.ushmm.org/wlc/en/article.php?ModuleId=10008193.

United States Holocaust Memorial Museum. "Jewish Population of Europe in 1945." *Holocaust Encyclopedia.* Last modified July 2, 2016. https://www.ushmm.org/wlc/en/article.php?ModuleId=10005687.

Weber, Dr. Ellen. "The Brain on Cortisol." *Brain Leaders and Learners*. Last modified September 22, 2008. http://www.brainleadersandlearners.com/general/the-brain-on-cortisol/ .

Weber, Dr. Ellen. "A Brain on Forgiveness." *Brain Leaders and Learners*: *Practical Tactics for Neuro Discoveries with Dr. Ellen Weber*. Last modified on September 17, 2011. http://www.brainleadersandlearners.com/amygdala/a-brain-on-forgiveness/.

"What it Takes to be Number One." *Vince Lombardi*. Acessed on September 26, 2016. http://www.vincelombardi.com/number-one.html.

"What Was the Jewish Holocaust?" *The Incredible Story of the Jewish People*. Accessed Sept. 19, 2016. http://www.the-jewish-story.org/holocaust1.html.

Willoughby, Martin. "Career Investment- T. Doug Dale finds success as shareholder at Security Ballew." *Mississippi Business Journal*. Last modified on June 20, 2014. http://msbusiness.com/2014/06/career-investment-t-doug-dale-finds-success-shareholder-security-ballew/.

20 Years of the Ethical Movement in New York and Other Cities, 1876-1896. Philadelphia, S. Burns Weston, 1896.

Ziglar, Zig. *Over the Top*. Rev. ed. Nashville: Thomas Nelson, Inc., 1997.

Zimmer, Carl. "100 Trillion Connections: New Efforts Probe and Map the Brain's Detailed Architechture." *Scientific American*. Last modified on Janary 1, 2011, https://www.scientificamerican.com/article/100-trillion-connections/.

ABOUT THE AUTHOR

Dr. Melodye Hilton works with individuals as well as workgroups around the globe as a Leadership Consultant, Behavioral Analyst, Executive Team and Personal Coach. Through years of leadership experience and consulting, she has developed a unique and personal approach to creating a positive, sustainable impact within her spheres of influence.

Her passion is in the development of people, which are the greatest resource of any organization. As individuals develop the soft skills internally, their ability for productivity exponentially increases, which creates worth in one's personal as well as professional environment.

Dr. Melodye's recognition extends throughout all ages, socio-economic, and educational backgrounds through her work in corporate and local business, government, not-for-profit organizations, as well as public and private educational sectors. She has served as Vice-President of a not-for-profit corporation for over 30 years and founded International Training Center: School of Emerging Leaders for the development and equipping of both emerging and established leaders.

She has also established the Voice of Justice Foundation to provide scholarships, nationally and internationally, for potential young leaders to receive training, aid in the rescue and care of orphans and children in developing nations, as well as partnering with other organizations to impact a generation with hope, vision, and purpose.

A core value for Dr. Melodye is justice— power used for the good of others and society— which is foundational to every leadership, consulting, and coaching practice she brings to the table.

Want to Learn More About Dr. Melodye or Contact Her?

Contact her by email at:

Contact@DrMelodye.com

Visit her website at:

www.DrMelodye.com

Follow her on social media at:

https://www.facebook.com/drmelodyehilton/

www.linkedin.com/in/melodye-hilton-904b9026

Check out the VOICE OF JUSTICE FOUNDATION at:

www.DrMelodye.com/voj

DR. MELODYE HILTON CONSULTING

Learn more at www.DrMelodye.com

LEADERSHIP CONSULTING AND TRAINING

Specialized and Customized Training Topics may include:

- Justice-centric Leadership
- Validation Quotient
- Higher Living Leadership
- Higher Thinking and Emotional Hijacking
- Values-Motivated Behavior
- Teambuilding
- Building Trust
- Conflict Resolution
- Communication
- Behavioral Consultation
- Corporate and Personal Purpose
- Shared Vision and Values
- Adapted vs Innate Contribution
- And many more....

EXECUTIVE TEAM AND PERSONAL COACHING

Dr. Melodye is a certified behavioral consultant with the Institute of Motivational Living since 1993 and often incorporates valuable profiling tools as part of her coaching.

Some of these profiles include:

The DISC Personality Style Workbook People Keys®

This profiling instrument identifies an individual's personality style, helps him or her understand the differences in people, providing a personal review of each individual's strengths and limitations.

The Values Style Profile People Keys®

The Values Profile is Dr. Melodye Hilton's favorite profiling instrument because every aspect of an individual's life and leadership is impacted by these invisible motivators. Individuals must choose to not live by needs alone, but by values that impact their professional and personal choices of life. Values drive choices—which drive behaviors—which drive results! Conflicts arise when we hold conflicting values which determine our perception of the situations and people around us.

The TEAMS Profile People Keys®

An outstanding corporate resource for team development, this TEAMS profile will give leadership the information to strategically position each person for the greatest efficiency. The roles of Theorist, Executor, Analyzer, Manager, or Strategist are key in developing a successful work group, starting a new business, or placing people in their most natural and effective role on the team. Team members will learn their role, value to the team, core strengths, and potential limitations for each style.

CORE VALUE INDEX™ (CVI™)

The Most Accurate and Reliable Human Assessment Available! 97.7%

A revolutionary assessment created by Taylor Protocols™. that bypasses personality and behavior revealing your unchanging motivational energies and sense for how you are wired to contribute to the world around you.

Discover your innate core values, your wired-in Human Operating System™, your six types of contribution, your negative conflict strategies, your deepest fears with 97% repeat score reliability so it is stable data that is diagnostic and prescribes change. Begin your discovery of Core Values Consciousness, a new pathway to personal excellence and happiness.

This assessment is one of the simplest, most versatile tools you can find for improving an individual's self-awareness and awareness of others. If you are an employee, business owner or someone who want to learn more about your core values, then the next few minutes could positive affect you, your friends and coworkers for years to come.

Spend less than ten minutes and discover in your profile report:

What causes you to conflict with others.

What values you base a majority of your decisions on.

Why you make the same mistakes over and over.

How you can improve your relationships with others.

Take a FREE CVI at: www.DrMelodye.com/cvi

VOICE OF JUSTICE FOUNDATION

Dr. Melodye Hilton's Voice of Justice Foundation is touching lives worldwide. We invite you to join us in releasing one voice for Justice!

Mission Statement:

To be a voice of hope, hands of rescue, and instruments of justice on behalf of the neglected, abused, or shamed.

Vision:

Injustice is simply an abuse of power, while justice is a righteous use of that power. The objective of the Voice of Justice Foundation is to use the influence and resources of its founders and supporters to be an instrument of justice, especially on the behalf of children and youth.

Already established is the International Training Center: School of Emerging Leaders where they train, equip, and activate young revolutionary leaders for platforms of influence. Our hearts have broken for young people nationally and internationally that have no one to assist them. We want the Voice of Justice Foundation to be a bridge of resources to help these young people that have amazing potential to be empowered to impact their world for good.

We have partnered with other not-for-profits in building schools, orphanages, and rescuing street children from abuse and prostitution. A young generation is crying out—our goal is to be an answer to its call! We are now making efforts to partner with others to see human trafficking ended and help the victims of its atrocities.

http://drmelodye.com/voj/

NOTES

INTRODUCTION: HIGHER LIVING LEADERS PURPOSE

[1] George W. Bush, "Remarks by the President on Corporate Responsibility" (speech, New York City, July 9, 2002), The White House George W. Bush Archives, https://georgewbush-whitehouse.archives.gov/news/releases/2002/07/20020709-4.html.

1. LEADERSHIP REFORMATION

[1] Edmund Burke, Public Domain.

[2] Martin Luther King, Jr., "I Have a Dream" (speech, Washington, D.C., August 28, 1963), National Archives, https://www.archives.gov/press/exhibits/dream-speech.pdf.

[3] James Kouzes and Barry Posner, *The Leadership Challenge,* 3rd ed. (San Francisco: Jossey-Bass, 2002), xxviii.

[4] Kent M. Keith, "Paradoxical Commandments," *Kent M. Keith.* Accessed 15 Sept. 2016. http://www.kentmkeith.com/mother_teresa.html. (Mother Theresa's sign paraphrased the original quote).

[5] Dr. Gary Allen, "The Healing of Nations: Healing the Wounds Inflicted by Injustice" (speech, United Nations, June 11, 1998), Christian Mission for the

United Nations Community, http://www.christianmission-un.org/resource-center/manuscripts/pdf/the-healing-of-nations-healing-the-wounds-inflicted-by-injustice.pdf.

[6] Ibid.

[7] Theodore Roosevelt, quoted in Dr. George Grant and Karen Grant, *Lost Causes: The Romantic Attraction of Defeated Yet Unvanquished Men and Movements* (Nashville: Cumberland House Publishing, Inc., 1999), 121.

[8] Unknown, quoted by Abraham Lincoln in William H. Herndon and Jesse W. Weik, *Herndon's Life of Lincoln: the History and Personal Recollections of Abraham Lincoln as originally written by William H. Herndon and Jesse W. Weik* (Cleveland, Ohio: The World Publishing Company, 1949), 355.

[9] Helen Keller, quoted in Helen Keller, *Helen Keller: Rebel Lives,* ed. John Davis (Melbourne New York: Ocean Press, 2003), 24.

[10] Lynn Ellsworth Taylor, *The Core Values Handbook, 3rd ed.* (Tukwila, WA: Elliott Bay Publishing, Inc., 2010), 11.

[11] Five Teams Preferences within the "TEAMS Profiling System" with the Institute of Motivational Living. Dr. Melodye Hilton has received her Certificate of Proficiency in April, 1993 in the Behavioral Analysis Consulting Program. You can learn more about the Institute as well as their resources at: www.peoplekeys.com

2. VALIDATION QUOTIENT: VALIDATION

[1] Albert Einstein, "On Education" (address, State University of New York at Albany, October 15, 1931), TODAYINSCI, http://todayinsci.com/E/Einstein_Albert/EinsteinAlbert-Life-Quotations.htm.

[2] Validation Quotient developed by Dr. Melodye Hilton in 2013

[3] Developed by Dr. Melodye Hilton, Consultant 2013 and is a term that is supported through her Higher Living Leaders training.

⁴United States Holocaust Memorial Museum, "Documenting Numbers of Victims of the Holocaust and Nazi Persecution," *Holocaust Encyclopedia,* last modified July 2, 2016, https://www.ushmm.org/wlc/en/article.php?ModuleId=10008193.

⁵ United States Holocaust Memorial Museum, "Jewish Population of Europe in 1945," *Holocaust Encyclopedia,* last modified July 2, 2016, https://www.ushmm.org/wlc/en/article.php?ModuleId=10005687.

⁶ "What Was the Jewish Holocaust?" *The Incredible Story of the Jewish People,* accessed Sept. 19, 2016, http://www.the-jewish-story.org/holocaust1.html.

⁷ "Big Lie," Wikipedia, accessed September 30, 2016, https://en.wikipedia.org/wiki/Big_lie. [This is an adaptation of Hitler's original words found in: Adolf Hitler, Mein Kempf, trans. James Murphy (Archive Media Publishing, Inc., 2011), 98.]

⁸ Deborah Gray White, Mia Bay, and Waldo E. Martin, Jr., *Freedom On My Mind: A History of African Americans* (Boston/New York:Bedford/ St. Martins, 2013), quoted in "Treatment of Slaves in the United States," *Wikipedia,* Accessed on Sept. 19, 2016, wikipedia.org/wiki/Treatment_of_slaves_in_the_United_States.

⁹ Mark Arabo, quoted in Barbara Boland, "Leader: ISIS is 'Systematically Beheading Children' in 'Christian Genocide'," *CNSNews,* last modified August 7, 2014, http://www.cnsnews.com/mrctv-blog/barbara-boland/leader-isis-systematically-beheading-children-christian-genocide.

¹⁰ "Caliphate, the political-religious state comprising the Muslim community and the lands and peoples under its dominion in the centuries following the death (632 ce) of the Prophet Muhammad. Ruled by a caliph (Arabic *khalīfah,* "successor"), who held temporal and sometimes a degree of spiritual authority…" *Britannica Academic,* s.v. "Caliphate," accessed September 20, 2016, http://0-academic.eb.com.library.regent.edu/levels/collegiate/article/18681.

¹¹ "Teaching to Kill: The Islamic State's Jihad Camps for Kids," *The Clarion Project,* last modified on August 28, 2014,

http://www.clarionproject.org/news/teaching-kill-Islamic-states-jihad-camps-kids.

[12] Roger Highfield, "DNA Survey Finds All Humans are 99.9pc the Same," *The Telegraph*, last modified on Dec. 20, 2002, http://www.telegraph.co.uk/news/worldnews/northamerica/usa/1416706/DNA-survey-finds-all-humans-are-99.9pc-the-same.html (emphasis added)

[13] Peter D. Demarest and Harvey J. Schoof, MS, *Answering the Central Question; How Science Reveals the Keys to Success in Life, Love, and Leadership* (Philadelphia: HeartLead Publishing, LLC, 2010), 19.

[14] Simon O. Sinek, "Simon Sinek, Creator of 'Discover Your Why' Course," *VerticalRising*, accessed on Sept. 20, 2016, http://verticalrising.com/about/simon-sinek/.

3. SIGNATURE OF VALUE

[1] Kyle McKinnon, "Will Malala's Influence Stretch to Europe?," *Deutsche Welle*, last modified on January 18, 2013, http://www.dw.com/en/will-malalas-influence-stretch-to-europe/a-16532149.

[2] Peter D. Demarest and Harvey J. Schoof, MS, *Answering the Central Question; How Science Reveals the Keys to Success in Life, Love, and Leadership* (Philadelphia: HeartLead Publishing, LLC, 2010), 4.

[3] Ibid., 47.

[4] Ibid., 5.

[5] Ibid. (First basic principle of Axiogenics)

[6] Ibid. (Second basic principle of Axiogenics)

[7] Ibid. (Third basic principle of Axiogenics)

[8] Ibid., 15.

[9] Matthew Lieberman, quoted in David Rock, "Managing With the Brain in Mind," *Strategy + Business*, last modified on August 27, 2009, http://www.strategy-business.com/article/09306?gko=5df7f.

[10] Demarest and Schoof, 47-48..

[11] Ibid., 77.

[12] Ibid.

[13] Ibid. 92.

[14] Ibid. 103.

[15] Henry Ward Beecher, quoted in William Drysdale, *Proverbs from Plymouth Pulpit (*New York: D. Appleton and Company, 1887), 37.

[16] Dr. Melodye Hilton has written about her life in a book entitled *Double Honor: Uprooting Shame in Your Life*, 1999.

[17] Cinderella, "Don't Know What You Got (Till It's Gone)," in *Long Cold Winter*, Mercury Records, 1988, Album.

[18] Demarest and Schoof, 93.

[19] Ibid., 98.

[20] Ibid., 118.

[21] Louis Nizer, *Between You and Me* (New York: Beechhurst Press, 1948).

4. HIGHER LIVING LEADERSHIP: HEAD-HAND-HEART

[1] Ken Olson, quoted in Gordon Goble, "The Top 10 Bad Tech Predictions," *Digital Trends*, last modified on November 4, 2012, http://www.digitaltrends.com/features/top-10-bad-tech-predictions/7/.

² Robert Metcalfe, quoted in Gordon Goble, "The Top 10 Bad Tech Predictions," *Digital Trends*, last modified on November 4, 2012, http://www.digitaltrends.com/features/top-10-bad-tech-predictions/7/.

³ "15 Ridiculous Predictions which didn't Come True!—Part 2," *History Rundown*, last modified on January 7, 2014, http://www.historyrundown.com/15-ridiculous-predictions-which-didnt-come-true-part-2/.

⁴ William Orton, quoted in, "15 Ridiculous Predictions which didn't Come True!—Part 2," *History Rundown*, last modified on January 7, 2014, http://www.historyrundown.com/15-ridiculous-predictions-which-didnt-come-true-part-2/.

⁵ Mary Somerville, quoted in "15 Ridiculous Predictions which didn't Come True!—Part 2," *History Rundown*, last modified on January 7, 2014, http://www.historyrundown.com/15-ridiculous-predictions-which-didnt-come-true-part-2/.

⁶ Daniel Goleman, *Working with Emotional Intelligence,* (New York: Bantam Books, 1998).

⁷ Daniel Goleman, *Working with Emotional Intelligence,* (New York: Bantam Books, 1998), 33.

⁸ Williams James, American Philosopher, Psychologist, and Physician, (1842-1910).

⁹ From Story of Cain and Abel in Genesis 4:9, paraphrase.

¹⁰Demarest and Schoof, 25.

¹¹ Winston Churchill, "The Gift of a Common Tongue," (speech, Harvard, September 6, 1943), The Churchill Centre, http://www.winstonchurchill.org/resources/speeches/1941-1945-war-leader/420-the-price-of-greatness-is-responsibility.

[12] Babe Ruth, "Babe Ruth Quotes," *Babe Ruth*, accessed September 24, 2016, http://www.baberuth.com/quotes/.

[13] Robert J. Morgan, *Real Stories for the Soul* (Nashville, TN: Thomas Nelson Inc., 2000), 53-55. "In December 1914, a great, sweeping fire destroyed Thomas Edison's laboratories in West Orange, New Jersey, wiping out two million dollars' worth of equipment and the record of much of his life's work. Edison's son Charles ran about frantically trying to find his father. Finally, he came upon him standing near the fire, his face ruddy in the glow, his white hair blown by the winter winds. 'My heart ached for him,' Charles Edison said. 'He was no longer young, and everything was being destroyed. He spotted me. 'Where's your mother?' he shouted. 'Find her. Bring her here. She'll never see anything like this again as long as she lives.'" The next morning, walking about the charred embers of so many of his hopes and dreams, the 67 year-old Edison said, 'There is great value in disaster. All our mistakes are burned up. Thank God we can start anew.'"

[14] Albert Einstein, quoted in "Albert Einstein Quotes- Humanity," *Albert Einstein Site Online*, accessed on September 24, 2106, htt[14] Albert Einstein, quoted in "Albert Einstein Quotes- Humanity," *Albert Einstein Site Online*, accessed on September 24, 2016, http://www.alberteinsteinsite.com/quotes/einsteinquotes.html.p://www.alberteinsteinsite.com/quotes/einsteinquotes.html.

[15] Albert Einstein, quoted in "Albert Einstein Quotes- Humanity," *Albert Einstein Site Online*, accessed on September 24, 2106, htt[15] Albert Einstein, quoted in "Albert Einstein Quotes- Humanity," *Albert Einstein Site Online*, accessed on September 24, 2016, http://www.alberteinsteinsite.com/quotes/einsteinquotes.html.p://www.alberteinsteinsite.com/quotes/einsteinquotes.html.

[16] Walt Disney, quoted in Lewis Howes, "20 Lessons from Walt Disney on Entrepreneurship, Innovation and Chasing Your Dreams," *Forbes*, last modified on July 17, 2012, http://www.forbes.com/sites/lewishowes/2012/07/17/20-business-quotes-and-lessons-from-walt-disney/#195f5e4d1f56.

[17] Os Hillman, *TGIF: Today God is First* (Grand Rapids: Revel, 2014), 16.

[18] Vince Lombardi, quoted in "What it Takes to be Number One," *Vince Lombardi*, acessed on September 26, 2016, http://www.vincelombardi.com/number-one.html.

[19] Robert T. Kiyosaki's Facebook Page, May 10, 2012, Accessed on September 26, 2016. https://www.facebook.com/RobertKiyosaki/posts/10150958481151788. (Robert Toru Kiyosaki is an American investor, businessman, self-help author, motivational speaker, financial literacy activist, and financial commentator. Kiyosaki is well known for his Rich Dad Poor Dad series of motivational books and other material published under the Rich Dad brand. He has written over 15 books which have combined sales of over 26 million copies).

5. INTRA-LEADERSHIP

[1] William James, American philosopher, psychologist, and physician, (1842-1910), public domain.

[2] This portion has been sourced from many neuroscientists, researches, etc. What areas are in quotes will be referenced. I am not a scientist, neuroscientist, nor do I claim to understand scientifically the aspects of the mind-brain. However, I have read, studied, and want to make the some complex principles simple to understand for application. Please note I am not using neuroscience to teach neuroscience but to apply the principles to leadership. I want to encourage the readers to google the different topics for further study as well as read the books, articles, etc. quoted in these writings. I want to thank my friend, Andrea Ham neuroscientist and microbiologist, who has listened to my trainings, reviewed and owns my presentation slides, and has read this book to ensure that the Higher Thinking, Intra-Leadership references to science are accurate.

[3] Neurons: "Join together 100 billion neurons-with 100 trillion connection-and you have yourself a human brain, capable of much, much more." Carl Zimmer, "100 Trillion Connections: New Efforts Probe and Map the Brain's Detailed Architechture," *Scientific American*, last modified on Janary 1, 2011, https://www.scientificamerican.com/article/100-trillion-connections/.

Dr. Caroline Leaf, *Who Switched Off My Brain? Series #1*, DVD.

Total number of synapse in cerebral cortex=6o trillion (yes, trillion) G.M. Shepherd, ed., *The Synaptic Organization of the Brain, 5th ed.* (New York: Oxford University Press, Inc, 2004), 7.

However, C. Koch lists the total synapses in the cerebral at "240 trillion." Christoph Koch, *Biophysics of Computation: Information Processing in Single Neurons*, 1st ed. (New York: Oxford University Press, 2004),87.

Branches (dendrites): "Dendrite is a highly branched, generally tapering extension of a neuron (nerve cell) that typically recives signals from other neurons and transmits the signals toward the cell body (soma) from which the dendrite protrudes...Although dendrites are where the majority of the input to the neuron occurs, in some cases dendrites may transmit signals from the cell body and release neurotransmitters to effect other neurons." "Dendrite," *New Word Encyclopedia*, accessed on September 26, 2016, http://www.newworldencyclopedia.org/entry/Dendrite.

"The human brain has about 100 billion neurons and 50 billion neuroglia." Michael S. Sweeney, *Brain: The complete Mind: How it Develops, How it Works, and How to Keep it Sharp* (National Geographic, 2009), 10.

[4] David Eagleman, *Incognito: The Secret Lives of the Brain*, 1st ed. (New York: Vintage Books, 2012), 1-2.

[5] Dr. Daniel G. Amen, *Making a Good Brain Great: The Amen Clinic Program for Achieving and Sustaining Optimal Mental Performance* (New York: Three Rivers Press, 2005), 147.

[6] Daniel T. Moore, Phd, "Six Ways to Help a Brain Heal," *Your Family Clinic*, accessed on September 26, 2016, http://www.yourfamilyclinic.com/trauma/heal.htm.

[7] Kevin S LaBar and Roberto Cabeza, "Cognitive neuroscience of emotional memory," *Nature Reviews: Neuroscience* 7, no. 1 (Jan. 2006): 54-64.

[8] Dr. Caroline Leaf, "Who Switched Off My Brain," LoveLife Conference video, youtube video, 1:00:54, posted July 29, 2014,

https://www.youtube.com/watch?v=1-goBWumIN4. (Her book by the same title is a must read to understand the process of thought more thoroughly).

[9] Dr. Caroline Leaf, *Who Switched off My Brain? Controlling Toxic Thoughts and Emotions* (Thomas Nelson Publishers, 2009), 14.

[10] The process of thought is complex. The portions written, though highly simplified, when understood will be effective in mind management. It's not my goal to teach science, but use it to demonstrate our innate ability to manage our thoughts, attitudes, emotions, and ultimately our decisions.

[11] Felix Adler, quoted in *20 Years of the Ethical Movement in New York and Other Cities*, 1876-1896 (Philadelphia, S. Burns Weston, 1896), 10.

[12] Dr. Ellen Weber, "The Brain on Cortisol," *Brain Leaders and Learners*, last modified September 22, 2008, http://www.brainleadersandlearners.com/general/the-brain-on-cortisol/ . (Dr. Ellen Weber recognized globally for brain-compatible communicating, learning and assessment renewal, lecturer, and author)

[13] Dr. Ellen Weber, "The Brain on Cortisol," *Brain Leaders and Learners*, last modified September 22, 2008, http://www.brainleadersandlearners.com/general/the-brain-on-cortisol/.

[14] Amunts K, Kedo O, Kindler M., Pieperhoff P, Mohlberg H. Shah N, Habel U, Schneider F, Ziles K, "Cytoarchitectonic Mapping of the Human Amygdala, Hippocampal Region and Entorhinal Cortex, Intersubject Visibility and Probability Maps." *Anat Embryol Berl*, (Dec 2005), 210 (5-6), 343-52, Quoted in "Amygdala," *Wikipedia*, accessed on September 25, 2016, https://en.wikipedia.org/wiki/Amygdala#cite_note-amyg-cytoarchitecture-3)

6. WHAT WAS I THINKING?

[1] Joseph Ledoux, quoted in Mary Lynn Hendrix, "The Emotional Brain: Lessons in Fear Conditioning," *NIH Record*, accessed on September 26, 2016, https://nihrecord.nih.gov/newsletters/06_03_97/story04.htm.

2 "Anger: Managing the Amygdala Hijack," *Life at the Bar*, last modified on May 11, 2007, https://lifeatthebar.wordpress.com/2007/05/11/anger-managing-the-amygdala-hijack/. (I encourage you to do a web search on "amygdala hijack" to learn more).

3 "Anger: Managing the Amygdala Hijack," *Life at the Bar*, last modified on May 11, 2007, https://lifeatthebar.wordpress.com/2007/05/11/anger-managing-the-amygdala-hijack/. (I encourage you to do a web search on "amygdala hijack" to learn more).

4 Dr. Ellen Weber, "A Brain on Forgiveness," *Brain Leaders and Learners: Practical Tactics for Neuro Discoveries with Dr. Ellen Weber,* last modified on September 17, 2011, http://www.brainleadersandlearners.com/amygdala/a-brain-on-forgiveness/.

5 Dr. Ellen Weber, "A Brain on Forgiveness," *Brain Leaders and Learners: Practical Tactics for Neuro Discoveries with Dr. Ellen Weber,* last modified on September 17, 2011, http://www.brainleadersandlearners.com/amygdala/a-brain-on-forgiveness/.

6 Dr. Ellen Weber, "A Brain on Forgiveness," *Brain Leaders and Learners: Practical Tactics for Neuro Discoveries with Dr. Ellen Weber,* last modified on September 17, 2011, http://www.brainleadersandlearners.com/amygdala/a-brain-on-forgiveness/.

7 Lewis B. Smedes, *The Art of Forgiving* (New York: Ballantine Books, 1996), 178.

8 Dr. Caroline Leaf, *Who Switched off My Brain? Series # 4,* DVD.

9 Dr. Ellen Weber, "A Brain on Forgiveness," *Brain Leaders and Learners: Practical Tactics for Neuro Discoveries with Dr. Ellen Weber,* last modified on September 17, 2011, http://www.brainleadersandlearners.com/amygdala/a-brain-on-forgiveness/.

10 Dr. Caroline Leaf, "The Perfect You: About," *Dr. Leaf,* Accessed on October 26, 2016, drleaf.com/about/the-perfect-you/.

[11] "Learn How to Increase Self Esteem," *Self Esteem Experts: Nurturing Vibrant Self Esteem*, accessed September 27, 2016, http://www.self-esteem-experts.com/how-to-increase-self-esteem.html.

[12] "How the Brain Works," *Self Esteem Experts: Nurturing Vibrant Self Esteem*, accessed September 27, 2016, http://www.self-esteem-experts.com/how-the-brain-works.html.

[13] Andrea L. Ham, M.S., email document to author, May 2013.

[14] Dr. Caroline Leaf, *Who Switched off My Brain?* Series #1, DVD.

[15] Demarest and Schoof, 50.

[16] Dr. Caroline Leaf, *Who Switched off My Brain?* Series #1, DVD.

[17] Andrea L. Ham, M.S., email document to author, May 2013.

[18] Albert Einstein, quoted in Morris Graham and Kevin Baize, *Executive Thinking: From Brightness to Brilliance* (Bloomington: iUniverse, Inc., 2011), 166.

7. INVISIBLE MOTIVATORS: VALUES

[1] Aspects of this section were sourced from "The Values Style Profile" and Dr. Melodye's training with the Institute of Motivational Living where she has received her Certificate of Proficiency in April, 1993 in the Behavioral Analysis Consulting Program. You can learn more about the Institute as well as their resources at: www.peoplekeys.com Direct quotes from the Values profile will be noted.

[2] The Values Style Profile, copyright 2010, The Institute of Motivational Living, Inc. New Castle, PA, USA.

[3] Demarest and Schoof, 44.

[4] Dr. Leon Pomeroy, *The New Science of Axiological Psychology*, ed. Rem. E. Edwards (Amsterdam:Rodopi, 2005), 38.

[5] The Values Style Profile, copyright 2010, The Institute of Motivational Living, Inc. New Castle, PA, USA

[6] Ayn Rand, *The Ayn Rand Lexicon: Objectivism from A to Z*, ed. Harry Binswanger (New York: Meridian, 1988), 198.

[7] The story is true in concept, but details were changed be protect confidentialities.

[8] "Resume Falsification Statistics," *Statistic Brain*, last modified October 1, 2015, http://www.statisticbrain.com/resume-falsification-statistics/.

[9] Lynn Ellsworth Taylor, *The Core Values Handbook, 3rd ed.* (Tukwila, WA: Elliott Bay Publishing, Inc., 2010), xvi. (Take free 10 minute self assessment to discover your innate core nature : www.DrMelodye.com/cvi).

8. DISCOVERING PERSONAL PURPOSE

[1] Lance Secretan, *Inspirational Leadership: Destiny, Calling, and Cause* (Canada: The Secretan Center, Inc., 1999), 83.

[2] The Leadership Challenge; Kouzes and Posner, pg 51, 52 Jossey-Bass, A Wiley Company, San Francisco, CA

[3] Unknown author

[4] Confucius

[5] Pius Ephenus, "Goal Setting: The Power of Writing Down Your Goals," *EzineArticles*, last modified on July 22, 2007, http://ezinearticles.com/?Goal-Setting---The-Power-Of-Writing-Down-Your-Goal&id=655551.

9. HIGHER LIVING LEADERS: EMPATHY

[1] Dr. Maya Angelou, interviewed by Trisha LaNae, "A Conversation with Dr. Maya Angelou" *Beautifully Said Magazine*, July 4, 2012, http://beautifullysmagazine.com/201207feature-of-the-month-3/.

[2] Dean Koontz, quoted in Harvey Deutschendorf, *The Other Kind of Smart: Simple Ways to Boost Your Emotional Intelligence for Greater Personal Effectiveness and Success* (New York: AMACOM, 2009), 112.

[3] Dr. Maya Angelou, quoted in Nagesh Belludi, "The Best Inspirational Quotations by Maya Angelou," *Right Attitudes: Ideas for Impact,* last modified April 4, 2015, http://www.rightattitudes.com/2015/04/04/inspirational-quotations-by-maya-angelou/.

[4] Matthew Lieberman, quoted in David Rock, "Managing With the Brain in Mind," *Strategy + Business*, last modified on August 27, 2009, http://www.strategy-business.com/article/09306?gko=5df7f.

[5] Daniel Goleman, PhD, quoted in Rhett Power, "7 Qualities of People with High Emotional Intelligence," *Success*, last modified on April 2, 2015, http://www.success.com/article/7-qualities-of-people-with-high-emotional-intelligence .

[6] Mike Bickle, quoted in Dr. Cindy Trim, *Reclaim Your Soul* (Shippensburg, PA: Destiny Image Publishers, Inc., 2014), 297.

[7] Dr. Thomas Lewis, "The Neuroscience of Empathy,"(presentation, Authors@Google Series, Google Headquarters Mountview, CA, December 5, 2007), Center for Building a Culture of Empathy, http://cultureofempathy.com/references/Experts/Thomas-Lewis.htm.

[8] L.R. Squire and S. Zola-Morgan, quoted in Yingchao Shi, Weiming Zeng, Nizhuan Wang, Shujiang Wang, and Zhijian Huang, "Early warning for human mental sub-health based on fMRI data analysis: an example from a seafarers' resting-data study," *Frontiers in Psychology*, last modified on July 23, 2015, http://journal.frontiersin.org/article/10.3389/fpsyg.2015.01030/full .

[9] Dr. Thomas Lewis, "The Neuroscience of Empathy,"(presentation, Authors@Google Series, Google Headquarters Mountview, CA, December 5, 2007), Center for Building a Culture of Empathy, http://cultureofempathy.com/references/Experts/Thomas-Lewis.htm.

[10] Demarest and Schoof, 32.

[11] Dr. Thomas Lewis, "The Neuroscience of Empathy,"(presentation, Authors@Google Series, Google Headquarters Mountview, CA, December 5, 2007), Center for Building a Culture of Empathy, http://cultureofempathy.com/references/Experts/Thomas-Lewis.htm.

[12] Dr. Thomas Lewis, "The Neuroscience of Empathy,"(presentation, Authors@Google Series, Google Headquarters Mountview, CA, December 5, 2007), Center for Building a Culture of Empathy, http://cultureofempathy.com/references/Experts/Thomas-Lewis.htm.

[13] *42*, directed by Brian Helgeland (2013; Burbank, CA: Warner Bros. Home Video, 2013), DVD.

[14] John C. Maxwell and Jim Dornan, *How to Influence People: Make a Difference in Your World* (Nashville: Thomas Nelson, 2013), 141.

[15] Dr. Caroline Leaf, *Who Switched off My Brain?* Series #4, DVD.

10. BUILDERS OF TRUST

[1] Stephen M.R. Covey and Rebecca R. Merrill, *The Speed of Trust: The One thing that Changes Everything* (New York, NY: Free Press, 2006).

[2] Stephen M.R. Covey and Rebecca R. Merrill, *The Speed of Trust: The One thing that Changes Everything* (New York, NY: Free Press, 2006), 10.

[3] Dr. Victor K. Fung, quoted in Stephen M.R. Covey and Rebecca R. Merrill, *The Speed of Trust: The One thing that Changes Everything* (New York, NY: Free Press, 2006), 55.

⁴ Gordon M. Bethune, interview by Adam Bryant, "Remember to Share the Stage," *The New York Times*, January 2, 2010, http://www.nytimes.com/2010/01/03/business/03corner.html.

⁵ Roy L. Smith, quoted in Zig Ziglar, *Over the Top*, Rev. ed. (Nashville: Thomas Nelson, Inc., 1997), 92.

⁶ Jim Rohn, quoted in John Rampton, "20 Quotes from Jim Rohn Putting Success and Life into Perspective," *Entrepreneur*, last modified on March 4, 2016, https://www.entrepreneur.com/article/271873.

⁷ Benjamin Disraeli, British Prime Minister and Novelist 1804-1881, public domain.

⁸ Denis Waitley, quoted in Martin Willoughby, "Career Investment- T. Doug Dale finds success as shareholder at Security Ballew," *Mississippi Business Journal*, last modified on June 20, 2014, http://msbusiness.com/2014/06/career-investment-t-doug-dale-finds-success-shareholder-security-ballew/.

⁹ John Luther, quoted in John C. Maxwell, *The Right to Lead: Learning Leadership Through Character and Courage* (Nashville: J. Countryman, 2010), 84.

¹⁰ Dwight D. Eisenhower, "First Inaugural Address of Dwight D. Eisenhower" (speech, Washington D.C., January 20, 1953), Dwight D. Eishenhower Presidential Library, Mueseum, and Boyhood Home, https://www.eisenhower.archives.gov/all_about_ike/speeches/1953_inaugural_address.pdf.

¹¹ Dr. Laura Schlessinger, quoted in Sean Covey, *The 6 Most Important Decisions You'll Ever Make: a Guide for Teens* (New York: Simon and Schuster, 2006), 277.

¹² Zig Ziglar, quoted in "Persuasion Tool," *Ziglar, Inc.*, accessed on September 29, 2016, https://www.ziglar.com/quotes/persuasion-tool/.

[13] W. Clement Stone, quoted in Anthony E. Jobe, Sr., *Discovering the Passion Thieves of Success and Unleashing the Real You* (Bloomington, IN, Authorhouse, 2012), 192.

[14] Albert Einstein, quoted in Gerald Holton and Yehuda Elkana, eds., *Albert Einstein: Historical and Cultural Perspectives* (Mineola, NY: Dover Publications, Inc., 1982), 388.

[15] Thomas Jefferson, (1743- 1826), public domain.

[16] Jean-Cyril Spinetta, quoted in Stephen R. Covey and Rebecca R. Merrill, *The Speed of Trust: The One Thing That Changes Everything* (New York: Free Press, 2006), 153.

[17] Hermann Hesse, *Narcissus and Goldmund: A Novel,* trans. Ursule Molinaro (New York: Picador, 1968), 43.

[18] James M. Kouzes and Barry Z. Posner, eds. *Christian Reflections on the Leadership Challenge* (San Francisco,:The Leadership Challenge, 2004), 124-125.

[19] Covey and Merrill, 222.

[20] Ernest Hemingway, quoted in Chris Oberbeck, "5 Ways a CEO Can Build a Culture of Trust," *Entrepreneur*, last modified on May 17, 2016, https://www.entrepreneur.com/article/273457.

[21] Graham Greene, *The Ministry of Fear* (London: Penguin Group, 1943), 43.

[22] Warren Buffet, quoted in James Berman, "The Three Essential Warren Buffet Quotes to Live By," *Forbes*, last modified on April 20, 2014, http://www.forbes.com/sites/jamesberman/2014/04/20/the-three-essential-warren-buffett-quotes-to-live-by/#765ed17732f5.

[23] James T. Byrnes, quoted in John F. Long, "There are No Federal Aid Funds Except Those Taken From Your Pockets," *Eerie Railroad Magazine* 45, no. 6 (August 1949): 3, accessed September 29, 2016,

https://books.google.com/books?id=m4szAAAAIAAJ&pg=RA15-PA3&lpg=RA15-PA3&dq=When+a+man+is+intoxicated+by+alcohol+he+can+recover,+but+when+intoxicated+by+power,+he+seldom+recovers.&source=bl&ots=GNUGYo3mM-&sig=4tt_AyG-Xlc6BxvGbxjhBFa7wcc&hl=en&sa=X&ved=0ahUKEwjy7azj97XPAhXJaz4KHVHAArUQ6AEINDAF#v=onepage&q=When%20a%20man%20is%20intoxicated%20by%20alcohol%20he%20can%20recover%2C%20but%20when%20intoxicated%20by%20power%2C%20he%20seldom%20recovers.&f=false.

[24] Unknown

[25] Johann Wolfgang von Goethe, German writer and statesmen, (1749-1832), public domain.

[26] *Braveheart*, directed by Mel Gibson (Hollywood, CA: Paramount, 1995)..

[27] Harry Truman, quoted in Robert Palestini, *No Laughing Matter: The Value of Humor in Educational Leadership* (Lanham: Rowman and Littlefield Education, 2013), 105.

[28] C.S. Lewis, quoted in Dr. Art Lindsley, "C.S. Lewis on Humility (and Pride) by Dr. Art Lindsley," *C.S. Lewis Institute*, last modified on October 8, 2012, http://www.cslewisinstitute.org/C.S._Lewis_on_Humility_and_Pride .

[29] Charles de Montesquieu, French Politician and philosopher, (1689-1755), public domain.

[30] Ralph Waldo Emerson, Poet, Lecturer and Essayist, (1803-1882), public domain.

[31] Donald T. Regan, quoted in Tom Hopkins, *Selling in Tough Times: Secrets to Selling When No One is Buying* (New York: Business Plus, 2010), 87.

[32] Stephen R. Covey, *The 7 Habits of Highly Effective Families* (New York: Golden Books, 1997),40. (original quote: "We then judge ourselves by our motives—and others by their behavior.").

11. THE GREATEST FORM OF HONOR

[1] Sonia Rumzi, quoted in "Sonia Rumzi Quotes," *Goodreads*, accessed on September 29, 2016, http://www.goodreads.com/quotes/345671-anyone-who-teaches-me-deserves-my-respect-honoring-and-attention.

[2] John Paul Warren, quoted in "John Paul Warren Quotes," *Goodreads*, accessed on September 29, 2016, https://www.goodreads.com/quotes/414326-you-will-never-reach-your-dreams-without-honoring-others-along.